THE OTHER JESUS

THE OTHER JESUS

Stories from World Religions

Todd Outcalt

ROWMAN & LITTLEFIELD
Lanham • Boulder • New York • London

Published by Rowman & Littlefield
A wholly owned subsidary of
The Rowman & Littlefield Publishing Group, Inc.
4501 Forbes Boulevard, Suite 200, Lanham, Maryland 20706
www.rowman.com

16 Carlisle Street, London W1D 3BT, United Kingdom

British Library Cataloguing in Publication Information Available

Library of Congress Cataloging-in-Publication Data
Outcalt, Todd.
The other Jesus : stories from world religions / Todd Outcalt.
pages cm
Includes bibliographical references and index.
ISBN 978-1-4422-2308-0 (cloth : alk. paper) — ISBN 978-1-4422-2309-7
(electronic)
1. Jesus Christ—Historicity. 2. Bible. Gospels—Extra-canonical parallels. 3.
Jesus Christ—Words—Extra-canonical parallels. I. Title.
BT303.2.O98 2014
232.9—dc23
2014025508

∞ ™ The paper used in this publication meets the minimum requirements of
American National Standard for Information Sciences Permanence of Paper
for Printed Library Materials, ANSI/NISO Z39.48-1992.

Printed in the United States of America

To the Bishops

Leroy Hodapp (1923–2006)
Woodie W. White
Michael J. Coyner

CONTENTS

PREFACE

I began working on this book soon after I completed the manuscript for *Candles in the Dark: A Collection of the World's Greatest Parables.* That was nearly fifteen years ago—but in some respects I have been working on this book for most of my life. As a nineteen-year-old college sophomore, I recall the thrill of discovering M. R. James's *The Apocryphal New Testament* among the stacks of the Indiana State University Library and reading, for the first time, other words and parables and sayings attributed to Jesus.

Soon after this, as part of a required assignment in an English class, I read D. H. Lawrence's essay "Christs in the Tyrol" and realized that there were, indeed, many ways that people had encountered and viewed Jesus through the centuries or had portrayed him in artistic expression and personal narrative.

During my seminary years at Duke University, I spent much time perusing the dry and dusty shelves devoted to ancient Near Eastern literature—complete with some ancient manuscripts—and there discovered additional expressions or stories about Jesus in texts ranging from the Gnostic, to the Islamic, to Jewish and early church. In those days I consumed books by David Margoliouth—a renowned "Orientalist" British scholar who researched and wrote at the turn of the nineteenth century—and the latest works forthcoming from then Duke scholar James Charlesworth, whose massive soon-to-be-published collection of *Old Testament Pseudepigrapha* was all the buzz.

I was also soaking in culture and background for this book, reading copious portions of the Talmud in Hebrew and Aramaic and many Greek texts, as well as translating legal documents discovered at Elephantine, Egypt. I also began reading Syriac and Arabic to round out my passion for the Semitic tongues. All the while, I continued to be amazed at the scope and profusion of the Jesus stories, and some of my research now harks back to those earlier times—and often entire days consumed—spent translating and compiling.

The reader will note that, in some instances throughout this book, I have provided my own (author's) rendition or retelling of a Jesus story or saying—as some of these were originally written or translated into language that doesn't sit well on the modern tongue. Wherever possible—and as my translation skills have allowed—I have attempted to shape others whole from the original texts or manuscripts. Most, however, are here presented from other authors who have accomplished the difficult work of researching and translating—and I am grateful to include them in this collection.

Throughout the book there are also references that will lead the reader to the Notes and Bibliography sections. Here the reader will find more detailed information about the particular Jesus narratives or find references to the books read and/or those that can provide deeper background for a particular idea.

My hope is that this book will be the most comprehensive collection of Jesus material published to date—but will also provide a much richer and fuller exploration of the various reasons why Jesus has occupied such a highly respected place among so many religious traditions . . . and some that are quite surprising. My hope is that the book will provide a kind of grand overture to the full slate of Jesus traditions while also being highly readable and, in the end, enjoyable as well as enlightening.

ACKNOWLEDGMENTS

In writing this book, I realize that it could not have been accomplished without the help of many people. Family and friends all played a role—if not vital to the pursuit—by providing support, assistance, and at times the space necessary to research and write. I am particularly indebted to my wife, Becky, and our children for their understanding and encouragement along the way. This one was a labor of love—if not a labor of long nights—and I'm grateful you shared so much coffee with me. I thank my parents for giving me those first typewriters (precomputer) and for compelling me to write. Thanks also to Bill and Marilyn as well as to my long list of family and friends. I love you all.

I am also grateful to my many teachers for providing inspiration and the climate that leads to learning. Here I need to thank Miss Wallace and Ron Kamman, along with Dr. E. Tarbox, Dr. Donald Jennerman, Dr. Lloyd R. Bailey, Dr. David Steinmetz, Dr. Orville Wintermute, and Dr. Eric Meyers.

Additionally, my heartfelt thanks to Sarah Stanton, Kathryn Knigge, and Janice Braunstein for editing my work—and to the publisher and staff at Rowman & Littlefield for allowing me the opportunity. The deficiencies that remain are mine, and I thank everyone involved for making this the best book possible.

INTRODUCTION

As Albert Schweitzer began his classic work *The Quest of the Historical Jesus*, he noted right off the difficulties of establishing a singular vantage point from which to view and study the life and teachings of Jesus. Any quest—as Schweitzer was about to undertake in his opus—would by definition be limited by both history and one's investigative methods. Ultimately, what every historian or believer would rest upon was what Schweitzer calls "intuition."

As Schweitzer accurately pointed out, any discussion of the Jesus of history—and certainly any books written about him—would necessitate a default to our own biases and preconceived notions of who Jesus was or who he has to be. Perhaps more than any personality in history, Jesus is revealed by many faces and names. The greatest difficulty—particularly for those who have faith in Jesus—is that we require him to be fashioned in our own image or we force him to be like the Jesus we need him to be. It is rare to find those individuals who are still forming an image of Jesus or who are open to new possibilities, images, and faces. Most everyone already has his or her own Jesus in tow, and it is a messy and delicate work to add ingredients to the pot.

But there have always been other Jesuses. Within the Bible we have the Jesus of the four gospels (similar but varied) and the Jesus of Paul the apostle. But there was also a Jesus of Judaism, a Jesus of the early church, and even a Jesus imagined and followed in Christian communities that developed in particular social structures and cultures—such as early monasticism. Later, there would be the Jesus of Islam and the

Jesus of Sufism. And in much later times, as Christian missionaries interacted with cultures and converts, there would develop a rich assortment of Jesuses, some more recently discovered, who would reveal how other faiths and philosophies adapted his life and teachings into other systems and practices.

This is what this book is about: the Other Jesus. The Jesus of many names and faces.

Schweitzer, however, notes well the difficulties:

> The problem of the life of Jesus has no analogue in the field of history. No historical school has ever laid down canons for the investigation of this problem, no professional historian has ever lent his aid to the theology in dealing with it. Every ordinary method of historical investigation proves inadequate to the complexity of the conditions. The historical study of the life of Jesus has had to create its own methods for itself.
>
> The cause of this lies in the nature of the sources of the life of Jesus and the character of our knowledge of the contemporary religious world of thought. It is not the sources that are themselves bad. When we have once made up our minds that we don't have the materials for a complete life of Jesus, but only for a picture of his public ministry, it must be admitted that there are few characters of antiquity about whom we possess so much indubitably historical information, of whom we have so many authentic discourses. Jesus stands much more immediately before us, because He was depicted by simple Christians without literary gift.[1]

Having heard the name of Jesus my entire life, I know that I, too, have a formed image of Jesus: the teaching Jesus, the authoritative Jesus, the suffering Jesus, the Jesus of earth and heaven. But as I have dialogued with others (even those of shared Christian faith) I have come to realize that all beliefs about and images of Jesus are, at best, shaded or colored by our own perceptions, needs, desires, and pursuits. We even use Jesus to justify our own ends—and create him in that manner—often with disastrous results.

Although I am not a scholar (but a seminary-trained pastor), I realize that I also bring my thoughts and persuasions to bear upon speaking about Jesus. I bring my deficiencies along with my strengths. I speak of the Jesus I know—but also realize that there is more of Jesus *to know*. Nevertheless, I am thankful that he remains, in many ways, a mystery to me—as one hidden and newly discovered each day through the nuance of his teaching and the testimony of his life. There is more to Jesus than I can write about, or uncover, or even speak to.

Nevertheless, for the past thirty-five years I have continued to search for Jesus in history, in other faiths and traditions, and in those new academic pursuits which uncover and astound. I am an academic (and pastor) at heart—but have always sought to write for the general reader. And so this book will be my attempt to bring together a trove of work from across academic disciplines and faiths, all the while offering the whole between two covers for the general reader.

I thank you for joining me in this pursuit to find The Other Jesus.

Let me also note that this quest to compile such a varied and comprehensive array about Jesus is by no means exhaustive. But in fact I have a weight of sadness in knowing that selections had to be made, that all of the teachings attributed to Jesus, the stories about him, the parables, the insights, the traditions, the images . . . could not possibly be collected. And certainly not all could be included here. I hope I have, nevertheless, assembled the best—and offered the appropriate commentary and connections along the way.

To get at another Jesus (other than our own Jesus), we must be willing to become a pilgrim again—a learner, a disciple. Perhaps this is what Jesus had in mind. It is as though we hear afresh the call of Jesus, "Follow me," and then bring to the journey no bag of books, no history, no tradition, no preconceived idea of where the trail will end or what we will discover about Jesus along the way. Whether one considers oneself a follower of Jesus (or not) has no bearing on a person's ability or willingness to learn about Jesus—or to encounter him.

I hope that this book will allow the reader to travel this type of journey with Jesus—to discover more of him or to leave behind our assumptions.

In many respects my own journey with Jesus has been one fraught with many plateaus and detours. My images of Jesus have changed through the years. I have, at various junctures, left behind certain ideas about him to embrace other ideas. And while some teachings of Jesus have broadened in scope and influence in my life, I have also felt the restrictions and narrowness of other sayings and parables—or been forced to admit defeat in understanding them. I might say that my concept of Jesus (or, I might say, *my faith*) has become more like music or art—a type of work in progress, a thing of beauty that is to be appreciated rather than understood purely through rational thought. I have learned more about Jesus, in fact, by writing about him than I have by merely believing in him—and certain of these beliefs have morphed, or wilted, or grown more pronounced through the years.

At the heart of my pursuits for this book, I note that certain teachings of Jesus—particularly those centered on compassion, or peace, or hospitality, or treating others with dignity and respect—are more universally known and thus carry more weight as we speak of Jesus or understand his impact across faiths and cultures. Beliefs are no longer as important as faith *when faith* is a way of life, a practice, the manner in which one lives in the awareness of God and neighbor.

There is no doubt that the Gospel writers themselves—these anonymous authors—were also taken with their respective images of Jesus and what they chose to communicate (or not) about him. Any writer can identify with these authors—who selectively used other documents, memories, traditions, and bits of information (both written and oral) to construct their respective Gospels.

In fact, the beginning of the Gospel of Luke says this plainly—and offers us the first image of a Jesus created for particular ends and purposes, if not for mere cause of celebration.

> Since many have undertaken to set down an orderly account of the events that have been fulfilled among us, just as they were handed on to us by those who from the beginning were eyewitnesses and servants of the word, I too decided, after investigating everything carefully from the first, to write an orderly account for you, most excellent Theophilus, so that you may know the truth concerning the things about which you have been instructed. (Luke 1:1–4, NRSV)

How telling that the Gospel writers themselves make note of their dependence upon other sources—and upon those who were the eyewitnesses—and not themselves, and also that they are attempting to construct a life of, and a body of work about, Jesus that is built upon the creative usage of words and the editorial process of selecting and omitting. I can identify—and in this I find one of the most compelling reasons to learn about Jesus . . . as everyone must begin to shape his/her own Jesus built of select pieces of memory, of spirit, of experience, and of choice pieces of history. The work of faith, then, is more like an act of

construction, of building or drawing or forming rather than mere intellectual ascent or buying into a set of beliefs.

I love this about Jesus, too, as I encounter him in other faiths and
traditions or discover him alongside the Tao or sitting beside the Buddha. Here I add another piece of clay. I get to use a different color. And
gradually a new or a brighter image of Jesus emerges.

I feel all the richer for it.

Likewise, the fourth Gospel—the ethereal Gospel built on the image
of a divine Jesus, the Logos, the Eternal One—offers no less than Luke
when it comes to constructing his Jesus. But rather than beginning with
a statement about editing and selecting—as the gospel of Luke does—
the fourth Gospel ends with a far more radical and universal concept of
discovering Jesus: an invitation to find him among all of the books that
have *not been written* about Jesus but which shall be.

> And there are also many other things which Jesus did, the which, if
> they should be written every one, I suppose that even the world itself
> could not contain the books that should be written. Amen. (John
> 21:25, KJV)

So many books about Jesus. And here another one.

During the years spent on researching the material for this book, I
was keenly aware that there is no lack of Jesus material. During seminary, I had access to the large and veritable trove of material available
to me through the Duke University Library system, and now, with the
rather instantaneous and near-ubiquitous availability of out-of-print
material through the Internet, the search has continued through small
capillaries of information and fingered out into tiny tributaries that, up
until a few years ago, would have been impossible to navigate. Writing
this book, I feel the stirrings of this unique place in history—as information, even about Jesus, is now transmitted with apparent ease and re-
sourcefulness.

As noted earlier, this book is for the general reader—though it is my
hope that I can contribute something to the larger circle of academic
discourse about Jesus. My gifts, such as they are, may perhaps be best
expressed as an "assembler" or "collector" of material, and where I can
offer commentary or thought to round out the edges, I have done so.

I have taken to writing this book, also, with some of my own questions. I am still finding Jesus—especially through conversation with others and not just in reading and research.

During my undergraduate college years I began to feel the stirrings of these questions through my warm and friendly conversations with two friends: one, a Jew from Iran, and the other, a Muslim from Iraq, who brought fresh perspectives about Jesus to bear upon my rather sheltered and limited pursuit of him. Whenever Jesus entered the conversation, I felt as though I were making progress in my own pilgrimage in the world, and without exception my ideas about Jesus were challenged, shattered, or affirmed. Discussing Jesus with friends—Christian, Jew, and Muslim—was a most exciting endeavor. At least it was for me.

But the world has changed. And so has, it seems, our ability and willingness to listen for the Other Jesus—the one we do not know. Many conversations about Jesus today are like prizefights—with Jesus as the spoils—and it is a rare thing to find those places and times and people who will sit in each other's presence, with Jesus as the centerpiece of conversation, and simply listen. I lament the loss of that earlier time in my life and hope to recapture it, in part, through sharing in these pages.

To everyone who picks up this book, my sincerest hope is that you will come with an open heart and an open mind. (Some, no doubt, will find even this invitation appalling.) But I'll leave Jesus at the center of conversation and allow the discoveries, the words, and the histories to represent themselves. There is no agenda for this book other than to offer what has been written about Jesus through the centuries—and to provide some framework for understanding the times and places from which these ideas and words originated.

I will allow my readers their own conclusions—and, in fact, have none to offer. Just the words.

But my hope is that every reader who makes a pilgrimage with me through Sufism, for example, or the Tao, or even the Gospels will come away with a deeper understanding of who Jesus is. I hope this will be so not just for those who profess to be his followers but also among the countless distant friends who embraced Jesus or his teachings or found in him some beautiful philosophy or life that inspired their own.

May we also be inspired.

And may we also discover Jesus—the Other Jesus—whom we have not known.

I

THE WORD MADE FLESH

The Jesus of the Early Church

But there are also many other things that Jesus did; if every one of them were written down, I suppose that the world itself could not contain the books that would be written. —John 21:25, NRSV

Jesus said, "Split a piece of wood, and I am there. Lift up the stone, and you will find me there." —The Gospel of Thomas

My son, first purify yourself toward the outward life in order that you may be able to purify the inward. And be not as the merchants of the Word of God. Put all words to the test before you utter them. Jesus Christ, Son of God, Savior (Ichthus). —The teachings of Silvanus[1]

Every book must have a beginning—and every story an ending.

Undertaking an exploration of Jesus, then, may automatically assume both the former and the latter. One could make a compelling argument that the Jesus of the early church saw Jesus as the culmination of a longer narrative and revelation that the Jewish people believed that God was unfolding among the people of Israel, the descendants of Abraham. In short, Jesus was the Jewish Messiah, the one who would redeem Israel from all its sins (Psalm 130). This was not the Jesus of Christendom—as Christianity had not yet become separated from Judaism by confession and by the inclusion of the Gentiles. Rather, this first- and second-generation Jesus still retained his rabbinical voice, his Jewishness. And those who followed him viewed Jesus as part of this longer Jewish narrative.

One could make a compelling argument that the apostle Paul—himself a Jewish Pharisee by birth and training and author of the bulk of the writings that make up the New Testament canon—saw Jesus in this light. And, as Paul's letters predate any of the four Gospels, one could make an argument that we glimpse in his letters a different Jesus than the one encountered in these later narratives. This is not to say that Paul contradicts the Gospels or did not know of their existence (quite the opposite)—but Paul's letters presume, in most cases, that he is writing about Jesus for a mostly Gentile audience, a people who may not know about the history of the Jewish people and the many formative narratives (chiefly the Exodus saga and Passover) that helped to explain the Jesus he was writing about.

These insights into the New Testament writings themselves are important, as they offer us a glimpse of Jesus as *subject*. Originally, the writers of the Gospels and Epistles did not presume that their audiences were necessarily knowledgeable about Jewish history—which would, in part, help to explain Jesus. The Gospel writer of Mark, for example, seems to assume a Gentile audience, while the Gospels of Matthew and John are more clearly focused on the Jewish. And most of Paul's letters—as one dissects them—bear out that Paul was attempting to explain Jewish concepts to his Gentile converts, with Jesus as the *subject* or centerpiece of faith. Romans is the primary example of this—the longest of Paul's sustained arguments for the faith—while letters like the Corinthian correspondence and Galatians mark Paul's liquid attempts to explain the practice of the Christian faith outside the bounds of the Jewish law.

These are complex issues—and far beyond the scope of this book—but as we begin to consider the many faces and forms of Jesus in the early church, it is worth noting that we might understand the New Testament itself as a kind of compilation of Jesus stories and teachings. Even in the canon we see a Jesus of varied focus. What the Gospel of Mark concentrates upon, for example, is quite different from the focus of the Gospel of John. And Luke, while most similar to Matthew, contains much material that is wholly unique to that Gospel, with an emphasis on a Jesus who reaches the poor, the outcast, and the marginalized of society—including women.

So Jesus, *as subject*, has many faces—and took many forms in the telling—from the very beginning.

The ending of the Gospel of Mark (most commonly regarded as the earliest Gospel of the four) offers, perhaps, a place from which to begin an exploration of the Jesus of the early church.

It is compelling to note that in most of the oldest surviving manuscripts of this Gospel, Mark ends abruptly. This Gospel, also the briefest of the Gospels at sixteen chapters (a short story, really), offers a fast-paced and exciting picture of Jesus as miracle worker, rabbi, and divinely appointed Messiah. Mark's profuse use of the word "immediately" hastens the narrative along and at the center shifts Jesus from Galilee to Judea and marches him toward the final days of his life. Jesus is arrested, given a mock trial at the hands of both Jewish and Roman authorities, and then crucified. Then, on the first day of the week (Sunday), women come to the tomb to anoint the body of Jesus for a proper (according to the Levitical law) burial, but they find that the body is missing. In the oldest versions of this Gospel, Mark ends with the words (16:8, NRSV): "So they went out and fled from the tomb, for terror and amazement had seized them; and they said nothing to anyone, for they were afraid."

It is doubtful, however, that this Gospel ended with these words in its original form. But given the nature of papyrus documents in those days and the manner in which the document would have been passed along and potentially torn, it is necessary to add other extant renderings from other ancient manuscripts of this Gospel to complete the narrative. And this, in fact, is precisely what happened.

But the variant endings of Mark's Gospel tell us about far more than the manner in which manuscripts were copied and shared in the first-century church. Mark is much more than a testimony to the manner in which these documents were cherished.

Rather, these various alternative endings to Mark's Gospel also allow us to glimpse how the Gospel was told (and in essence *retold*)—how the gospel was transmitted and rendered—in the early church. For our purposes here, we can see that other unique stories about Jesus—and in Mark's case stories about the resurrected Jesus—were told and transmitted in order to complete a narrative that otherwise ends abruptly and, shall we say, without satisfaction.

That a longer ending to the Gospel of Mark once existed (and one perhaps more akin to the ending of Matthew?) is evidenced by earlier references within Mark's Gospel to the forthcoming resurrection. Earlier in this same Gospel, for example, we have Jesus saying (14:28, NRSV): "But after I am raised up, I will go before you to Galilee." And just verses before the curt ending, we find the angel telling the women (16:7, NRSV): "But go, tell his disciples and Peter that he is going ahead of you to Galilee."

These two references inside Mark's Gospel foreshadow a different ending from the abrupt one. The women flee the tomb in fear and trembling (this is noted in the other Gospels, too, along with either amazement or awe). But Mark's shorter version surely didn't end there. Otherwise, how would one read the earlier instructions of Jesus for his followers to return to Galilee in anticipation of seeing him again?

So, when and how the two longer endings of Mark's Gospel came about, we cannot say. But Mark's Gospel, perhaps more than the other three, does reveal the many faces of Jesus—and his teachings—that were used in the early church to produce and instruct a community of faith. This early community that shared Mark's Gospel, at least, felt compelled to add and/or subtract material about Jesus—the *subject* of the Gospel.

These longer endings to the Gospel of Mark, then, represent one of the earliest efforts to extrapolate Jesus from unique sources (and these are unique!). Again, as Luke points out in the beginning of his Gospel, many sources are used—as are other gospels—in the retelling of the story of Jesus, even in the resurrection narratives.

Hence, we can begin with the longer endings of Mark's Gospel (my translation) as our first image of the Other Jesus in the early church.

Everything they had received as commands they [the women] told to the others and to Peter. And afterwards Jesus used them as emissaries, proclaiming from east to west the holy and undying message of eternal salvation.

Now after Jesus rose up on the first day of the week, he had appeared first to Mary Magdalene, from whom he had exorcised seven demons. She was the one who boldly proclaimed—and to those who, though they had been with him, were still mourning. But when they heard the news that he was alive, and considered it was Mary who told them, they would not believe it.

But soon after he appeared in another form to two others as they were walking out in the country. These two went back and told the others, too, but they wouldn't believe them, either.

Later Jesus appeared to the eleven disciples themselves as they were still sitting at a table together. Jesus scolded them for their lack of faith and stubbornness, because they had not believed any of the others who had seen him after his resurrection. But he did tell them, "Go throughout the world and tell this good news to the whole creation! Whoever believes and is baptized will be saved; but the one who doesn't believe will be condemned. And as for signs—these will be present among those who believe: they will speak my name and cast out demons; they will preach in other languages; they will be able to pick up snakes, and even if they drink a deadly poison they won't be harmed; they will touch the sick and these will be healed of illnesses."

After the Lord Jesus had spoken these things he was taken up to heaven where he sits at God's right hand. But these went out and told the good news everywhere, even while the Lord continued to work with them by confirming the message through these various signs.

(And still other ancient manuscripts of Mark add . . .)

They all attempted to make excuses for their work by pointing out: "This present age is one of lawlessness and unbelief, and is clearly under Satan, who won't allow God's truth and power to prevail over these unclean spirits. So you need to reveal your righteousness now!" This is what they said to Christ!

And Christ replied, "Listen, Satan's years of power have come to an end, although there are other terrible events soon to come. I was handed over to death for those who have sinned, so that they could return to the truth and sin no more and thus inherit the spiritual and undying glory of the righteousness found in heaven. Amen."

These longer endings to the gospel of Mark reveal how the early church used a plethora of stories, teachings, and narratives about Jesus to create a satisfying ending to an abrupt Gospel. Again, this is not to say that another ending to this Gospel did not originally exist, but once lost, other communities and circumstances picked up where it left off.

This Gospel, unlike any of the other three—or even Paul's Epistles—
offers an image of Jesus who is still working miracles in the lives of the
faithful. The Gospel of Mark, which moves quickly through its paces
with miracle after miracle at the hands of Jesus, now ends with speaking
of the disciples' hands. They continue to perform the miracles of Jesus,
who has been raised. The disciples' hands become the hands of the
resurrected Jesus. That seems to be the message of the longer version
of Mark, and this Gospel ending is unique among the Gospels. Perhaps
it was so unique it had to be expunged from some manuscripts.

Mark's message is that these same hands of Jesus are now found
among those who exorcise demons, exhort, pick up serpents, and quaff
deadly potions.

But we cannot miss the image of Jesus being portrayed here, either.
This Jesus is much different, resurrected, from the same living Christ of
Matthew, Luke, or John. And his inclusion can help us to see that the
Jesus of the early church was far more varied and diffuse than we are
often led to believe. Jesus, to those first communities, became a type of
everyman—yet ever present in the trials and struggles of the sinful
world. The greatest testimony to the power of Jesus was not necessarily
his miracles, but his miraculous power to transform lives and offer
meaning and significance regardless of the circumstances, culture, or
resistances (even persecutions). That the Gospels emerged through a
cloud of Roman persecution of the Jews (the temple was destroyed in
70 CE) is highly significant and cannot be overlooked. Mark's Gospel,
and to a lesser extent the other three, seems deeply aware of these
persecutions and the need for a message of hope.

Consequently, the Jesus of the early church, by necessity, had to
have many faces, many hopes, many teachings, and many nuances in
order to address the magnanimity of the forces allayed against the small
band of believers. Jesus could not be just a Galilean rabbi from an
obscure village, or a miracle worker, or a remarkable teacher. Nor could
he be simply a peasant carpenter, an exorcist, or a provocative prophet
who challenged the power structures of Judea and Rome. The Jesus of
the first and second centuries, while obscure, is also revealed in a myriad of ways through these early communities and the struggles they
faced in order to *tell the story* of Jesus. And as the very early church
began to form its own identity apart from Judaism, one can see how the
images of Jesus changed from suffering Jew to triumphant king of the

universe. A Jewish rabbi/Messiah would not play well in a predominantly Gentile church—and we shall see how, over time, these images of Jesus morphed from obscurity to powerful king.

As for this story—we can turn our attentions now to this diversity. And we shall see how, in just a few generations, Jesus developed from a humble Jewish Messiah to Lord of the Universe. Jesus was *the subject*—and by the fourth century, the church would make a bold attempt to bundle Jesus into one image.

THE JESUS OF THE MASSES

Perhaps it was inevitable that Jesus would evolve as the first generation of disciples died and others, who had not walked with him through the dusty hills of Galilee and Judea, would continue to speak of him in words and images drawn through the lenses of history. While it was not important to the Gospel writers to describe the physical appearance of Jesus, for example, later generations would be aroused by curious questions concerning the childhood of Jesus, or the missing years not noted in the Gospels, or even those miracles and teachings not described elsewhere or passed along in the oral traditions of the ever-growing church.

Infancy gospels—no doubt born and bred of this intrigue—were written to address some of these new questions. There is an infancy *Gospel of Thomas* (not to be confused with the Nag Hammadi *Gospel of Thomas*), now widely known and published, that describes the boy Jesus as a creator of clay birds—which he promptly turns into living things by clapping his hands . . . and another episode where the young Jesus, in a fit of rage, transforms some unruly children into goats.[2]

Another account in this same infancy gospel—reminiscent of John's Gospel where Jesus turns water into wine—has the boy Jesus performing a miracle on a vat of dye. And like the singular childhood account from Luke—where Jesus is discovered in the temple by his parents, teaching the elders at the age of twelve—this episode in *Thomas* is a cause for celebration.

> It came to pass that one day the Virgin Mary went to visit a neighbor—a man who happened to be a dyer by trade. And although she

was unaware, her son Jesus was following close behind as boys will often do. While Mary wasn't looking, Jesus slipped into the shop where this man practiced his trade—and where he was in the process of dying some strips of cloth into various colors. But Jesus, when he noticed the beautiful colors of the various cloths, took them all, bundled them together as one, and tossed them into a vat of black dye.

Later, when the thing became known to the man who operated the business, he was angry and brought a complaint against Mary. "Look what your son has done!" he said. "He's ruined a day's labor for me. I'm not letting him go until you pay the damages."

When Mary heard it, she said to Jesus, "My beloved son, what have you done? I had always hoped to receive nothing but joy from you, but you have made me sad."

But Jesus asked, "What have I done to make you grieve?"

Mary answered, "You've destroyed this man's labors."

Jesus again asked, "But how have I destroyed it?"

Mary said, "The strips of cloth were all of varied color. But you bundled them together and tossed them all into a single vat of black dye. They are ruined and now I will have to make restitution for your troubles."

When Jesus heard this he walked over to the vat of black dye and began to draw strips of cloth from it—one by one. As he pulled each strip of cloth from the black dye, it was restored to its original color, and he handed them back to the man.

When the man and Mary saw this they glorified Jesus and held him in great admiration. Then the Virgin Mary embraced her son, kissed him, and returned, rejoicing, to her house. [3]

These infancy gospels—at their heart—demonstrate the innate curiosity with the missing years of the Gospels themselves. Not much is written about the infant or boy Jesus after all, and people of early generations, like our own, naturally wonder: What was happening in those early years? Many of the images and stories about Jesus from this time period reflect both an awareness of the Christian writings and a desire to fill in the missing pieces. Jesus—as subject—continued to occupy a central place in many of these early forms, or pseudoforms, of Christian writing.

Indeed, there is no lack of Christian literature—or various approaches to Jesus—that one can now dredge from the profusion of these manuscripts. As the Gospels and certain letters of the apostle Paul began to have greater prominence within the worshipping communities (and as these Christian writings began to supplement the reading and study of the Hebrew Bible), it is apparent that other writings sprang up, their authors using the style and form of the Gospel writers and the apostle himself.

Gospels, Acts, and Epistles attributed to the growing pantheon of Christian leaders became the norm. And the works of some second-generation Christians—such as Clement, who accompanied Paul on some of his missionary journeys—began to gain nearly equal prominence in the church as sacred writing and were used for both study and worship in the early church.

Clement himself, who was probably both a Gentile and a Roman, wrote follow-up epistles to the church at Corinth—the most lengthy of Paul's surviving correspondences to the churches in the New Testament canon. Like Paul's letters before, Clement's epistles gained a foothold among these populated Christian communities and both Eusebius (born in 260, and a Roman who wrote the first history of the church) and Origen (an early Christian interpreter and theologian) note that Clement's epistle to the Corinthian church was still being read widely by the churches in their respective eras.

Reading Clement's epistle, we can see how the images of Jesus and some of the illustrations used to describe his life and teachings had evolved from the Jewish origins and were extrapolated through the lenses of Greek philosophy and myth to describe Jesus for his time. The use of Greek philosophy, and in particular the writings of Plato, had a profound impact upon the development of the Jesus taught and preached during the age of the ecumenical councils (as we shall see). But in Clement's time (late second century) Jesus was still imagined as the Jewish Messiah who, through his triumphant resurrection, had redeemed humanity and through this victory offered the hope of eternal life. But the emphasis on the resurrection of the body was waning even as the Greek philosophy of the eternal soul was taking a firm root. We see this clearly in Clement's epistle to the Corinthian church, where he turns his attentions to these matters—where he combines the Jewish tradition of the resurrection with various observances of nature and one prominent Near Eastern myth.

Let us consider, beloved, how the Lord continually proves to us that there shall be a future resurrection, of which He has rendered the Lord Jesus Christ the first-fruits, by raising Him from the dead. Let us contemplate, beloved, the resurrection which is at all times taking place. Day and night declare to us a resurrection. The night sinks to sleep, and the day arises; the day departs and night comes on. Let us behold the fruits of the earth, how the sowing of grain takes place. The sower goes forth, and casts it into the ground; and the seed being thus scattered, though dry and naked when it fell upon the earth, is gradually dissolved. Then out of its dissolution the mighty power of the providence of the Lord raises it up again, and from one seed many arise and bring forth fruit.

Let us also consider the wonderful sign which takes place in Eastern lands, that is, in Arabia and the countries round about. There is a certain bird which is called a phoenix. This is the only one of its kind, and lives five hundred years. And when the time of its death draws near that it must die, it builds itself a nest of frankincense and myrrh and other spices into which, when the time is fulfilled, it enters and dies. But as the flesh decays a certain kind of worm is produced, which, being nourished by the juices of the dead bird, brings forth feathers. Then, when it has acquired strength, it takes up that nest in which are the bones of its parent, and bearing these it passes from the land of Arabia into Egypt, to the city called Heliopolis. And, in open day, flying in the sight of all, it places them on the altar of the sun, and having done this, hastens back to its former abode. The priests then inspect the registers of the dates, and find that it has returned exactly as the five hundredth year was completed.

Do we then deem it any great and wonderful thing for the Maker of all things to raise up again those that have piously served Him in the assurance of a good faith, when even by a bird He shows us the mightiness of His power to fulfill his promise?[4]

It is difficult to imagine the apostle Paul—Jew and convert—using a mythological illustration to speak of the resurrection of Jesus. And yet we can see how, in just one generation, the resurrection has taken a mighty leap from body to spirit—and the greatest triumph of God through Jesus has now to be explained in other ways, as the Jewish connections are being lost and the Greek concepts are becoming more prominent in the church influenced by Greco-Roman thought.

But the tide would turn again—as concepts of Jesus would migrate into other communities and new interpretations of the Christian faith would spring up. Early challenges to the mainstream Christian faith in these first two centuries would include Docetism—the belief that Jesus only appeared to be human, that he was not flesh and blood but purely divine—and also Gnosticism—which included long and winding expressions of faith, some of which had Christian overtones and others not. Although it is difficult, if not impossible, to describe the forms of Gnosticism succinctly, in essence the Gnostic tendencies leaned toward the idea of dualism: the notion that spirit was good and matter (the created world) was evil. Some forms of Gnosticism even saw the body and creation as an illusion—and a person could gain salvation from the created order only by employing secret knowledge (thus gaining access to the spiritual realm of the true God).[5]

What makes the Gnostic conversation so difficult, however, is that while this was certainly a controversy that engulfed much of the early church writings, it was also difficult to pin down, as certain creative expressions of the Christian faith—and new descriptions and tendencies to describe the person and work of Jesus—had already crept into the churches.

Irenaeus, a second-century bishop of Lyon, wrote extensively about these and other controversies—and in fact seemed infatuated with them, if not infuriated and frustrated by them. Having been a young disciple of the former bishop, Polycarp, who was martyred for the faith, Irenaeus filled the vacancy right off and eventually wrote his opus, *Against Heresies*, which described in abundant theological detail the various misinterpretations that Irenaeus believed had crept into the church (or at least threatened it). Irenaeus was one of the first theologians to begin forming a doctrine of the dual nature of Christ—a God-man—who represented the best of both the divine and the human.

While many apologists would later read Irenaeus as support for their own interpretations of Christ, in his day the bishop's writings demonstrate that there was, even by the second century, a diversity of thought about Jesus in and around the church which was not yet unified by any doctrines or creeds. Rather, one might say that the teachings and concepts about Jesus continued to broaden to the point where some ideas were being roundly rejected by some Christians and other ideas, proffered by still other Christian groups, accepted as truth.

This was also true in the interpretation of the life and teachings of Jesus.

Irenaeus himself, who quotes from the earlier Papas (a prominent Christian teacher of the previous generation), also provides some fodder for seeing how the teachings of Jesus, including the parables, had been extrapolated and explained by later generations. Note how the parable of the talents is retold by this early Christian leader:

> The days will come when the vines will grow and each will have ten thousand branches, and on each branch there will be ten thousand shoots, and on each shoot ten thousand clusters, and on each cluster ten thousand grapes, and each grape, when pressed, will yield twenty-five measures of wine. And when any holy one takes hold of one of the clusters, another one will cry out, "I am a better cluster! Take me! Bless the Lord through me!"
>
> In the same way a grain of wheat will bring forth ten thousand ears, and every ear will have ten thousand grains, and every grain will give five quarts of the best flour. And all of the other fruits and seeds and plants will yield by the same proportion, and all animals that use these foods will be at peace and harmony with one another, and in obedient submission to humanity.[6]

Irenaeus, extrapolating Jesus's parable of the talents, makes a bold play for harmony in the church while subtly renouncing those who would propagate their own interpretation of Jesus at the expense of others. This citation also demonstrates how the early church was beginning to use the teachings of Jesus to teach the church of later generations—and shows how the teachings of Jesus, in and of themselves, were regarded as needing a little help, or at the very least, an interpretation. One couldn't just quote Jesus. Rather, great leaders like Irenaeus were expected to expand upon the teachings, to essentially preach from them. Interpretation was born. And with it—new images of Jesus.

Other ideas about Jesus would also show the diversity of the early church.

Clement of Alexandria, a teacher in the second and third centuries who taught in the catechetical school, was a prolific writer. His *Stromata* ("miscellanies") contains hundreds of quotations from the Gospels—but with new wording and "twists" in them—demonstrating how the early church used the teachings of Jesus in a fluid, even organic fashion. For example, note how Clement takes the story of Zacchaeus (found in Luke 19) and provides an aside concerning another tradition related to this episode—namely that Zacchaeus was not the tax collector, but Matthew himself (which, in Clement's mind, may provide a clue as to why this story is not included in Matthew's gospel):

> Then Zacchaeus, a head tax collector (though some say Matthew), when he heard that the Lord was coming to visit him, said, "Lord, I have given half my possessions as alms and if I have taken anything from someone by extortion, I will pay it back quadrupled." Then the Lord said, "The son of man came today and found that which was lost."[7]

Clement also adds a new twist to Jesus's teachings on divorce and marriage (compare with Matthew 5:31–32), here showing how the growing tendency toward male celibacy was impacting church leaders—perhaps because pastors and bishops were desiring to marry. Note how the attribution to Jesus has become a primary method of teaching in Clement's time and culture (northern Egypt).

> Whoever is married should not send away his wife, and whoever is not married should not marry; whoever has determined not to marry because of abstinence should remain unmarried.[8]

It should be noted that Clement of Alexandria lived in one of the largest and most influential cities of his day. The environment of northern Africa was flourishing under the Roman influence (think Antony and Cleopatra). Alexandria was not only home to the largest Jewish population in the world, but also populated by Babylonians, Persians, and philosophies and religions of such variety that this city might be considered the first melting pot. We can scarcely imagine this type of diversity today—and the round-robin philosophical and religious conversations of such a diverse and close-living population—all made possible through the auspices of the Peace of Rome.

Based on the journeys that the apostle Paul notes in his Epistles and as they are recorded in the book of Acts, we know that Paul did not bring Christianity to Alexandria. The arrival and propagation of Christianity in Alexandria is something of a mystery.

However, the book of Acts does note a man named Apollos, who was a native of the city and an early convert. Acts 18:24–27 describes him thus:

> He was an eloquent man, well-versed in the scriptures. He had been instructed in the Way of the Lord; and he spoke with burning enthusiasm and taught accurately the things concerning Jesus, though he knew only the baptism of John. He began to speak boldly in the synagogue [at Ephesus]; but when Priscilla and Aquila heard him, they took him aside and explained the Way of God to him more accurately. And when he wished to cross over to Achaia, the believers encouraged him and wrote to the disciples to welcome him. On his arrival he greatly helped those who through grace had become believers.

Here, from the Bible, we gather a glimpse of an Alexandrian disciple—a mysterious convert who knew only the baptism "of John." How Apollos had made his way to the Judean wilderness is unknown, and when—but the fact that he was "eloquent" and "well-versed" demonstrates his Alexandrian connections and shows that the city was regarded as a place of learning and high culture even in the mid-second century.

Clement, who preceded Origen (his star pupil), was a somewhat mystical teacher—and he prepared candidates for baptism into the Christian faith. Again, we can see how he used Jesus—in fact, gave him a new face and image not completely found in the Gospels—to prepare these candidates. Note how Clement here quotes from the *Gospel of the Egyptians* (a gospel used by the church in Alexandria) and also provides altered teachings of Jesus to instruct the faithful:

> I have come to destroy the works of the female.[9]
>> My mystery is for me and for the children of my house.[10]
>> Blessed are those who are persecuted for my sake, for they will have a place where they will not be persecuted.[11]
>> Blessed are they who are persecuted for righteousness, for they shall be perfect.[12]
>> Blessed are you when others shall hate you, when they shall separate you, when they shall cast out your name as evil, for the Son of Man's sake.[13]

Here we can see how the use of scripture was fluid in those early days—and, in fact, the sacred writings were conversational as well as treasured. There was not yet any doctrine of "inspiration" or "infallibility" as some in the church would describe the scriptures today—but the words of Jesus, in particular, had a robust appeal for various types of instruction and interpretation. Different cultures cherished slightly different scriptures. The four Gospels were mainstays, as were some of the letters of Paul, but beyond that there was an ebb and flow in those early years. Some other writings were used in worship. Others not. And the canon of the times varied from place to place, depending upon the culture and the prevailing winds.

Again, these variations were not always significant. But they are worth noting.

Clement also wrote hymns—as the church was by now developing liturgies and orders of worship. Hymns have always been a rich source of theology, but they also reveal how the church views Jesus of the time. Clement's hymns are no disappointment. This hymn to Christ is one that uses many biblical images but also portrays Jesus through the lenses of one leader's faith, or perhaps a community's understanding. Note the juxtaposition of the royal imagery with the humble shepherd—common metaphors of the time that were reminiscent of the Psalms.

> Bridle of colts untamed, over our will presiding,
> Wing of unwandering birds, our flight securely guiding.
> Rudder of youth unbending, firm against adverse shock.
> Shepherd, with wisdom tending Lambs of the royal flock.
> The simple children bring, in one that they may sing,
> In solemn lays their hymns of praise
> With guiltless lips to Christ their King.
>
> King of saints, almighty Word, of the Father highest Lord,
> Wisdom's head and chief, assuagement of all grief,
> Lord of all time and space, Jesus, Savior of our race.
> Shepherd, who dost us keep, Husbandman, who tillest,
> Bit to restrain us, Rudder, to guide us as thou willest.
> All the holy flock celestial wing, Fisher of Men who thou life dost bring.

By the time of Clement we can see that Jesus was being elevated to the image of the *Pantocrator*—the creator of life. Jesus was no longer just an obscure Jewish rabbi/Messiah but by now was being interpreted through new metaphors and words. Some of these interpretations were accepted as the Jesus for their times. And others were used to counter various pseudo-Christianities or false teachings. Jesus, *as subject*, was used to address a variety of community questions and concerns.

The writings of Clement show how the images of Jesus were, in fact, morphing. As a leader of a school, Clement was instrumental in forming many of these new ideas about Jesus.

But there was a greater teacher yet. Origen, the star pupil of the great teacher Clement of Alexandria (150–216), developed a new allegorical approach to scripture. Origen had been trained in the classical Greek way as a child and was reared by a devout Christian mother after his father was martyred for his faith. As Origen grew older and experienced the first pangs of struggle in the faith, he took a literal approach to Jesus's instructions, "If your hand offends you, cut it off," and, after wrestling with his own sexual desires, castrated himself.

But Origen's study methods were rigorous, and as he studied and fasted, he also developed a unique style of prayer and devotional life as a meditation on scripture. He also began to speak of levels of interpretation of scripture—from literal, to historical, to allegorical—with the former literal approach being regarded for "simple believers of simple mind."[14]

Origen's allegorical approach to the whole of the Bible—even the life and teachings of Jesus—was a form he borrowed from Greek literary theory, where a piece of writing would say one thing but speak on another level of a deeper truth. One of the reasons for Origen's allegorical interpretation of Jesus was that he believed the literal interpretation was open to attack from those who could easily point out the discrepancies within the Gospels or even the theological differences that one could note when certain of Paul's teachings are compared to the teachings of Jesus. As Origen's Bible study and devotional methods caught on, this method of interpreting Jesus also gained momentum. Origen created a new form of study—and, one might say, another type of Jesus.

Although Origen had as many critics as adherents, his path to teaching and preaching was not an easy one. At one point, after having left Alexandria as the head of the school there, Origen traveled to Caesarea, where he established yet another school and also began preaching. Later, after his ordination as an elder, he was exiled by the bishop of

Alexandria and not allowed to return. Soon after, Origen did follow in his father's path and became a martyr himself. But one thing is for certain about this prominent teacher and his approach to Jesus: the new images and ideas he produced through his allegorical method brought still more images of Jesus to the mix of the early church.

But Origen also gives us glimpses into the manner in which those outside the Christian faith were impacted by the words of Jesus. We can see that even in these early years, Jesus had taken on a larger persona and had become part of culture. In our time, we might use the term "pop culture" to describe this phenomenon—as Jesus was no longer an obscure Jewish prophet but had entered into the popular mix of cultural and religious debate . . . even among those outside the church who had something to say about this Christian philosophy and way of life. Basically, Jesus was now becoming known by those outside the church or by others who had at least heard of him, and they had their opinions about Jesus, too.

In one treatise, Origen wrote a counterargument against a man named Celsus—a pagan critic of the faith who had written to Origen claiming that he had heard people in Phoenicia and Palestine using Jesus's teachings to claim a divine status for themselves. This is an astounding turn, really, as Celsus's criticisms of the Christian proclamation—and Jesus himself—do provide one of the earliest glimpses of the counterclaims about Jesus and show how the teachings of Jesus provided fodder for all manner of interpreters. Celsus writes:

> [Some are heard saying] I am a Son of God. And I have come. Already the world is being destroyed. And you will perish because of your sins. But I wish to save you. And you shall see me returning with heavenly power. Blessed is he who worships me now! And I will cast everlasting fire upon the rest. But I will preserve forever those who have been convinced of me![15]

Origen's prolific writings become all the more important for historians, especially in attempting to understand how those in the second and third centuries interpreted scripture or used the Gospels. This would especially hold true for the development of Christology. Origen's commentaries on the Gospels are some of the earliest—and certainly the most detailed—from this period (or from any period, for that matter). His commentary on the Gospel of John, in fact, may be the first

true Gospel commentary of any value, especially as a detailed and sys-
tematic attempt to comment on the Gospel verse by verse. Origen's
volumes on John and Matthew are revealing—and they show a theologian's reason as well as his heart.

Origen's commentaries also establish that by the early second century, the four Gospels were firmly established as formative to the church
and were esteemed, even, as being of superior value to the Acts of the
Apostles and Paul's Epistles, which were also read widely in the worshipping communities. Origen noted that Paul did not seem to regard
his own letters as on the same par as the Gospels, as Paul includes
phrases in his Epistles such as "*I say*, and not the Lord" or "So *I ordain*
in all the churches" or "What things *I suffered* in Antioch."[16]

So Origen's writing also shows that the early church did not necessarily regard all Christian writings as equal or on the same par. There
was a type of hierarchy of scripture, with highest value being placed
upon the Gospels and lesser value upon the letters of Paul, for example.
This valuation, then, was much like that of the Hebrew Bible, where
Torah took a more prominent and important place over the Prophets
and the Writings (the other two "portions" of the Hebrew Bible following the books of Moses). In subsequent generations—and certainly in
the modern church—this hierarchy of New Testament scripture cannot
be found, as Christians generally regard all of the New Testament writings as being of equal authority. But through the first four centuries of
the church, these equal levels of authority and inspiration did not seem
to be in tow.

Rather, this early valuation of Christian scriptures has all but been
lost in the church today—and the whole of the New Testament lumped
together in terms of "inspiration" or "importance." But again, it was not
so in the early centuries of the church, as teachers such as Clement and
Origen demonstrate.

Various teachers also had their favorites—and played favorites.

When Origen notes the Gospels, he expresses his favor for the
fourth Gospel—indeed a favorite during this period because of its util-
ity for expressing Jesus in allegorical or spiritual terms.

> The gospels then, being four, I deem the first fruits of the gospel [to
> be] John. For Matthew, writing for the Hebrews who looked for Him
> who was to come in the line of Abraham and David . . . and Mark,
> knowing what he writes, narrates the beginning of the Gospel; but

Luke, though he says at the beginning of Acts, "The former treatise did I make about all that Jesus began to do and to teach," yet leaves to him who lay on Jesus' breast the greatest and most complete discourse about Jesus. For none of these [other three Gospels] makes Him say, "I am the light of the world," "I am the way the truth and the life," "I am the resurrection," "I am the door," "I am the Good Shepherd," and in the Apocalypse, "I am the Alpha and Omega, the beginning and the end, the first and the last." [17]

Origen's commentary on John then proceeds along the lines of interpreting Jesus on several "levels"—beginning with what Origen calls the somatic (or fleshy) and proceeding toward the deeper levels, or the spiritual. Throughout these commentaries we gain a sense of how the teachers in the early church used the Gospels to interpret the persona and work of Jesus—and we dare not forget that Origen was leading a school of thought, first at Alexandria and later in Caesarea. These methods and interpretations that he taught became, in many ways, the widely accepted practice.

But with an ever-widening circle of both disciples and critics, the ideas proffered about Jesus were becoming wildly divergent. As the church grew in different cultures and other tongues, new forms of the faith—such as worship style, prayer style, and scriptures used in worship—also diversified considerably.

One Christian community in Egypt, certainly one of the earliest and longest-enduring expressions of the church (Coptic), was particularly enamored of a gospel entitled *The Gospel of the Hebrews*. Both Jerome and Origen note this gospel as having been prominent in their time among the Egyptian Christians—but it was a book that did not win broad favor in the church, in large part because of its unusual doctrine of the Holy Spirit. Here in *The Gospel of the Hebrews* the Spirit, named Michael, comes from God to impart power to Christ and Mary.

When Christ wished to come upon the earth to men, the Good Father summoned a mighty power in heaven, which was called Michael, and entrusted Christ to his care. And the power came into the world and it was called Mary, and Christ was in her womb seven months. [18]

But Jerome notes another version of *The Gospel of the Hebrews* and a much different doctrine when he quotes from its passage regarding the baptism of Jesus:

> And it happened when the Lord was come out of the water the whole fount of the Holy Spirit descended upon him and rested upon him and said, "My son, in all the prophets I am waiting for you that you might come and I might rest in you. For you are my rest; you are first-begotten Son who reigns forever. [19]

What we can make of these varied ideas about Jesus and his relationship with God is that the church—pre-Nicaea—had many expressions for the same Jesus. The reasons for this, of course, are debated—but passage of time and diversity of culture were certainly factors. The further Christianity developed apart from its Jewish origins, the broader the sweeps into Greek philosophy and varied interpretation.

But this was not simply a Gnostic or heretical practice. The church, too, was using the words of Jesus to create new images and instructions. The teachings of Jesus began to take on a layered meaning, with some words being added or others subtracted, in order to place emphasis on the prevailing needs of the time—and thus preserve some truth for the church. Nearly all of the church fathers took this approach—and when they are quoting Jesus we can see how Christ's teachings were extrapolated and expanded to meet the latest challenge of the day.

From this time were also written other gospels that—although not accepted by the early church—do show how others chose to express Jesus or counter with a theology of their own, including Docetism, the idea that Jesus only "appeared" to be a human being, the notion that Christ was, in actuality, a spiritual being who came to release people from the bondage of human flesh.

One such early Docetic gospel was *The Gospel according to Peter*. Both Origen (around 253) and Eusebius note the existence of this gospel in certain circles. The gospel, however, did not have wide notoriety or appreciation, as the Passion narrative in particular offered the following additions to the scene of the Crucifixion:

- "But Jesus held his peace [on the cross] as though having no pain."
- "Jesus cried from the cross, 'My power! My power!'"

- "[Jesus was taken up to heaven] and a voice came from heaven saying, 'Thou has preached to them that sleep.'"[20]

Gospels such as these—and other writings—offered both a challenge to early Christianity and a forum for deepening a theology of Jesus, though this early Christology was by no means consistent or uniform. Although Docetism was one such early theology that the church countered, there were others that had broader appeal—especially Gnosticism.

The writings associated with this form of spirituality—some of them in more prominent Christian expression—is now widely affirmed and noted. Jesus was becoming many things to many people.

But for this exploration of Jesus we turn now to a deeper understanding of Gnosticism and the plethora of scriptures associated with these various expressions.

GNOSTICISM AND THE ONE FAITH

Elaine Pagels, in her quintessential book on Gnosticism, *The Gnostic Gospels*, completes her exploration of these developments and early Christianity with a series of observations. On the one hand, she notes that it is always the "winners" who write history—and thus this becomes the history we know and believe.

But on the other hand, she points out that Christianity may not have survived if it had become a hodge-podge of varying beliefs or traditions—just a philosophical amalgam. Rather, the fact that Christianity not only survived but thrived in the midst of such religious and social diversity and resistance is a testimony to "the organizational and theological structure that the emerging church developed."[21]

She also notes that one early theologian by the name of Tertullian discovered that "heretics and philosophers," no less than brilliant Christian theologians themselves, were essentially asking the same set of questions—questions such as: *Where did humanity come from and how? What is the origin of evil?* Tertullian believed that the church had succeeded and gained power and momentum because the church provided superior truths or answers to these questions. Gnosticism then, as a moral and religious force, simply couldn't win the day against the truth.

Tertullian was onto something . . . but for some centuries the various Gnostic expressions may have been equally forceful, and they certainly provided some crossover between Christianity and the growing tendencies to compile tenets for an orthodox faith. The discovery of the Nag Hammadi library—a vast collection of Coptic gospels, letters, prayers, and apocalyptic literature—is now well documented. But the significance of these works is still being written about and dissected from a number of vantage points—including their impact on Christianity.

While this Nag Hammadi library is far too vast to comment on for our purposes, one gospel in particular has shown a remarkable ability to stand alongside the four Gospels of the New Testament and was even included in the Jesus Seminar's opus, *Five Gospels*. In this work, scholars compared the four New Testament Gospels among themselves but also added the *Gospel of Thomas* to the mix—the one gospel of the Nag Hammadi library that is most similar in style and structure to the synoptics and John. [22]

Indeed, *The Gospel of Thomas* is a remarkable work (and should not be confused with an infancy gospel bearing the same name). This gospel, which does not have the ultra-Gnostic overtones of the other works in this library, at first blush reads very much like one of the synoptic Gospels—especially Matthew or Luke—and comprises 114 "sayings." The gospel has no narrative per se but reads much like a collection of the sayings that many scholars assume existed in a "Q" (*Quelle*) document that Gospel writers used to compose portions of their Gospels. (Remember: Luke says he is using other sources, and the ending of the Gospel of John also alludes to other books and untold stories.)

Many sayings found in the synoptic Gospels are also found in *The Gospel of Thomas*, or slightly different variations. But there are also sayings unique to *Thomas* which many scholars would attribute to the historical Jesus, including: "Jesus said, 'Become passers-by.'"

Or: "Jesus said, 'The kingdom of the father is like a certain woman who was carrying a jar full of meal. While she was walking on the road, still some distance from home, the handle of the jar broke and the meal emptied out behind her on the road. She did not realize it. When she reached her house, she set the jar down and found it empty.'"

Or: "Jesus said, 'He who will drink from my mouth will become like me. I myself shall become he, and the things that are hidden will be revealed to him.'"[23]

As Elaine Pagels and others have pointed out, even within Gnosticism there was a diversity of thought—with certain schools of thought seeing themselves as Christian in belief and principle, and other communities more heavily weighted toward the mystical, dualistic beliefs that were part and parcel of the heretical teachings that the early Christian theologians countered in so many treatises and letters. *The Gospel of Thomas* seems to fall outside the pure Gnostic thought and is heavily centered, if not wholly dependent, upon preserving the teachings of Jesus. In fact, this gospel contains the longest single collection of Jesus sayings that we find anywhere and, as stated previously, has many verbatim or near-verbatim sayings found in Matthew and Luke.

Standing on its own, *The Gospel of Thomas* is the single longest (and wholly dedicated) collection of Jesus's sayings/teachings that exists. Even if one doesn't attribute these sayings directly to the historical Jesus, *The Gospel of Thomas* does provide a glimpse into the manner in which Jesus material—and images of Jesus—was used in a worshipping community in northern Egypt. Jesus was clearly at the center of this community, and his name was used as a source of teaching and hope. And the fact that *The Gospel of Thomas* also contains so much material found in Matthew, Mark, and Luke is evidence that this community had, at the very least, certain Christian beliefs in the mix—or knew of these gospels. The teachings of Jesus that formed this community were not just found in the synoptic Gospels but in this fifth gospel as well.

Regardless of how one studies Gnosticism today, it remains apparent that this system of belief(s) had an impact on the church—especially as it pertained to what the early church said about Jesus and the images and teachings used to describe him. Even as an outward force, Gnosticism impacted what was written about Jesus—so nothing is lost either from the perspective of the church (as it became) or the church (as it countered other philosophies).

Gnosticism was, however, only one of several forces that shaped the church as it grew into the fourth century.

FROM MANY VOICES TO ONE

We also know that Jesus had many faces in those early years because of what came later. There were other Jesuses before there was the One Jesus.

Early in the fourth century CE, around the year 320, a controversy about Jesus had engulfed the church east and west. Those embroiled in this controversy—namely learned men from across the newly formed Christian empire headed now by Constantine—all believed that they were representing Jesus, proclaiming the Gospel through their teachings about him. By now the books of the New Testament were nearly universally accepted—though not officially canonized until later—and with three hundred years of theology under the belt, the beliefs about Jesus had become diverse and resilient, with various communities in their respective parts of the church holding out for certain concepts and images, while others parted ways for other philosophical differences and beliefs about him.

But broadly speaking, the two camps that developed were represented by Arius—a Christian elder in Alexandria—and Athanasius, an assistant to the bishop who took up the charge of arguing on behalf of the other view. While Arius and Athanasius certainly agreed on many things about Jesus—that Christ had saved them from sin and death, that he was life, and that Jesus shared an existence with God in some fashion—they differed on the latter point over the "how" of the relationship between Jesus (the Son) and the Creator (the Father).

Arius, using many scriptural references to support his view, believed that Christ was a creation, a person like ourselves, who had been elevated to the status of Son of God via his faithfulness and sinlessness. Arius represented literally millions of people who shared his same view across the church. Arius stressed that Jesus was humble, weak, and vulnerable. But he also emphasized that God had created all things through the Logos (the prelude to John's Gospel)—meaning that God had also created Christ, his Son, and that one day Christ would give the creation back to the Father, and God would be all in all (see 1 Corinthians 15:20–26 as one such text). Arius in no way saw his view as a denigration of Christ but as an exaltation, as Jesus had been exalted above all names through his faithfulness, even to the point of death, and raised to victory over sin and death, ensuring our salvation as human beings.

On the other hand, Athanasius—who again represented millions of people in the same church—blazed a different theological trail. He did not share Arius's seemingly optimistic view of humanity. No sinful creature, no person, he argued, could overcome sin and death and be exalted to divine Sonship. Rather, Athanasius argued that Creator and Redeemer were one and the same—though different persons—within the same Godhead. Creator and Redeemer were of the same substance (Greek: *ousia*), and though Jesus was begotten, he was not created. Using scripture and Greek philosophical terms, Athanasius made an argument in Nicaea in 325 that sought to resolve this simmering debate in the church, and, with all bishops present and under orders of the emperor Constantine, bring about a theological cohesion in the church and empire. The result was the Nicaean Creed—an attempt to unify the church in its expression, principally regarding the person and work of Jesus. But there had already been developing splits in the church— some theological, others in practice—which would eventually lead to an East/West break.

This history of the creeds is beyond the scope of this book.

But there was one early theological divide that centered on a single word in the creed. This *ousia* debate was in essence a debate about the image of Jesus and was at the heart of the controversy, namely: Could various ideas about Jesus be accepted within the one church? Would various interpretations of scripture be tolerated? Could the church endure, and even expand, if Christological diversity was affirmed? These were the questions at the heart of the debate . . . and Nicaea and the councils that followed essentially answered "no" to these questions.

The bulk of the creed, now recited by hundreds of millions of Christians (even billions through history), is predominantly focused on Jesus and these early theological debates about who he is and how the church is to see him. This became orthodoxy for both East and West churches (with variables). Although the first four centuries had a diversity of thought regarding Jesus, the creed represented the one view of Jesus that could be taught. Precision was important—and one couldn't dance around Christology any longer by using allegory, symbolism, metaphor, or inexactitude.

As such, the creed (or the one below produced by the Council of Constantinople nearly fifty years later) represents the one expression of

Jesus that Western Christians (Catholics and most Protestants) have
used since the fourth century.

> We believe in one God,
> the Father, the Almighty,
> maker of heaven and earth,
> of all that is, seen and unseen.
> We believe in one Lord, Jesus Christ,
> the only Son of God,
> eternally begotten of the Father,
> God from God, Light from Light,
> true God from true God,
> begotten, not made,
> of one Being (ousia) with the Father.
> Through him all things were made.
> For us and for our salvation
> he came down from heaven:
> by the power of the Holy Spirit
> he became incarnate from the Virgin Mary,
> and was made man.
> For our sake he was crucified under Pontius Pilate;
> he suffered death and was buried.
> On the third day he rose again
> in accordance with the Scriptures;
> he ascended into heaven
> and is seated at the right hand of the Father.
> He will come again in glory to judge the living and the dead,
> and his kingdom will have no end.
> We believe in the Holy Spirit, the Lord, the giver of life,
> who proceeds from the Father and the Son.
> With the Father and the Son he is worshiped and glorified.
> He has spoken through the Prophets.
> We believe in one holy catholic and apostolic Church.
> We acknowledge one baptism for the forgiveness of sins.
> We look for the resurrection of the dead,
> and the life of the world to come. Amen.

The creed, however, at its inception, was difficult to sell . . . and even
more difficult to enforce throughout the church—which had by now
grown to immense and bureaucratic proportions from its humble beginnings as a tiny Jewish sect. Although Athanasius seemed to win the day
in Nicaea, Arius eventually gained imperial favor, and Athanasius was

exiled at least five times over the course of his life. But fifty years after the creed was produced, those in the church who would not affirm these particular beliefs about Jesus could be excommunicated—or worse.

That the creed was difficult to infuse into the majority of churches is testimony to the diversity that existed in those early days. There were, in fact, many ideas about Jesus that were at play—some that were not represented by either Arius or Athanasius. After Nicaea, the church began to lose this diversity of thought as power was centralized, and the creed eventually took hold as the true interpretation of all things biblical and theological.

Though the church divided in starts and stops over a variety of issues (East vs. West)—with one theologian noting that the split was over a Greek diphthong at that—the debates leading up to the formation of the official beliefs about Jesus certainly reveal that prior to the ecumenical councils there was a much wider array of beliefs about Jesus—and expressions of faith in him. To be sure, many of these images of Jesus were built upon esoteric extrapolations of distant communities intent on making their own forms of faith—but others were more clearly centered on what would become the creedal faith in Jesus but had to be rejected by rule once faith was welded to political power. One had to express faith in Jesus via formula, with only certain words and expressions being tolerated. As the creed took hold, only those willing to express Jesus in strict creedal wording would be accepted. Any slight deviation, any other ideas about Jesus or expressions of him, were regarded as anathema.

As with the formation of the creed, alternative images of Jesus—and ways of expressing the faith—were also codified via the selection of the New Testament canon. Prior to the canonization, there were several other books that were used by hundreds of churches—and were well known and beloved. As noted earlier, the epistle of Clement was one such book that was highly regarded. Clement, probably written toward the end of the first century, was a widely distributed letter that continued on the apostle Paul's themes within the Corinthian church.

Other early books most certainly included *The Gospel of Thomas* (or some form of it based upon the teachings of Jesus), *The Gospel of the Hebrews* (of which no manuscripts exist but which is a gospel noted in the writings of no fewer than seven of the church fathers),[24] other sayings collections, a miracle collection, *The Gospel of the Egyptians* (again noted only in patristic writings), the *Didache* (which we shall review in chapter 3), and *The Shepherd of Hermas*.

This latter book—the *Shepherd*—is noteworthy because it was a most unique book among those used in the early churches. Possessing an apocalyptic vision, this book offered a moralistic view of the faith set among a series of allegorical parables. But books like the *Shepherd* did not fare well amid the Trinitarian controversies of the councils, as they possessed little Christology and did not have an apostolic tradition attached to them.

The councils were looking to establish a faith that could be expressed consistently in theology and practice. Diversity was not valued nearly as much as form and function and unity.

The councils also established the New Testament canon as we know it today—and with it, the accompanying ideas about Jesus that form our concepts of his life and teachings. Many books (now included in the canon) were marginal, including Revelation, James, and 2 Peter. These were included—but with much discussion. Other books, such as *The Shepherd of Hermas*, were rejected, though the *Shepherd* was widely used in the church in earlier times. Although this latter book was used throughout the church and known by many prominent church leaders such as Irenaeus—it was likely rejected by the councils because of its strong Arian-like tendencies toward "adoptionist" theology. Nevertheless, it did exist, and it did occupy a central place in the pantheon of scriptures before the fourth century, and in certain communities it played a much stronger role than either Revelation or 2 Peter.

Looking more deeply at *The Shepherd of Hermas*, we can see where the appeal lay. It is a metaphorical book, layered with meaning, and would have had a broad appeal for those who enjoyed the allegorical methods of Clement of Alexandria and Origen. It also brings a unique image of Jesus to the mix—provided one can get beneath the layers.

The Shepherd of Hermas is a series of parables, devotional in nature, offered up by a disciple, a shepherd who speaks of Jesus in broad and poetic terms—much as the Song of Songs of the Hebrew Bible has been interpreted as a love song between God and his people. But the fifth parable, in particular, offers an image of Jesus not found in other early scriptures and gives indication that the poetic expressions of Jesus were much more pronounced during these earlier centuries.

As I was fasting and seated on a certain mountain, and giving thanks to the Lord for all that He had done unto me, I see the shepherd seated by me and saying; "Why hast thou come hither in the early morn?" "Because, Sir," say I, "I am keeping a station."

"What," saith he, "is a station?" "I am fasting, Sir," say I. "And what," saith he, "is this fast [that ye are fasting]?" "As I was accustomed, Sir," say I, "so I fast."

"Ye know not," saith he, "how to fast unto the Lord, neither is this a fast, this unprofitable fast which ye make unto Him." "Wherefore, Sir," say I, "sayest thou this?" "I tell thee," saith he, "that this is not a fast, wherein ye think to fast; but I will teach thee what is a complete fast and acceptable to the Lord. Listen," saith he;

"God desireth not such a vain fast; for by so fasting unto God thou shalt do nothing for righteousness. But fast thou [unto God] such a fast as this: do no wickedness in thy life, and serve the Lord with a pure heart; observe His commandments and walk in His ordinances, and let no evil desire rise up in thy heart; but believe God. Then, if thou shalt do these things, and fear Him, and control thyself from every evil deed, thou shalt live unto God; and if thou do these things, thou shalt accomplish a great fast, and one acceptable to God.

"Hear the parable which I shall tell thee relating to fasting.

A certain man had an estate, and many slaves, and a portion of his estate he planted as a vineyard; and choosing out a certain slave who was trusty and well-pleasing (and) held in honor, he called him to him and saith unto him; "Take this vineyard [which I have planted], and fence it [till I come], but do nothing else to the vineyard. Now keep this my commandment, and thou shalt be free in my house." Then the master of the servant went away to travel abroad.

When then he had gone away, the servant took and fenced the vineyard; and having finished the fencing of the vineyard, he noticed that the vineyard was full of weeds.

So he reasoned within himself, saying, "This command of my lord I have carried out I will next dig this vineyard, and it shall be neater when it is digged; and when it hath no weeds it will yield more fruit, because not choked by the weeds." He took and digged the vineyard, and all the weeds that were in the vineyard he plucked up. And that vineyard became very neat and flourishing, when it had no weeds to choke it.

After a time the master of the servant [and of the estate] came, and he went into the vineyard. And seeing the vineyard fenced neat-ly, and digged as well, and [all] the weeds plucked up, and the vines flourishing, he rejoiced [exceedingly] at what his servant had done.

So he called his beloved son, who was his heir, and the friends who were his advisers, and told them what he had commanded his servant, and how much he had found done. And they rejoiced with the servant at the testimony which his master had borne to him.

And he saith to them; "I promised this servant his freedom, if he should keep the commandment which I commanded him; but he kept my commandment and did a good work besides to my vineyard, and pleased me greatly. For this work therefore which he has done, I desire to make him joint-heir with my son, because, when the good thought struck him, he did not neglect it, but fulfilled it."

In this purpose the son of the master agreed with him, that the servant should be made joint-heir with the son.

After some few days, his master made a feast, and sent to him many dainties from the feast. But when the servant received [the dainties sent to him by the master], he took what was sufficient for him, and distributed the rest to his fellow servants.

And his fellow-servants, when they received the dainties, rejoiced, and began to pray for him, that he might find greater favor with the master, because he had treated them so handsomely.

All these things which had taken place his master heard, and again rejoiced greatly at his deed. So the master called together again his friends and his son, and announced to them the deed that he had done with regard to his dainties which he had received; and they still more approved of his resolve, that his servant should be made joint-heir with his son."

I say, "Sir, I understand not these parables, neither can I apprehend them, unless thou explain them for me."

"I will explain everything to thee," saith he; "and will show thee whatsoever things I shall speak with thee. Keep the commandments of the Lord, and thou shalt be well-pleasing to God, and shalt be enrolled among the number of them that keep His commandments.

But if thou do any good thing outside the commandment of God, thou shalt win for thyself more exceeding glory, and shalt be more glorious in the sight of God than thou wouldest otherwise have been. If then, while thou keepest the commandments of God, thou add these services likewise, thou shalt rejoice, if thou observe them according to my commandment."

I say to him, "Sir, whatsoever thou commandest me, I will keep it; for I know that thou art with me." "I will be with thee," saith he, "because thou hast so great zeal for doing good; yea, and I will be with all," saith he, "whosoever have such zeal as this.

This fasting," saith he, "if the commandments of the Lord are kept, is very good. This then is the way, that thou shalt keep this fast which thou art about to observe].

First of all, keep thyself from every evil word and every evil desire, and purify thy heart from all the vanities of this world. If thou keep these things, this fast shall be perfect for thee.

And thus shalt thou do. Having fulfilled what is written, on that day on which thou fastest thou shalt taste nothing but bread and water; and from thy meats, which thou wouldest have eaten, thou shalt reckon up the amount of that day's expenditure, which thou wouldest have incurred, and shalt give it to a widow, or an orphan, or to one in want, and so shalt thou humble thy soul, that he that hath received from thy humiliation may satisfy his own soul, and may pray for thee to the Lord.

If then thou shalt so accomplish this fast, as I have commanded thee, thy sacrifice shall be acceptable in the sight of God, and this fasting shall be recorded; and the service so performed is beautiful and joyous and acceptable to the Lord.

These things thou shalt so observe, thou and thy children and thy whole household; and, observing them, thou shalt be blessed; yea, and all those, who shall hear and observe them, shall be blessed, and whatsoever things they shall ask of the Lord, they shall receive."

I entreated him earnestly, that he would show me the parable of the estate, and of the master, and of the vineyard, and of the servant that fenced the vineyard, [and of the fence,] and of the weeds which were plucked up out of the vineyard, and of the son, and of the friends, the advisers. For I understood that all these things are a parable.

But he answered and said unto me; "Thou art exceedingly importunate in enquiries. Thou oughtest not," [saith he,] "to make any enquiry at all; for if it be right that a thing be explained unto thee, it shall be explained." I say to him; "Sir, whatsoever things thou showest unto me and dost not explain, I shall have seen them in vain, and without understanding what they are. In like manner also, if thou speak parables to me and interpret them not, I shall have heard a thing in vain from thee."

But he again answered, and said unto me; "Whosoever," saith he, "is a servant of God, and hath his own Lord in his heart, asketh understanding of Him, and receiveth it, and interpreteth every parable, and the words of the Lord which are spoken in parables are made known unto him. But as many as are sluggish and idle in intercession, these hesitate to ask of the Lord.

But the Lord is abundant in compassion, and giveth to them that ask of Him without ceasing. But thou who hast been strengthened by the holy angel, and hast received from him such (powers of intercession and art not idle, wherefore dost thou not ask understanding of the Lord, and obtain it from Him)."

I say to him, "Sir, I that have thee with me have (but) need to ask thee and enquire of thee; for thou showest me all things, and speakest with me; but if I had seen or heard them apart from thee I should have asked of the Lord, that they might be shown to me."

"I told thee just now," saith he, "that thou art unscrupulous and importunate, in enquiring for the interpretations of the parables. But since thou art so obstinate, I will interpret to thee the parable of the estate and all the accompaniments thereof, that thou mayest make them known unto all. Hear now," saith he, "and understand them.

The estate is this world, and the lord of the estate is He that created all things, and set them in order, and endowed them with power; and the servant is the Son of God, and the vines are this people whom He Himself planted; and the fences are the [holy] angels of the Lord who keep together His people; and the weeds, which are plucked up from the vineyard, are the transgressions of the servants of God; and the dainties which He sent to him from the feast are the commandments which He gave to His people through His Son; and the friends and advisers are the holy angels which were first created; and the absence of the master is the time which remaineth over until His coming."

I say to him; "Sir, great and marvelous are all things and all things are glorious; was it likely then," say I, "that I could have apprehended them?" "Nay, nor can any other man, though he be full of understanding, apprehend them." "Yet again, Sir," say I, "explain to me what I am about to enquire of thee."

"Say on," he saith, "if thou desirest anything." "Wherefore, Sir," say I, "is the Son of God represented in the parable in the guise of a servant?"

"Listen," said he; "the Son of God is not represented in the guise of a servant, but is represented in great power and lordship." "How, Sir?" say I; "I comprehend not."

"Because," saith he, "God planted the vineyard, that is, He created the people, and delivered them over to His Son. And the Son placed the angels in charge of them, to watch over them; and the Son Himself cleansed their sins, by laboring much and enduring many toils; for no one can dig without toil or labor.

Having Himself then cleansed the sins of His people, He showed them the paths of life, giving them the law which He received from His Father. Thou seest," saith he, "that He is Himself Lord of the people, having received all power from His Father.

But how that the lord took his son and the glorious angels as advisers concerning the inheritance of the servant, listen.

The Holy Pre-existent Spirit. Which created the whole creation, God made to dwell in flesh that He desired. This flesh, therefore, in which the Holy Spirit dwelt, was subject unto the Spirit, walking honorably in holiness and purity, without in any way defiling the Spirit.

When then it had lived honorably in chastity, and had labored with the Spirit, and had cooperated with it in everything, behaving itself boldly and bravely, He chose it as a partner with the Holy Spirit; for the career of this flesh pleased [the Lord], seeing that, as possessing the Holy Spirit, it was not defiled upon the earth.

He therefore took the son as adviser and the glorious angels also, that this flesh too, having served the Spirit unblamably, might have some place of sojourn, and might not seem to have lost the reward for its service; for all flesh, which is found undefiled and unspotted, wherein the Holy Spirit dwelt, shall receive a reward.

Now thou hast the interpretation of this parable also."

"I was right glad, Sir," say I, "to hear this interpretation." "Listen now," saith he, "Keep this thy flesh pure and undefiled, that the Spirit which dwelleth in it may bear witness to it, and thy flesh may be justified.

See that it never enter into thine heart that this flesh of thine is perishable, and so thou abuse it in some defilement. [For] if thou defile thy flesh, thou shalt defile the Holy Spirit also; but if thou defile the flesh, thou shalt not live."

"But if, Sir," say I, "there has been any ignorance in times past, before these words were heard, how shall a man who has defiled his flesh be saved?" "For the former deeds of ignorance," saith he, "God alone hath power to give healing; for all authority is His.

[But now keep thyself, and the Lord Almighty, Who is full of compassion, will give healing for thy former deeds of ignorance,] if henceforth thou defile not thy flesh, neither the Spirit; for both share

in common, and the one cannot be defiled without the other. Therefore keep both pure, and thou shalt live unto God."[25]

This particular parable from *The Shepherd of Hermas* is abundant with
imagery from the gospels—particularly taken with the image of Jesus as
the Good Shepherd and teller of parables. This passage is full of references to the prophets and their injunctions to be a pure people and care
for the widow and orphan, as well as references from many parables of
Jesus found in the Gospels. That *Hermas* was used so widely in the early
church is no surprise—but it ultimately didn't win favor in the canon
because of its dualist tendencies regarding spirit and creation, its limited appeal among the bishops, and even its somewhat odd-man-out approach to speaking of Jesus.

Although *The Shepherd of Hermas* is but one example of other
books that narrowly missed inclusion into the canon (yes, *1 Clement* was
also considered) the formation of the New Testament was actually
something of a winnowing process. By the fourth century certain books
were no doubt established as holy scriptures, including the four Gospels
as we now have them, the Acts of the Apostles, and most of the Epistles
of Paul. But again, some of the debated books included James and
Hebrews, 2 Peter, and even Revelation.

Regardless, the formation of the canon and the acceptance of the
creed solidified the image of Jesus, too—as other images, teachings,
nuances, and voices were cast aside for those scriptures and creedal
expressions which would become formative for all Christians in the
centuries ahead. Or perhaps, as Elaine Pagels has suggested, Christianity could not have survived with such diversity—and having a centralized and politicized scripture and creed was what saved the faith from
obscurity.

But to get at these other conversations about Jesus—and the ways
that others saw him—we may have to backtrack a bit and consider how
Judaism itself, which birthed the Messiah, also countered the Messianic
image and proclamation of this small but influential sect.

2

THE JEWISH JESUS

Yeshuah and the Rabbis

Bless them that curse you. —Jesus, Matthew 5:44

Be rather of the accursed than of those who curse. —Rabbi Yehudah, Talmud, Sanhedrin 98

Throughout the canonical Gospels there are references to the tensions between Jesus and the Jewish leaders. In the Gospels we see that as Jesus, a peasant Jew from an obscure village (Nazareth) in Galilee, interacts with the religious authorities, he quickly encounters resistance to his methods and message. Certainly the Gospels—written through the lenses of a post-Easter faith—preserve these tensions for a number of reasons.

Principal among them would be the Jewish backlash against this new sect—a group that was proclaiming that not only did Jesus have a special relationship with God, but he was also raised from the dead following his brutal crucifixion at the hands of Roman authorities, a form of death that was considered by the Jewish leaders to be a curse and a certain sign of God's disfavor. This same Jesus was also being proclaimed as Messiah. So when we read the Gospels, and particularly the Gospels of Matthew and John, we are also reading commentary on the tensions that had developed between traditional Judaism and the new Jewish community that believed in Jesus as Messiah and savior.

In time, the Jesus followers would be identified—and would, in fact, identify themselves—in the nomenclature of *Christian* rather than *Jew*. But it was not so in first-century Judea, and much of the dichotomy between the two faiths did not pull to the extremes until Gentile converts began to be included in the movement. Paul's letters, especially his letter to the churches of Galatia and his early correspondences with the Corinthian church, indicate at many points these growing tensions. Paul addresses these difficulties time and again:

- We ourselves are Jews by birth and not Gentile sinners; yet we know that a person is justified not by works of the [Jewish] law but through faith in Jesus Christ. (Galatians 2:15–16)
- For all who rely upon the works of the [Jewish] law are under a curse. (Galatians 3:10)
- Christ redeemed us from the curse of the law. (Galatians 3:13)
- Tell me, you who desire to be subject to the law, will you not listen to the law? (Galatians 4:21)
- Listen! I, Paul, am telling you that if you let yourselves be circumcised, Christ will be of no benefit to you. (Galatians 5:2)
- For Jews demand signs and Greeks desire wisdom, but we proclaim Christ crucified, a stumbling block to Jews and foolishness to Gentiles. (1 Corinthians 1:22–23)

Paul's many references to Judaism and the law, however, are argumentative and theological rather than anti-Jewish, for Paul himself makes much of his training as a Pharisee and the zeal he has for the Mosaic law. Christians reading Paul's letters today can miss this point. These are not Christian writings, after all, but Jewish letters written in the style of rabbinic argument—and Paul, in most of his Epistles, is making his case for recognizing Jesus as the Messiah and for opening the covenant wide for the inclusion of the Gentiles.

But the Gospels, which were written later than Paul's letters, reflect to a greater degree these mounting tensions between Jew and Christ believer—both historical and theological—and indicate that there was a fair amount of name calling and one-upmanship in these early years when both ideologies were attempting to live side by side under Roman rule. Likewise, the first century (and early second century) also paralleled the writing of the New Testament canon (both Paul's letters and the Gospels) and the Talmud—a massive collection of oral and written rabbinic teachings, much of which emerged from this same time period.

When considering the Jewish image of Jesus, it is of no small consequence that both the New Testament writings and the Talmud emerged together, because many of the same issues were at play for both Jews and those who believed in Jesus as Messiah. Following the Jewish revolt and the fall of Jerusalem in 70 CE, influential rabbis such as Yohanan ben Zakkai and Akiva set out to collect the oral teachings on the Mosaic law, which became known as the Mishnah. These rabbis, who lived in both Palestine and Babylonia, were known as the *tannaim*, and they essentially codified these rabbinic discourses on the law and brought them up to date. Soon after, another set of scholars known as the *amoraim* would codify the various commentaries on the Mishnah (known as the Gemara)—and the two commentaries taken as a whole became known as the Talmud.

Beyond this history, however, both first-century Jews and early Christians were struggling with questions of identity and with their respective theologies of God. The rabbis, who were able to live out their faith without the complex laws and practices of the destroyed temple, essentially created a new Judaism built around the concept of a transcendent and ever-present Creator who did not need brick and stone to lead and shape a people. Likewise, those who first believed in Jesus as Messiah were proclaiming this very presence of God as witnessed in the life and death of a Nazarene prophet.

Early Jewish images of Jesus, then, were in no way foreign to the prevailing (and, in fact, necessary) theological realities of living without a temple. The earliest and most predominant image of Jesus, in fact, was that of the sacrificial lamb—the centerpiece of the Passover meal, which harked back to the Exodus from Egypt and God's instructions:

> They are to take a lamb . . . for each household. . . . Your lamb shall be without blemish. Then the whole assembled congregation . . . shall slaughter it at twilight. They shall take some of the blood and put it on the two doorposts and the lintel of the houses in which they eat it. The blood shall be a sign for you on the houses where you live: when I see the blood, I will pass over you, and no plague shall destroy you when I strike the land of Egypt. (Exodus 12:4, 5, 7, 13, NRSV)

Early images of Jesus featured these theological and historical connections with Passover—and especially the idea of sacrifice. But while the atonement of Jesus (or *how* his death actually atones for sin) is never fully explained by the Gospel writers or by Paul, there was the proclamation that Jesus had died for the sins of humanity. Later generations—and the ecumenical councils (see chapter 3)—would do the bulk of the work of explaining atonement in philosophical terms that would, essentially, define the "three-in-one" deity.

But the fact that both the Talmud and the New Testament emerged during the period immediately preceding and following the destruction of Jerusalem and the Second Temple is of paramount importance to these Jewish ideas about Jesus. After the destruction of the temple, all things changed for Judaism—and consequently, also for those who believed that Jesus was the Messiah.

This rabbinic period—marked by the rise of the Pharisees—had already demonstrated that Jews did not need a temple in order to worship God or fulfill the law. This tension was already in the air before the destruction of the temple, as evidenced by the two principal sects of the Sadducees (who were literalists and believed in worshipping at the temple) and the Pharisees (who worshipped in synagogues and debated fine nuances of the written and oral law).

There is a famous rabbinic story from this period that demonstrates the differences:

> One day Rabbi Yohannan ben Zakkai was leaving Jerusalem and Rabbi Joshua followed after him as they beheld the Temple in its ruin.
>
> "Woe be unto us," Rabbi Joshua said, "for this, the place where the sins of Israel were atoned for is now laid to waste."
>
> Rabbi Yohannan responded, "My son, don't grieve. We have another atonement that is as effective as [the temple]. And what is it? It is acts of loving kindness, as it is written, 'For I desire mercy and not sacrifice.'"[1]

Both the New Testament and the Talmud could be said to reflect this rabbinic period—the age between the First and Second Jerusalem Temple—when rabbis readily debated in the synagogues and among the people, when various rabbinic schools developed and disciples were plentiful. Protected within the confines of the Pax Romana, rabbinic

Judaism emerged as a wonderful and diverse expression of the Jewish faith. Jesus could clearly be said to represent this rabbinic expression, as could Paul and more famous rabbis such as Hillel—an older contemporary.

In fact, the rabbis contemporary with and succeeding the first century spoke similar themes. The rabbis had already begun to speak of God's imminent Holy Spirit as well as the transcendent *shekinah*, which was God's glory. Following the destruction of the temple, this glory, this spirit, would have to guide the people. The faithful would be required to follow the law and the prophets' teachings in everyday living—to see God in the smallest of details and in the created order.

Jesus tackles these very themes with gusto in his discourse which has traditionally been known as the "Sermon on the Mount" (Matthew 5–7) and, again, how Jesus speaks and the manner in which he teaches is typical rabbinic. But the rabbis debated. Schools of thought developed. And there was rarely agreement on the interpretation of the finer points of the law.

Because of these realities in first-century Judea, differences of opinion were going to develop between traditional Jews and those who believed in Jesus as Messiah.

Taken on the whole—and understanding both the New Testament and the Talmud as reflecting the tensions that were growing between Christian and Jew—one should not be surprised to find negative references to the Jewish leaders in the New Testament and negative references to Jesus and his followers in the Talmud. These tensions are, in fact, recorded in both.

While some in years past have looked to the Talmud as proof of an anti-Christian bias among the Jews, it should be equally noted that Jews can easily see an anti-Semitic message in the New Testament. But if we take all of these references from both in their historic context, what we discover is a fascinating glimpse into a time and culture where survival of ideology and community was of paramount importance and wars were often fought in words before they were inflicted (as, sadly, they subsequently were) in actual violence.

For our purposes here, my hope is that both the New Testament and the Talmud (and other Jewish expressions of Jesus, positive or negative) can demonstrate the deeper truths common to both and which can be found in the underlayment of teaching. I also hope that as we explore

the Jewish image of Jesus that we can see similarities among the rabbis—including Jesus and Hillel, two first-century teachers who taught
many similar concepts and ideas.

There is, in fact, a Jewish Jesus—and the images of him vary from
admiration to contempt. But whether regarded as a great teacher or a
prophet or healer, Jesus obviously holds a place in the Jewish history
and mind-set because he was Jewish. And most often, what we encounter in the tensions between the New Testament and the early Jewish
literature is not a hatred expressed *by Jesus* or *toward Jesus*, but the
hatreds expressed by the disciples of either camp. In other words, we
don't primarily see Jesus as he was, but Jesus as his followers and critics
spoke of him in relation to the other.

Following the destruction of the Second Temple in 70 CE, these
tensions among the various Jewish sects grew all the more pronounced,
with Jesus followers being one of these. Some Jewish sects, such as the
Essenes, disappeared almost immediately, while others, such as the
Sadducees, essentially slipped underground and attempted, at other
junctures over the next century, to revive a Jewish state. Only the Pharisees—to which Jesus aligned himself most closely in theology and spirit—survived as teachers of the law. And Paul was also among them.

So we can see why there would have been varied opinions about
Jesus and his followers—and why so much of this tension can be found
in the early Christian writings and the Talmud.

The New Testament Gospels, therefore, do reflect some of these
early opinions and *images* about Jesus. The underlying message at certain junctures in the Gospels is that the Jewish leaders, and sometimes
other rabbis, had evil designs against Jesus. At other junctures the opinion is that the Jewish leaders were blind. And sometimes there is name
calling and the pointing of fingers, even blame.

One of the earliest references can be found in Mark, chapter 3, and
may reflect some of the prevailing theology of first-century Judaism that
attached exorcism and false teaching to the work of the devil. Mark
records this tension on the side of Jesus, attempting to show the hard-
ness of the Jewish elders (scribes) who have brought a charge of insanity
and divination against Jesus:

> Then he went home; and the crowd came together again, so that they
> could not even eat. When his family heard it, they went out to re-

strain him, for people were saying, "He has gone out of his mind." And the scribes who came down from Jerusalem said, "He has Beelzebul, and by the rulers of the demons he casts out demons." (Mark 3:19–22, NRSV)

Contemporary to this time, we find many negative references to Jesus in the Talmud. Some of these references, which some Christian communities later used to spout negative polemic against Jews or which became fodder for anti-Semitic movements, do have a marked anti-Jesus sentiment—but again, this was part and parcel of the rabbinic discourse and shows the mounting tensions between Jew and Christian in certain communities of the first and second centuries.

The Gospels also contain other tension references with regard to Jesus eating and drinking with sinners, the charge that he was a Sabbath breaker, and the charge that he did not keep the dietary laws but was seeking to abolish the requirements of clean and unclean food. Other invectives in the Gospels are references that seek to explain how the Jewish leaders interpreted the empty tomb:

> While they were going, some of the guard went into the city and told the chief priests everything that had happened. After the priests had assembled with the elders, they devised a plan to give a large sum of money to the soldiers, telling them, "You must say, 'His disciples came by night and stole him away while we were asleep.' If this comes to the governor's ears, we will satisfy him and keep you out of trouble." So they took the money and did as they were directed. And this story is still told among the Jews to this day. (Matthew 28:11–15)

In various places in the Talmud, we see counters to the Gospel claim or, in a better light, rabbinic explanations that consist of their opinions about Jesus's teachings and his death. Many of these Talmudic traditions regard Jesus as a false teacher, one who practiced magic and whose death was indicative of one who had blasphemed against God. As such, these Talmudic traditions seek to counter the Gospels' claims that Jesus was a prophet, a great teacher, and that his subsequent resurrection vindicated his life and teachings and revealed him as the Messianic Son of God. The Talmud, at the points where it notes Jesus, expresses the counteropinion that Jesus made claims for himself, or set himself up as God, and that he led Israel astray through his teaching.

Note that the claims against the Talmudic Jesus are often attached to rabbis who want to make a point—an insight that may indicate that Jesus was often imagined as a foil or a personality through which one could make a counterargument. The Hebrew prophet Balaam fits nicely into this category throughout the Talmud and is even used in this manner in the New Testament (2 Peter 2:15, Jude 11, Revelation 2:14). Rabbinic teachings were often balanced by counterweight personalities and often-used stories that were recycled to fit the point.

The Talmudic references to Jesus hold some of this ballast as well. And the fact that Jesus is noted within the massive corpus of the Talmud is a testament to the prevalent (though marginalized) impact that Jesus had within this era of Judaism (even as a foil).

There are many Talmudic references to Jesus, and these illustrate how Jesus was interjected into the rabbinic debates:

Our Rabbis teach, "Ever let the left hand repel and the right hand invite, not like Elisha who repulsed Gehazi with both hands, and not like Rabbi Joshua ben Perachjah who repulsed Jeshu the Nazarene with both hands."

He came and found himself in a certain inn; they showed him great honor. He said, "How beautiful is this Ascania!" [Jesus] said to him, "Rabbi, she has narrow eyes." He said, "Wretch, dost thou employ thyself thus?" He sent out 400 trumpets and excommunicated him. He [Jesus] came before him many times and said to him, "Receive me." But he would not notice him. One day he [Joshua] was reciting the Shema [i.e., the words: "Hear, O Israel," Deuteronomy 6:4] and he [Jesus] came before him. He [Jesus] thought that he had repelled him. He went and hung up a tile and worshipped it. Joshua said to him, "Return." He replied, "Thus I have received from thee, that everyone who sins and causes the multitude to sin, they give him not the chance to repent." And the teacher has said, "Jesus the Nazarene practiced magic and led astray and deceived Israel." (Sanhedrin 107a)[2]

Did not Ben Stada [Jesus] bring spells from Egypt in a cut which was upon his flesh? (Sabbath 104a)[3]

There shall be no evil befall thee—which means that evil dreams and bad fantasies shall not vex thee; and Neither shall any plague come nigh thy tent—which means that thou shalt not have a son or disciple who burns his food publicly like Jeshu the Nazarene. (Sanhedrin 103a)[4]

Rabbi Avin said in the name of Rabbi Hilkiah: The minds of those liars who say that the Holy One, blessed by He, has a son are truly dense. Consider what happened to Abraham's son. When God saw that Abraham was about to slaughter him, He could not bear to see him in pain, but immediately cried out, "Do not put forth your hand" (Genesis 22:12). Now, if God had a son, would He have allowed him to be crucified? Would He not have turned the world upside down, reducing it to chaos and desolation? Solomon said, "There is One that is alone, and He hath not a second; yea, He had neither son nor brother." (Ecclesiastes 4:8)[5]

It is tradition: On the eve of the Passover they hung Jeshu the Nazarene. And the crier went forth before him forty days saying, "Jeshu the Nazarene goeth forth to be stoned, because he has practiced magic and deceived and led astray Israel. Anyone who knoweth aught in his favor, let him come and declare concerning him. And they found naught in his favor. And they hung him on the eve of the Passover. Ulla said, "Would it be supposed that Jeshu the Nazarene a revolutionary, had aught in his favor?" He was a deceiver, and the Merciful [God] has said (Deuteronomy 13:8), "Thou shalt not spare, neither shalt thou conceal him." But it was different with Jeshu the Nazarene, for he was near to the kingdom.[6]

Elsewhere in the Talmud we find references to the followers of Jesus, to the Christian scriptures, and even to traditions about Mary—who, as is affirmed in the Gospel accounts, is noted for having birthed Jesus out of wedlock. The inclusion of these references to the followers of Jesus also makes evident that the early Christian community had enough clout to warrant commentary among the Jewish rabbis and presupposes that the claims made by Christ followers should be countered by the weight of the Hebrew scriptures, which were then, and have always been, regarded as authority within the church, too. So the Talmud attempts to counter the Christ claims by citing scriptural passages that might appeal to the higher authority of the Bible or perhaps sway some of the Messianic believers back into the fold of the true Israel.

While the image of Jesus in the Talmud is a negative one—even excruciatingly harsh—Christians can look back into this history now with an appreciation for the arguments that existed then rather than taking offense at the argumentative manner in which Jesus was cited in the Talmud. The New Testament, then, may be seen in the same light by the Jewish community—as references to the Jewish leadership were marked by this ongoing debate between Jew and Christ follower. Much of what we read can be attributed to the rabbinic discourse, which was the manner in which Jesus and his contemporaries taught and debated one another.

Likewise, as many Christians read the New Testament Gospels today, they assume that the debates between Jesus and the Pharisees (or Sadducees) were contentious to the point of hatred. But in many instances, Christians may be interjecting their preconceived notions about debating—ideas that may more accurately reflect contemporary political animosities or the modern-day polemic rather than the spirit of a first-century rabbinic culture. Many of the conversations that Jesus had with the Pharisees (as recorded in the Gospels) are not contentious at all but simply reflect how various schools of thought debated in the yeshiva manner. The discourse between Jesus and Nicodemus (a Pharisee) as recorded in John 3 is a prime example of this style of teaching.

Although the direct references to Jesus in the Talmud form a negative image, one might see an altogether different Jesus in regard to his teachings when compared to the rabbis of his day. Here, perhaps, we see Jesus as he was—an itinerant healer and teacher who, in the aftermath of Easter, was proclaimed to be Messiah and Savior. His teachings stand nicely against the prevailing wisdom of his age—and echo other rabbinic voices who were, in many instances, his contemporaries.

THE RABBI JESUS

As the Christian community emerged from the historic ranks of Judaism and became a separate faith altogether, the voices within the church became increasingly focused on the polemic against Jesus. The early church fathers, including Justin Martyr (who died in 163) and Tertullian, who just decades later wrote profusely at the turn of the second century, each had their go at one heresy or another. Both Justin Martyr and Tertullian had much to say about the Jewish response to Jesus as well—by now a relationship which had grown harsher through the passing of time, with new written and oral traditions about Jesus also being added to the Talmud—particularly the Gemara, which was the rabbinic commentary on the Mishnah (again, the whole of the Talmud comprising the two).

Justin Martyr, in his *Dialogue with Trypho 117*, accuses

> the high priests of your nation and your teachers to have caused the name of Jesus to be profaned and reviled through the whole world. And added thereto, that Christ taught those impious, unlawful, and horrible actions, which you disseminate as charges above all against those who acknowledge Christ as Teacher and as the Son of God . . . and your teachers exhort you to permit yourselves no conversation whatever with us . . . regarding us as foes and opponents, and kill, and torture us if they have the power. In the lately-ended Jewish war, Bar Kokh'ba, the instigator of the Jewish revolt, caused Christians alone to be dragged to terrible tortures, whenever they would not deny and revile Jesus Christ. [And] in your synagogues ye curse all who have become Christians, and the same is done by the other nations, who give a practical turn to the curse, in that when any one acknowledges himself a Christian, they put him to death.[7]

Here we see that by the second century, the Jewish response to Jesus was not a favorable one—and Jesus was imagined now as a teacher who was completely outside the bounds of Judaism. If Jesus is recognized as having any connection with Judaism, he is regarded primarily as a false teacher, a rabbi with low credentials and a dabbler in magical arts. There is no longer any conversation and close proximity built on a common history or heritage between Christian and Jew (at least according to Martyr).

Tertullian, writing a few decades later in his *De Spectaculis*, imagines the second coming of Christ as a final vindication and triumph of Christian belief, with Jesus returning, in essence, to punish the Jews and counter their litany of disbelief. He imagines Jesus saying to the Jews: "This is your carpenter's son, your Sabbath-breaker, your Samaritan, your demon-possessed! This is He whom ye bought from Judas; this is He who was struck with reeds and fists, dishonored with spittle, and given a draught of gall and vinegar! This is He whom His disciples have stolen secretly, that it may be said He is risen, or the gardener abstracted that his lettuces might not be damaged by the crowds of visitors!"[8]

But what we have in Justin Martyr and Tertullian is the proclivity toward doctrine *about Jesus* rather than a recognition of any common ground with Judaism that can be found in the teachings *of Jesus*. True, there was no longer any attempt in Judaism to find the commonalities, to see Jesus as a rabbi among rabbis. But neither was the church attempting to offer Jesus as a rabbi or to hold up his authority as a teacher under the light and scrutiny of the Talmud. Rather, the beliefs of both Judaism and Christianity had become too extreme for either faith to recognize its own face in the other. Christianity and Judaism, however, continue to share much in common—including shared concepts of God the Creator, the same Hebrew scriptures, and a dynamic conversation about themes of justice, peace, and mercy—all of which can be found among the prophets and in the teachings of Jesus.

But if we look back—and peer deeper—we can see that Jesus holds much in common with the rabbis of his time as well. In the Gospels, for example, Jesus is more widely accepted by the Pharisee tradition, those teachers who believed in resurrection, than he is by the Sadducees, who were traditionalists, and literalists who saw no biblical indication of a life to come. As such, Jesus falls squarely into the camp of the rabbinic Judaism of the first century, whose lines were drawn by Pharisaic Judaism and the houses of prayer (synagogues) instead of the temple complex in Jerusalem (which was overseen and maintained by the Sadducees). A large part of the gospel tradition—and especially as indicated by works such as *The Gospel of Thomas* and the now lost Q document containing a running list of Jesus's teachings—was, in fact, centered on the oral presentations of Jesus. These teachings don't just fall into the category of lengthy extrapolations about life (Matthew 5–7) but also include the parables—a story method which was used widely by the rabbis of all traditions and mind-sets to make their points and confound their adversaries.

Moving into the Talmudic record, we can see how the rabbis of the first and second centuries taught much as Jesus did—or, we should say, how Jesus *taught like them*. There is much here to consider and to remember as we consider the image of Jesus as a rabbi.

But the comparisons are legion—and when taken as a whole, an entirely different image of the Jewish Jesus emerges from this rabbinic core. Here are some extrapolations that have direct correspondence with the teachings of Jesus—but which also demonstrate that these themes were consistent and pronounced within the Jewish communities of these early centuries.

He who is merciful toward his fellow creatures shall receive mercy from heaven above; but he who is unmerciful toward his fellow creatures shall find no mercy in heaven. (Rabbi Beribbi, third century, Shabbath 151:2)
Blessed are the merciful, for they shall obtain mercy. (Jesus, Matthew 5:7)

Be rather one of the persecuted than of the persecutors. (Rabbi Abahu, 279–310 CE, Baba Kamma 93:1)
Blessed are they which are persecuted for righteousness' sake, for theirs is the kingdom of heaven. (Jesus, Matthew 5:10)

Be equally attentive to the light and weighty commandments. (from Aboth 2:1)
Be prompt in the performance of even a light precept. (Ben Azai, Aboth 4:2)
Whosoever shall break one of the least of these commandments, and teaches others to do the same, will be called least in the kingdom of heaven; but whoever does them and teaches them will be called great in the kingdom of heaven. (Jesus, Matthew 5:19)

Whosoever lifts up his hand against a neighbor, though he do not strike him, is called an offender and sinner. (Resh Lakesh, Sanhedrin 98:1)
But I say unto you, that whosoever is angry with his brother without cause shall be in danger of the judgment. (Jesus, Matthew 5:29)

Whosoever looketh on the little finger of a woman with a lustful eye is considered as having committed adultery. (Rabbi Shesheth, Berachoth 24:1)
But I say to you, that whoever looketh on a woman to lust after her, committeth adultery. (Jesus, Matthew 5:28)

To teach that your yea by yea, and your nay be just. (Rabbi Jose berabbi Jehudah, Baba Mezia 49:1)

But let your communication be Yea, yea; Nay, nay. (Jesus, Matthew 5:37)

How is that popular saying: If any one ask for thy ass, give him also the saddle? (Rabba, Baba Kamma 92:2)
And if any man will sue thee at the law, and take away thy coat, let him have thy cloak as well. (Jesus, Matthew 5:40)

As for giving alms in a public manner: You had better not give anything; in the way you gave it to him you must have hurt his feelings. (Rabbi Yanai, Chagiga 5:1)
Take heed that you do not give alms before men to be seen by them. (Jesus, Matthew 6:1)

Whoever forgives the wrong done to him, God will also forgive his sins. (Rabba, Massecheth Derech Erez sutta, 8:4)
For if ye forgive men their trespasses, your heavenly father will also forgive you. (Jesus, Matthew 6:14)

Hast thou ever seen a beast or a bird that followed a trade, and yet they are fed without toil. But these were only created to minister to me, while I was created to minister to my Maker. (Rabbi Simon ben Eleazar, Kidushin 82:2)
Behold the fowls of the air, for they sow not, neither do they reap. But your heavenly Father cares for them. (Jesus, Matthew 6:26)

With the measure a man metes it shall be measured to him from heaven. (Rabbi Meir, Sanhedrin 100:1)
With what measure ye mete, it shall be measured to you again. (Jesus, Matthew 7:2)

If he be admonished to take the splinter out of his eye, he would answer: Take the beam out of thine own. (Rabbi Tarphon, Arachin 16:2)
How will you say to your brother, "Let me pull out the mote out of thine eye," and behold, a beam is in thine own eye? (Jesus, Matthew 7:4)

He whose knowledge surpasses his good deeds may be compared to a tree with many branches and a scanty root—every wind shakes and uproots it. But he whose good deeds excel his knowledge may be compared to a tree with a few branches and strong roots; if all the hurricanes of the world should come and storm against it they would not move it from its place. (Rabbi Eliezer ben Azariah, Pirke Aboth 3:17)

Therefore whosoever heareth these sayings of mine and doeth them I will liken to a wise man which built his house upon a rock. The rains fell, the floods came, and the winds blew and beat upon that house, but it did not fall, because it had been built on rock. (Jesus, Matthew 7:24–25)

The day is short and the task is great, and the workmen are sluggish, and the reward is great and the master of the house is urgent. (Rabbi Tarphon, Aboth 2:15)

The harvest is plenteous, but the laborers are few. (Jesus, Matthew 9:37)

In the world to come there is neither eating or drinking, neither fruitfulness nor increase, neither trade nor business, neither envy, hatred, nor strife; but the righteous sit with their crowns on their heads, and feast themselves on the splendor of the Shechinah. (Rab, Berachoth 17:1)

For in the resurrection they neither marry nor are given in marriage, but are as the angels of God in heaven. (Jesus, Matthew 22:30)

Whoever makes himself little in this world for the sake of the word of the law will be great in the world to come, and whosoever makes himself a slave in this world for the sake of the word of the law will be made free in the world to come. (Rabbi Jeremiah, Baba Meziah 85:2)

Whoever shall exalt himself shall be abased; and he that shall humble himself shall be exalted. (Jesus, Matthew 23:12)

There are a number of insights from these common teachings that one can make. First, it may presuppose that Jesus's teachings as found in Matthew 5–7 or known from some earlier document, such as Q, form the basis of much of the crossover teaching among the rabbis. But one could just as easily be convinced that Jesus was not teaching original material but speaking those words that he had received from other teachers—a kind of common corpus of oral material that may have floated about on the winds of Galilee and Judea. In a first-century

Jewish culture, Jesus's words then would not have been unique or even original. While he certainly added his own voice and authority, the scope of Jesus's teachings and the subject matter was part of the rabbinic discourse of the age.

One might also deduce from these ideas that, if taken in the context of the rabbinic, most of the teachings of Jesus would not have been outside the purview of the age or even controversial. At those points where Jesus makes an observation about life or teaches some moral context from the law, most Jews would have heard his words with a ring of the familiar.

One might also come to regard this collection of teachings in Matthew 5–7 as a rabbinic commentary on other rabbinic traditions. We cannot, after all, overlook the recurring line in the Sermon on the Mount: "You have heard it said."

Indeed, Jesus is debating. He would not even have been drawing outside of the lines, though the Gospel writer does make the claim that Jesus taught "with authority"—which was a characteristic the Gospel writer claims was not present among other rabbis of the Pharisaic school. But there was certainly authority among the Pharisees—for they were able to gather about them a variety of disciples and the debates of the time were often heated, though certainly playful as well.

We can imagine Jesus debating points with the rabbis along these other lines found in the Talmud:

Rabbi Jacob once said: "Whoever is studying as he travels and then, suddenly, stops studying to observe—'Wow, that's a beautiful tree, and look how pretty this hill is'—is going to be guilty against himself, according to the Scriptures."[9]

Rabbi Eleazer the Moabite said: "Whoever dismisses holy acts and despises festivals and embarrasses a friend in public, and makes a mockery of the covenant of Abraham our father, and offers interpretations of the Torah that are not in accordance with halachah—even if he knows the Torah and has good deeds—he will have no inheritance in the life to come."[10]

Jesus was clearly a rabbi among rabbis—and this is an image we should not overlook as we read the Gospels or the Talmud.

So as the Christian faith began to distance itself from the roots of Judaism, one might conclude that early Jewish images of Jesus would have consisted of teacher, preacher, sage, and rabbi. But as the teachings of Jesus became layered with history and the postresurrection *kerygma* (original Christian message), Jesus's teachings did not have appeal to many Jews. Those who could not accept the message proclaiming Jesus as Messiah retreated further into the distance (as some of Paul's inferences indicate that many Christ believers returned to their former righteousness in the law and the Jewish rituals). And so the teachings of Jesus took on less of a Jewish air and more of the Gentile as the years progressed and the connections between church and synagogue grew more disparate.

To be sure, Jesus was always on the periphery as far as the Jewish discourse was concerned—even in the first century—but that is not to say that he had no impact on Judaism, even as Judaism sought to counter the fledgling movement that was proclaiming him as Lord. The Talmud does indicate that the rabbis weighed in on Jesus himself but also that many of his teachings were not so far afield from those precepts taught by many others. Even if one doesn't recognize Jesus as Messiah, there can be a mutual appreciation of his insights into the law and the prophets. And, in fact, this has always been the case.

Again, in the Talmud, we encounter many rabbinic teachings which are not unlike those taught by Jesus. Rather, we see that Jesus received many of his teachings from these older rabbinic authorities—and may have offered his own authority to later rabbinic discourses. For example, similarities can be noted in the following:

> Rabbi Eleazer of Bartotha said, "Give to [God] what is [God's], for you and what you possess are His. Didn't David say in the scriptures [1 Chronicles 29:14]: 'For all things come from You, O God, and we have given to You what is already Yours.'"[11]
> Rabbi Ishmael said, "Submit to the ruler, be patient when oppressed, and receive everyone graciously."[12]
> Jesus: Give to Caesar what belongs to Caesar and to God what belongs to God. (Luke 20:25)

> [Rabbi Akiva] used to say: "Everything is a pledge, and a net is spread over the world. The store is open and the owner is giving credit. The account book is open and a hand is recording. So everyone who wants to borrow, come and borrow . . . for all things are being made ready for the banquet."

Jesus: Someone gave a great dinner and invited many. At the time for the dinner he sent his slave to say to those who had been invited, "Come, for everything is ready." (Luke 14:17)

Rabbi Johanan ben Barokah said, "Whoever curses the Name in Heaven in secret will be penalized in the light of day."[13]
Jesus: Do not swear at all, either by heaven, for it is the throne of God, or by earth, for it is God's footstool (Matthew 5:34). And your father who sees in secret will reward you. (Matthew 6:18)

Rabbi Zadok used to say, "Don't separate yourself from the congregation and don't be like those who are prepared to judge."[14]
Rabbi Ishmael ben Jose used to say: "Whoever shuns the office of the judge escapes from hardship, theft and perjury."[15]
He also said, "Don't judge alone . . . for there is only One who can judge alone."[16]
Jesus: Do not judge. (Matthew 7:1)

Rabbi Jonathan used to say, "Whoever lives by Torah when he is poor will live by Torah when he is rich."[17]
Jesus: Whoever is faithful over a little will also be faithful over much. (Luke 16:10)

Rabbi Jacob used to say, "This existence is like a front porch to the world to come. Prepare yourself on the porch so you may enter into the banquet hall."[18]
Jesus: Enter through the narrow gate. (Matthew 7:13)

The rabbi said, "Don't look at the pitcher but consider what is inside of it. There is a new pitcher which is filled with old wine and an old pitcher which has no new wine inside of it."[19]
Jesus: Neither is new wine put into old wineskins. (Matthew 9:17)

As the Gospels attest, Jesus was often called "rabbi"—and it is apparent that the earliest Jewish recollections of Jesus consisted of those of teacher. He gathered disciples around him—another rabbinic practice. And he sat down to teach—which was the posture of rabbinic authority.

Later, as Christianity blossomed and the Gospels were proliferated in manuscript form and various tongues, it also becomes apparent that the Gospel of Matthew—or at least Matthew 5–7 (The Sermon on the

Mount)—holds up as the most influential of the four Gospels as it intersected with Jewish and, later, Islamic cultures. The teachings of Jesus found in this section of the Gospel relate very well to the rabbinic style of the first century and relate even more keenly to the Islamic expression of Jesus after the seventh century.

There are many comparisons to be made between Gospel and Talmud.

But among Jesus's near-contemporaries, perhaps no comparisons have greater weight than with the famous rabbi Hillel.

A RABBI AMONG RABBIS

There are many traditions associated with Hillel and his teachings— some found in the Talmud and others elsewhere. Among them is one story about Hillel sitting at the city gate (a common place for elders and sages to interact with people). Here, as people come in and out of the city, Hillel inquires as to their purpose. Most reply that they are going into the world to make money for the basic necessities of life. Hillel responds, "Come with me, and I will show you how to gain heaven as well."[20]

A similar teaching is found in Matthew 6:33, where Jesus says, "Seek first the kingdom of God and His righteousness, and all these things shall be given to you as well."

Hillel, who represented a more liberal slant on the law than did his opponent, Shammai, was an earlier contemporary of Jesus but was, in his day, far more heralded and famous than the prophet from Nazareth. Hillel likely came from Babylon, and he studied under Shemaiah and Abtalion. He married, and his descendants were famous in founding a new school of rabbinic Judaism, namely his grandson, Gamaliel I, who is mentioned in Acts 22:3 as having been Paul's teacher.

Both Hillel and Jesus possessed an openness to Torah interpretation—not a strict or literal approach—and both were practical in their application to daily life. However, whereas Hillel was primarily concerned with *halacha* (the interpretation of the Torah and practice), Jesus seems to be equally, if not more, enamored of *haggadah* (the use of stories and parables to illustrate Torah teaching).

Although the teachings of Hillel and Jesus have remarkable similarities in that both were of a liberal bent toward Torah interpretation, their lives could not have been more dissimilar. Hillel was linked to the powerful Jewish establishment in Jerusalem—a group that Jesus seemed to oppose and through whom he encountered much resistance and difficulty. Hillel lived in relative ease, while Jesus was an itinerant peasant rabbi. Hillel also taught in the courtyards of Jerusalem and had many disciples in his school, while Jesus labored predominantly in the relative obscurity of the upper Galilee and gathered about him a small contingency of students who attempted to put his teachings into practice.

But as far as their teachings are concerned, there are other similarities. Both Jesus and Hillel seem to have rejected the strict legalisms of the Essenes—one of the three main sects of Judaism in the first century. According to Josephus, the Essenes were found on the outskirts of most cities, as well as in large desert compounds adjacent to the Dead Sea. Both Hillel and Jesus reject the predestination theology of this sect and the sectarian attitude that hailed the Essene community as the true Israel, the only "sons of light." Likewise, both Hillel and Jesus rejected the austere demands of the Essenes with regard to the Sabbath but possessed a more rounded and flexible interpretation of what the Sabbath represented and how to live through it.

One famous teaching of Hillel's goes like this:

> On another occasion, it happened that a certain heathen came before Shammai and said to him, "Take me as a proselyte, but on condition that you teach me the entire Torah, all of it, while I stand on one foot." Shammai instantly drove him away with a builder's measuring rod he happened to have in his hand. When the heathen came before Hillel, Hillel said to him, "What is hateful to you, do not do to your fellow man. This is the entire Torah, all of it; the rest is commentary. Go and study it."[21]

This, of course, closely resembles the teaching of Jesus: "Do unto others as you would have others do unto you."

Very likely this was a saying—or some derivative of it—that did not originate with either Hillel or Jesus but was part of a wider circle or rabbinic insight shared in various forms. But there are other similarities to be found between Hillel and Jesus also. These similar teachings may, again, point to the wide circle of rabbinic discourse that existed in these centuries when the Mishnah was being composed, but they can demonstrate how Jesus used rabbinic traditions to formulate his unique voice.

It has long been noted that these similarities exist. Even a cursory glance at the variety and breadth of these two rabbis will produce a wealth of parallel teachings.

> If a man has gained a good name he has gained for himself, but if he has gained for himself words of the Torah he has gained for himself life in the world to come. (Hillel, Aboth 2:7)
> In my father's house are many rooms. (Jesus, John 14:2)

> Do not judge another person until you have stood in his place. (Hillel, Aboth 2:5)
> Judge not, that ye be not judged. For with the judgment you make will be the measure by which you are judged. (Jesus, Matthew 7:1)

> More Torah, more life. More study, more wisdom. More counsel, more discernment. More righteousness, more peace. (Hillel, Aboth 2:8)
> Do not think that I have come to abolish the law or the prophets; I have come not to abolish, but to fulfill. (Jesus, Matthew 5:17)

> If I am not for myself, who is for me? But if I am only for myself, what am I? And if not now, when? (Hillel, Aboth 1:14)
> You shall love the Lord your God with all of your heart, and with all of your soul, and with all of your mind, and with all of your strength. The second commandment is: You shall love your neighbor as you love yourself. There is no commandment greater than these. (Jesus, Mark 12:29–31)

> Be disciples of Aaron: love peace, pursue peace, love others, and bring them near to the Torah. (Hillel, Aboth 1:12)
> Blessed are the peacemakers, for they shall be called sons of God. (Jesus, Matthew 5:9)

Had Jesus and Hillel interfaced in first-century Judea, they may have recognized each other through such similar teachings. The one would not have excluded the other from being a true son of the Torah.

Observed from the vantage point of the Torah teaching, Jewish concepts of Jesus range from viewing him as a heretic to viewing him as a rabbi in the liberal school of thought who was not enamored of the temple rules and regulations. Jesus was likely regarded—especially among those who disagreed with him at the beginning—as an obscure rabbi/healer who lived an ascetic life of prayer. From the Gospels, we find indications that Jesus was not highly regarded because he not only came from an obscure village but also had no formal training and had studied under no famous teacher. In time, the teachings and signs which Jesus performed would give rise to bolder opposition, especially as Jesus moved from Galilee to Judea. The Gospels reflect this post-Easter memory of the opposition but are set in the light of deeper rifts that had since developed between Jews and adherents of the new Jesus movement.

Although Hillel and Jesus did not invent new forms of teaching, each brought his unique approach and persistence to the study of Torah and the life of prayer. The Jewish Jesus, then, is not an image that would be entirely foreign to Jewish life and faith—not in the essence of the teaching itself. Rather, Jesus could be recognized through his *haggadah*, as most of his parables do not articulate a doctrine or creed that would be threatening to the existence of Judaism. Within the Gospels, then, we discover early images of the Jewish Jesus as a *haggadah* rabbi.

Among the parables that scholars identify as entirely Jewish (without later Christian interpretation or commentary) are:

- The parable of the sower—less the commentary at the end (Matthew 13:18ff)
- The parable of the vineyard (Luke 13:6–9)
- The parable of the mustard seed (Matthew 13:31–32)
- The parable of the dragnet (Matthew 13:47–50)
- The parable of the pearl and the treasure (Matthew 13:44–45)
- The parable of the wheat and the tares (Matthew 13:24–30)
- The parable of the shepherd and the lost sheep/the lost coin (Luke 15:3–10)
- The parable of the lamp stand (Luke 11:33–36)
- The parable of the good Samaritan (Luke 10:29–37)
- The parable of the prodigal son (Luke 15:11–32)
- The parable of the rich man and Lazarus (Luke 16:19–30)

- The parable of the Pharisee and the tax collector (Luke 18:9–14)

Through these parables especially we imagine Jesus as a moralistic teacher, a rabbi of some persuasion and power who was able through his expertise with *haggadah* to create a vision of the kingdom of God and Torah faithfulness. As Jesus himself noted, he did not come to abolish the Torah but to fulfill it (or make it full and evident). Like Hillel, Jesus had enough disciples to say that he had created a school of followers. It was only later that the Jesus *haggadah* developed into a movement separate from the finer points of Judaism and traditional Torah interpretation. And in time, even the Jewish flavor of these parables would be lost on those who called themselves Christian.

Perhaps the deepest cuts in the Jewish image of Jesus were eventually found in his protests. First-century Judea was a volatile time amid the Roman and Jewish conflicts. However, Jesus manages to stay above the fray in his commentary on Roman rule—at least as we have record of his comments in the Gospels. When faced with an opportunity to weigh in on the debate and potential for revolution, Jesus finds a loophole.

> Then the Pharisees went and plotted to entrap him in what he had said. So they sent their disciples to him, along with the Herodians, saying, "Teacher, we know that you are sincere, and teach the way of God in accordance with truth, and show deference to no one; for you do not regard people with partiality. Tell us, then, what you think. Is it lawful to pay taxes to the emperor, or not?" But Jesus, aware of their malice, said, "Why are you putting me to the test, you hypocrites? Show me the coin used for the tax." And they brought him a denarius. Then he said to them, "Whose head is this, and whose title?" They answered, "The emperor's." Then he said to them, "Give therefore to the emperor the things that are the emperor's, and to God the things that are God's." (Matthew 22:15–22, NRSV)

But the Jewish image of Jesus in regard to his protests internally are far more problematic. Jesus at various junctures has conflict with two of the major sects—the Pharisees and Sadducees. The Sadducees, representing the temple establishment and a strict interpretation of the written Torah, were frequently at odds with the more liberal Jesus, this rabbi who (like the Pharisees) believed in a resurrection of the dead and taught through the oral traditions. These conflicts with the Sadducees were especially problematic as they eventually led to Jesus's arrest and crucifixion. Among these conflicts, however, we can see that the Sadducees regard him as a troublemaker and potential threat to the security of the nation, for instance, in Matthew 3:7 and following verses, Matthew 16:1–12, Matthew 22:23–34, and Luke 20:27 and following verses.

These conflicts were not uncommon in first-century Judea. For in fact, Josephus records many such "false Messiahs" and movements that led to the crucifixion or expulsion of those leaders. Often, the Sadducees and the temple establishment were at the center of these arrests. Jesus was not a solitary figure on the Roman front.

But although more closely aligned with Pharisaic thought (belief in resurrection, oral teaching and authority, rabbinic schools, belief in prayer as well as sacrifice), Jesus has his protests among the Pharisees also, and the Gospel record with these conflicts is far more pronounced and evident. Matthew's Gospel records no less than six such conflicts, Mark, at least four, and Luke, seven. The Gospel of John, while frequently regarded as being the most anti-Semitic of the four, is surprisingly beneficent toward the Pharisees at many turns.

In the fourth Gospel, for example, we find the friendly conversation and relationship that develops between Nicodemus (a leader of the Pharisees) and Jesus. In rabbinic fashion, Jesus and Nicodemus discuss the nature of spiritual birth and the mercy of God. John 7:48 also notes that many Pharisees believed in Jesus. And at the end of the Gospel of John, it is Joseph of Arimathea and Nicodemus who return (secret disciples?) to claim the body of Jesus for burial:

> After these things, Joseph of Arimathea, who was a disciple of Jesus, though a secret one because of fear of the Jews, asked Pilate to let him take away the body of Jesus. Pilate gave him permission; so he came and removed his body. Nicodemus, who had at first come to Jesus by night, also came, bringing a mixture of myrrh and aloes, weighing about a hundred pounds. They took the body of Jesus and wrapped it with the spices in linen cloths, according to the burial custom of the Jews. Now there was a garden in the place where he was crucified, and in the garden there was a new tomb in which no one had ever been laid. And so, because it was the Jewish day of Preparation, and the tomb was nearby, they laid Jesus there. (John 19:38–42, NRSV)

What we can make of these references (especially as they come from John) is that Jesus was not entirely viewed in a bad light—even among the Pharisees of the day. John, at least, is willing to concede that many among the Pharisees did receive the teaching of Jesus in a favorable light and did not regard him as a revolutionary or a threat. Although John is fond of the phrase "the Jews" to describe the opposition to Jesus (though this could be a later church addition to the Gospel), he also paints a picture of a Jesus who was able to speak eloquently and persuasively to certain Jewish leaders. But whether these inclusions served to appease or inflame the Jewish-Christian relations toward the end of the first century (or beginning of the second century) is another matter.

Although Hillel is never mentioned in the Gospels—and, in fact, no rabbis are mentioned by name—we know that Jesus did interact with many. He debated other rabbis, appealed to some, and was castigated by others. This was the culture. This was the time. Rabbis abounded. The discourse and debate was deep and ever present.

What we can take away from the Hillel-Jesus comparisons is a richer image of Jesus as rabbi and storyteller. While Hillel focused on his commentary of Torah in daily life, Jesus used the *haggadah* methods in a far more extravagant way, extrapolating new and recycled stories to build an image of the kingdom of God. This image of kingdom and Torah, however, was not unlike others of the time—but it was Jesus's actions and pronouncements toward the Jewish powers, not his teachings, that eventually led to his demise.

It is not easy to get at these images from the Gospels alone—but through the Talmud and through some of the early literature that crossed the line between Jew and Gentile—we can view still other faces.

JEWISH JESUS, GENTILE CONVERT

Most scholars date the Acts of the Apostles (the second installment of Luke) to either late first century or early to mid-second century. But regardless of dating, Acts—unlike its predecessor Luke—is more insightful when it comes to Jewish-Christian relations. Early in the work, we see a famous rabbi, Gamaliel, interacting with an angry Jewish mob that has just heard the preaching of Peter regarding Jesus—a sermon in which Peter proclaims the resurrection and the authority of Jesus. Gamaliel's approach to quieting the crowd and dispersing them offers a touch of the rabbinic argument of the day.

> When they heard this, they were enraged and wanted to kill them. But a Pharisee in the council named Gamaliel, a teacher of the law, respected by all the people, stood up and ordered the men to be put outside for a short time. Then he said to them, "Fellow Israelites, consider carefully what you propose to do to these men. For some time ago Theudas rose up, claiming to be somebody, and a number of men, about four hundred, joined him; but he was killed, and all who followed him were dispersed or disappeared. After him Judas the Galilean rose up at the time of the census and got people to follow him; he also perished, and all who followed him were scattered. So in the present case, I tell you, keep away from these men and let them alone; because if this plan or this undertaking is of human origin, it will fail; but if it is of God, you will not be able to overthrow them—in that case you may even be found fighting against God!" (Acts 5:33–39, NRSV)

Josephus, in his *Antiquities of the Jews*, mentions this same Judas the Galilean as being the leader of the "fourth sect of Judaism" (the first three, which Josephus describes in detail, being the Pharisees, Sadducees, and Essenes). He notes Judas the Galilean as promoting the following ideas:

> But of the fourth sect of Jewish philosophy, Judas the Galilean was the author. These men agree in all other things with the Pharisaic notions; but they have an inviolable attachment to liberty; and they say that God is to be their only Ruler and Lord. They also do not value dying any kinds of death, nor indeed do they heed the deaths of their relations and friends, nor can any such fear make them call any man Lord; and since this immoveable resolution of theirs is well known to a great many, I shall speak not further about the matter [only to say that it caused] the Jews to go wild with it by the abuse of his authority, and to make them revolt from the Romans. [22]

Josephus, in his history, informs us additionally that there were many such ideologies and zealots of the time. In fact, there were many who set themselves up as Messiahs, who gathered adherents and, sometimes, small armies in an attempt to overthrow Roman occupation. All were squelched, with the final blow being dealt in 70 CE, when Jerusalem and the Second Temple complex were razed and thousands crucified.

To read the Gospels then—including the book of Acts—one is likely reading about Jesus from the vantage point of the end of Torah Judaism. With the temple destroyed, there was no longer any sacrificial law that could be followed, and so the Sadducees quickly dispersed and disappeared. The Essenes, for the most part unwilling to marry, also died away (and their philosophy with them) in the deep regions of the Dead Sea wilderness. Only the Pharisees and the houses of prayer remained—and also the rabbinic methods that carried forward into modern-day Jewish practices.

But these events and realities also forced both Jews and Christians to reimagine Jesus in the light of the catastrophes. Followers of Jesus felt, perhaps, vindicated by the fall of Jerusalem—while traditional Jewish thought was forced to reimagine life without temple and literal Torah.

The Gospel writers assume a Jewish life is possible through the recognition of Christ's Messiahship. So does Paul. But the foundation of the vantage point did shift after the fall of Jerusalem. After 70 CE, Jesus is no longer seen as simply the fulfillment of the prophets but also as the promise of spiritual restoration in the soon-coming kingdom of God.

The passage from Acts, as well as the many accounts in Josephus, assume that the Jewish revolt was costly in a myriad of ways. The writer of Acts (Luke) writes under the assumption that the fall of Jerusalem was, in some way, a vindication of and announcement for the Messiahship of Jesus. Luke reasons that since the Jesus movement still stands but much of the Jewish landscape has been destroyed, it must be because God has willed it so and has ascended Christ to the throne.

These realities—and these thoughts post–70 CE—may be the source of much of the anti-Semitic rhetoric sprinkled in the Gospels, and we may begin to understand how references to Jesus in the Talmud took on a negative tone as well. When there are winners and losers there is often sparring before and after.

But what are we to make of these early images of Jesus?

John Dominic Crossan, in his epic biography, *The Historical Jesus: The Life of a Mediterranean Peasant Jew*, offers many of these images of Jesus through a series of marvelous couplets that describe how a first-century audience could have heard and received Jesus. These ideas could have ranged among:

- Slave and patron
- Visionary and teacher
- Peasant and protester
- Magician and prophet
- Bandit and Messiah
- Rebel and revolutionary
- Resurrection and authority

Bearing in mind the latter, we need not automatically assume that the resurrection and authority of Jesus were clearly evident to those who knew him or were especially evident to those who had heard of Jesus or once listened to his teachings. How a first-century Judean audience would have responded to Jesus would more likely have embraced the former ideas of rabbi and healer. It would have taken a true "leap of faith" to trust in Jesus through the *kerygma* of the first apostles and their testimony about him.

But this is the wonder of history and of faith.

Images cannot be proved, only lived. What Jesus taught, therefore, is only a portion of his life. What people have done with what remained of his memory and spirit is the difference between the various images. While some regarded Jesus as authority, others were unable to accept that his teachings—while valid and full of Torah truth—were meant to elicit a faith *in Jesus*. And this became the difference, ultimately, between Christian and Jew—and later, between Christian and Jew and Muslim.

3

THE CHURCH SPEAKS

Jesus and Alternative Communities

The kingdom of heaven is like unto a treasure hidden in a field; the like of which when a man finds it, he hides it, and for the joy thereof, goes and sells all that he has, and buys it. —Matthew 13:44

He that findeth Jesus finds a good treasure, yes—a Good above All. —The Imitation of Christ 2:8

Prior to the time of Constantine, when Christianity was not recognized and supported by the Roman state, many Christians viewed martyrdom as the ultimate form of devotion to Jesus. Several well-known theologians and teachers, such as Origen, were eventually martyred for their faith, as were hundreds of followers of more simple and humble means. In Christian communities where no earthly happiness could be found it was easier—and deemed more noble and acceptable—to simply slip away into the Pauline adage: *For me to live is Christ, to die is gain.*

However, as happens to any religion, as time passes and as generations cede interpretation and practicality to a new batch of adherents, new expressions emerge. Christianity was no different. New images of Jesus began to enter the frame. Or, more accurately, the variety of ways that one could choose to live out the Christian faith took new forms.

Some of these forms could be described in individual terms—with each person deciding what it meant to be a follower of Jesus. But at the same time, there were also new expressions of community—new sacrifices, new forms of living.

One of these new expressions of community was monasticism. Unlike the more urban expressions of Christianity, the monastic movement called people to a life of asceticism built around rules of order and communal living.

During the early eras of persecution, primarily under Roman authority, there began a movement toward the African desert. This migration, credited to Anthony the Great (around 270 CE), was the first formalized ascetic movement in the Christian faith, and those who made their home in the wilderness became known as the desert fathers (though there were women, too). Anthony had first taken to the desert after hearing the words of Jesus, "Sell all of your possessions, give it to the poor, and you shall have treasure in heaven" (Luke 18:18–25). Anthony followed this command and began a life of self-denial and devotion. No longer worried for possessions, he lived a simple life of prayer, fasting, and study. In time, a rather large community gathered around him. Various desert communities sprang up in places like Syria, Egypt, and points in northern Africa.

After the rise of Constantine, when it was safe to practice Christianity, even more people crossed over into these desert communities—perhaps because this form of asceticism was now seen as the new martyrdom. Whereas it was now safe to profess faith openly in the cities of the empire, the faith soon became sterile and influenced by the prevailing winds of culture. Many found the desert communities to be places of self-denial, hardship, and struggle—a form of Christianity that proved to be an alternative to the formalized worship style now gathering in large buildings of the cities, with an array of professional priests and leaders leading congregations.

There were other great desert fathers following Anthony—including Macarius and Pachomius, who is credited with having formalized the rituals and prayers practiced in many of these communities, the forerunners of the Lectio Divina and Hours of Prayer.

The desert fathers, so called, also provide a glimpse into the lesser-known history of the Jesus movement. From the second to fourth centuries CE there was a plethora of writings (very well preserved) by the church fathers, the ecumenical councils, and the liturgies. There were also dozens—if not hundreds—of other documents from this time period. Many were of Gnostic origin and theology and were patterned after those books that were, by now, generally accepted by the church. Alternative gospels such as *The Gospel of Peter*, *The Gospel of the Hebrews*, *The Gospel of Thomas* (infancy), and *The Gospel of the Nazoreans* were written and circulated. And there was a circus of esoteric books such as *The Revelation of Peter*, *The Vision of Paul*, *The Testament of Abraham*, and a corpus of pseudo-epistles written under Paul's name. Much of the literature of the early church fathers has been preserved as arguments against the theologies represented in these books (far too many to list here).[1]

But at the same time the church was becoming unified in belief and expression, there were alternative communities that preferred lifestyle instead of creed. These communities, represented by the desert fathers, were more concerned about devotion *to Jesus* than discourse *about Jesus*. The literature of the desert fathers offers a portrait of Jesus that is more akin to a family history than to church history. In these desert communities, Jesus was loved, adored, worshipped, and honored. Perhaps the same was happening in the large urban centers where the great cathedrals would be built, but the desert fathers were not nearly so concerned about liturgy *expressing Jesus* as they were with rules for living in community *with Jesus*.

As such, the large corpus of material preserved in the Greek and Latin texts (*Patrologia Graeka* and *Patrologia Latina*, respectively) is an astounding collection of Jesus material—though one has to dissect the parables and teachings to get at the manner in which this community saw Jesus in its midst. The desert fathers could be seen, therefore, as a kind of resurrection community where hermits, sages, abbots, and pilgrims attempted to live out the teachings of Christ and thus perpetuate his presence.

The desert communities—found predominantly in Egypt and Syria at this time—were not for everyone. Indeed, few could live in the marginalized faith, and certainly few could attain the rule of life that was defined by sacrifice, poverty, utter devotion, and, at times, shocking solitude. That this literature survives, however, is a testimony to the pull and importance of this way of life—and the Jesus these works taught.

To say that there was only one image of Jesus during these formative centuries is to renege on the weight of evidence against it. There were by now many images of Jesus—some populated in the new iconography and theological literature of the church fathers who lived in the urban centers, and others being formed in the crucible of alternative communities and common expressions of life. Sometimes the two could be melded. At other times, not.

The literature of the desert fathers (or at least attributed to them) shows—perhaps for the first time in the faith—how Jesus was interpreted *into a community*. Unlike the apostle Paul's letters, where he addresses questions and concerns of the early churches, the literature of the desert fathers often assumes the form of parable. But these are unlike the parables that Jesus told. Rather, instead of pointing to the kingdom of God or attempting to make a point, the stories are frequently playful, even humorous, and often seek to engage the community in interpreting its own existence.

The desert fathers saw their way of life, their practices and methods, as being a kind of communion with Jesus himself. The goal was to stay in conversation with Jesus, not to lose sight of him, and to expunge from the community those thoughts and ideas that would entice followers back to the trappings and tragedies of the other life—even other expressions in the church.

It is not entirely clear if the desert fathers regarded their community as the true church (much like the Essenes of the Dead Sea wilderness regarded themselves as the pure Israel). But they certainly had an ability to imagine Jesus within their community, sometimes taking sides. Whether Jesus would only be found in the desert as opposed to the city is debatable, but they had no doubt that Jesus was still informing them. Jesus was a teacher. A friend. A guide. And as this parable reveals, Jesus was envisioned within the circle of devotion and friendship—or, as he said, "wherever two or three are gathered." Yet this circle was also regarded as part of the larger framework of the church, bowing at times to ecclesiastical authority.

Ultimately, Jesus is viewed as the supreme abbot, as this parable shows.

> It happened one day that abbot Schnoudi was holding conversation with our Savior Jesus Christ, when the bishop Schmin arrived at the monastery. He sent to ask the abbot to come to him that he might talk to him. But Schnoudi sent back word to the bishop, "Schnoudi at this time has no leisure." When the servant had given this message to the bishop, he sent again saying, "Bid him come to me, for I have

come here with the purpose of knowing him." But Schnoudi again sent word, "Tell him again I have no leisure to see him."

Then the bishop was vexed and said, "Say to him, 'If you do not come, I shall excommunicate you.'" Schnoudi, when he heard this message smiled and said, "Behold the folly of this man of flesh and blood. Behold, I have with me here the Creator of Heaven and Earth and I shall abide with him."

Then the Savior said, "Oh, Schnoudi, rise and go to the bishop, lest he excommunicate you. If he does, I shall not receive you into heaven, for the Father promised saying, 'Whatsoever you shall bind on earth shall be bound in heaven, and whatsoever you loose on earth shall be loosed in heaven.'" When the abbot heard these words he hastened to the bishop.[2]

Many stories from the desert fathers demonstrate adaptability with the teachings of Jesus. Here is one that could have been used to address Jesus's injunction: "And when you fast, do not look dismal like the hypocrites" (Matthew 6:16). Many such parables show a lively ability to adapt the teachings of Jesus to changing times and circumstances—a huge jump for any religious community that is based on rules or order. Although Jesus is not mentioned specifically in this parable, we hear the echo of his voice among the community which was asking: *Which teaching takes precedence when we encounter a paradox?*

There was a certain brother who practiced abstinence from various kinds of food, and especially refused to eat bread. He went once to visit a renowned elder. As it happened, while he was there, some strangers arrived, and the old man prepared a scanty meal for them. When they sat down to eat, the brother who practiced abstinence would eat nothing except a single bean. When they rose from the table the elder took him apart privately and said to him, "Brother, when you are in the company of others do not be anxious or display your own way of living. If you really wish to keep your rule unbroken, sit in your own cell and never leave it." When he heard these words he felt the elder was right. Therefore ever afterwards he conformed his ways to those brethren among whom he found himself.

In certain respects, the desert fathers offer us a glimpse of an early Christian community that was beginning to think on its feet. Now generations away from Jesus of Nazareth, from the oral traditions and the writing of the Gospels, the desert communities and their leaders are beginning to diverge in their ideas and concepts about Jesus. Jesus is becoming more than an object of devotion, an exemplar of a living faith—a most excellent friend who has something to say about any situation that can be encountered in life.

Not all of this literature is of this vein, but much of it shows how the image of Jesus was again being transfigured into a contemporary world. The desert fathers were unwilling to leave Jesus in the shroud of dogma and history. Instead, they brought him along for the journey and included him in their various disciplines and philosophies of living.

So it is not so much Jesus as "the way, the truth, and the life" that concerns them . . . but living the way with Jesus and finding his truth and life among them that is paramount. It is the difference between adhering to a set of beliefs (creeds) and actually living a life patterned after Jesus. The desert fathers chose the latter course, and much of their literature abounds with fresh voices and interpretations of the teachings of Jesus—but brought into their place and time.

Here is a brief story detailing how the community struggled with Jesus's words of Matthew 6:24: "You cannot serve God and mammon" (money).

> A certain brother once came to an elder and said, "My father, of your kindness tell me, I beseech you, what I ought to strive for in my youth, that I may own something in my old age." The old man replied to him, "You may either gain Christ or gain money. It is for you to choose whether you will have for your God the Lord or mammon."

In the New Testament Gospels we find Jesus instructing his disciples about the end of days. In Matthew 24:5, 23–24: "For many will come in my name saying, 'I am the Messiah.' Then if anyone says to you, 'Look! Here is the Messiah!' or 'There he is!'—do not believe it. For false messiahs and prophets will appear."

Even isolated communities struggled with these teachings—but now in new ways. As these next two stories demonstrate, the temptation of the church has often been to see Jesus as a possession, as a commodity with which we can barter and broker power or self-importance. But if Jesus isn't available to the faithful in these ways but is with the community in spirit only—then one is freed from the temptation to see Jesus as a talisman against sin and evil. Rather, Jesus is gone, and his spirit lives among the community desirous to live in his love and strength.

> They tell about a certain old man that sometimes in his struggles against temptations he saw the devils, who surrounded him, with his bodily eyes. Nevertheless, he despised them and their temptations. Seeing that he was being vanquished, the devil came and showed himself to the old man saying, "I am Christ." But when the old man beheld him he shut his eyes. Then the devil said again, "I am Christ; why have you shut your eyes?" The old man answered him, "I neither expect nor wish to behold Christ in this present life. I look to see Him only in the life beyond." Hearing these words, the devil straightway vanished from his sight.

> There was another old man whom the devils wished to seduce. They said to him, "Do you wish to behold Christ?" He replied, "May you be accursed for the words you speak. I believe my Christ when he says to me, 'If anyone shall say unto you, Lo, here is Christ or lo there, believe him not.'" When they heard him answer them thus the devils immediately vanished.

Among those teachings of Jesus most difficult to fulfill are the ones on forgiveness: Matthew 18:21–22, Luke 17:4. The early desert communities were not immune from these same struggles, but in fact, solitude often exacerbated or heightened the tension. There are many stories that touch upon this—and the willingness to forgive is of paramount importance in any community seeking unity and love.

As this story demonstrates, perhaps the greater struggle is the need to forgive oneself.

> A brother asked the abbot, "I have committed a great sin. Shall I do penance for three years?" The abbot replied, "That is too long." Then the brother said, "Do you advise one year?" The abbot said, "That is too long." Those who were standing by asked, "Is forty days sufficient?" Abbot said again, "It is too long." Then he added, "If a man repent with all his heart, and fully determine not to commit again the sin which he deplores, God will receive his repentance though it endure but three days."

A story extrapolating Jesus's teaching on prayer (Matthew 6:5–18):

Certain brothers asked Macarius how they ought to pray. He answered them, "There is no need of much speaking in our prayers. Stretch out your hands and say, 'Lord, have mercy upon me as you see best and as you will.' If your mind is disquieted, say, 'Help me!' He knows what is best for us, and of his own will he grants us mercy."

The desert fathers are not always easy to read, but they do provide that alternative face of Jesus during a time when expressions about him were becoming philosophical and intellectually removed from the common person. As such, the literature of the desert fathers flows out of the heart more profusely than from the mind or the seat of academia. That is not to say that these leaders were void of intellect—quite the contrary. Their intelligence and perceptions were keen.

As the following stories show, the literature of the desert fathers is a rich source of Christian imagery. Some stories, no doubt patterned after the parable forms that Jesus used, demonstrate how these early communities interpreted Jesus for their generation.

A brother once came to abbot Macarius and said to him, "Master, speak some word of exhortation to me, that, obeying it, I may be saved." St. Macarius answered him, "Go to the tombs and attack the dead with insults." The brother wondered at this advice, but nevertheless went to the tombs, casting stones at the dead and railing against them. He returned to Macarius and told him what he had done. Macarius asked him, "Did the dead notice what you did?" The brother admitted the dead did not notice him. "Go again then," said Macarius, "and this time praise them." The brother wondered about this word but did return to the tombs, this time praising the dead, calling them saints and apostles. He returned to Macarius and told him what he had done. "And did the dead reply to you?" asked Macarius. "They did not reply to me," answered the brother. Then Macarius said to him, "You know what insults you have heaped upon them and with what praises you have flattered them, and yet they never spoke to you. If you desire salvation you must be like the dead. You must think nothing of the wrongs others do to you, nor of the praises they offer to you. Be like the dead. And so you will be saved." (*Wisdom of the Desert*)

The abbot John once told a parable: "There was a very beautiful woman who lived in a certain city and had a multitude of lovers. A great man—one of the nobles of the city—came to her and said, 'Promise that you will be mine and I will marry you.' She gladly promised, and after being married, went to the palace to live. But afterwards her many lovers came seeking her, but could not find her. When they heard that she had become the nobleman's wife they said to one another, 'If we go to the palace and ask for her, it will be apparent that we are seeking her, and without a doubt we will be punished. So let's go back to the house and whistle for her, just like we used to do when she was free. When she hears us whistling, she will certainly come down to us.' They did as they had planned and the woman heard their whistling. Hating greatly even to hear them, she went with haste to the interior of the palace and shut the doors and windows. Now the woman is the human soul. Her husband, the nobleman, is Christ. The palace is the eternal mansion. Those who whistle to her are the demons." (*Wisdom of the Desert*)

Certain brothers once came to St. Antony and asked him to speak some word through which they might attain the perfection of salvation. But Antony said to them, "You have heard the scriptures. The words which you have heard from the lips of Christ are sufficient for you." When they pressed him harder, still asking him to speak a word, he said, "It is taught in the gospel that if someone strikes you on the one cheek you are to turn the other also." Then they confessed that they were not able to do this. St. Antony answered, "Is this too hard for you? Are you willing to let the same person strike you on the same cheek again?" They said, "We are not willing." They hoped to hear some easier thing. Then he said to them, "If this is too hard for you, then at least do not render evil for evil." Again they answered him as they had before. Then St. Antony turned to his disciple nearby and said, "Prepare some food and give it to these men, for they are weak." But to the brothers who had inquired of him he said, "If you cannot do one thing or the other, then why have you come seeking a word of exhortation from me? To me it seems that what you need most is to pray. By prayer perhaps you will be healed of your infirmity." (*Wisdom of the Desert*)

The abbot Macarius, when he dwelt in Egypt, once had occasion to leave his cell for a little while. At his return he found a robber stealing what was in his cell. St. Macarius stood and watched him, as one who was a stranger might watch as having no interest in what was stolen. Then he loaded the robber's horse for him and led him forth saying, "We brought nothing into this world. The Lord giveth and the Lord taketh away. According to his will so things happen. Blessed be the name of the Lord." (*Wisdom of the Desert*)

The movement toward asceticism worked for many Christians because it offered a personal Jesus. Whereas much of the church had migrated toward those expressions of Jesus born of liturgy and ritual, the monastic movement offered an opportunity for people to live individually within a wider circle of like-minded community. The weights of social convention and culture could be shed—and life was lived in an environment of essential labor and prayer. Devotion was born of reflection and study. Solitude—if not admired—was at least advised from time to time, and the desert fathers birthed a new way of approaching the faith and, essentially, approaching Jesus. Not always understood, monasticism was difficult because it called forward an introspective life—which fewer and fewer were able to achieve amid the larger urban centers such as Alexandria.

Much of the Jesus material of the desert fathers is deeply personal, with advice bordering on the mystical. As noted in the following stories, the manners and means of living the faith have both personal and profound impact—and see Jesus as the guardian of the soul. In monasticism, one perfected the faith through practice and by looking to Jesus as an example of humility, forgiveness, and sacrifice.

The abbot Allois said, "Except a man say in his heart, 'Christ and I are alone in the world' he will not find peace." (my translation)

Father Samartas said, "I prefer a person who has sinned—but knows he has sinned and has repented—over a person who has sinned and yet believes he is righteous." (my translation)

Father Poemen said to Father Joseph, "Tell me how I can become a Monk." Father Joseph said, "If you want to be at peace now as well as in eternity, say in every occasion, 'Whom am I?' and do not judge anyone." (my translation)

One time two brothers visited an old man by surprise. The old man was in the habit of fasting every other day, but when he saw his guests he said to himself, "Fasting is rewarding, but if I eat for the sake of love I shall satisfy two commandments: Giving to others and offering sustenance to those who are hungry." (my translation)

Father Poemen once said, "Teach your mouth to speak what is in your heart." (my translation)

Father Epiphanus said, "God sells righteousness cheaply for those who are willing to buy: consider a piece of bread, used clothes, a cup of water, or a coin." (my translation)

Father Sisoes said: "Seek God, and not where God lives." (my translation)

A soldier asked Father Mios if God would forgive a sinner. Following instruction, Father Mios asked him, "If your coat were torn would you toss it away?" "I would not," the soldier said. "I would repair it and wear it." Then Father Mios said, "If a sinner can show care for his coat, cannot God show care for the one he has created?" (my translation)

Father Evagrius told the story about a brother who did not own anything except a manuscript of the Gospel—and this he sold to feed the poor. He also said this: "I have sold even the words that told me, 'Sell everything and give to the poor.'" (my translation)

The abbot Pastor said, "It is written in the gospel, He who has a coat let him sell it and buy a sword. This word [of Jesus] is to be understood in this manner: He who has peace let him cast it away, and in its place let him take up strife. But now our strife is against the devil." (*Wisdom of the Desert*)

Although no iconography or art exists from the desert father period, there are certainly images created through words. Unlike some of the austere and stern images of Jesus that were beginning to emerge throughout the new Roman church, the monastic life pictured a softer Jesus, almost beckoning with love and humility. As much of the literature reflects, biblical stories and themes were revisited in order to paint a welcoming image of Jesus.

Even the elders could be superseded by the younger—and everyone was regarded as a learner, a disciple. In many respects, the desert orders could be seen as an attempt to return to Galilee, to get back to something which the abbots believed the church had lost in the succeeding generations. A church was being birthed. But what kind of church?

As these stories demonstrate, these were the questions at the heart of the movement—and the desert fathers believed they represented that element in the church who were answering the call to follow Jesus.

> A certain elder once asked, "What is the meaning of this which is written: 'Strait is the way and narrow is the way that leads to life?'" He answered, "The straight and narrow way is this: that a man do violence to his thoughts and destroy his own will for God's sake. This is what we are told the apostles did, of whom it is written: 'Lo, we have left all and followed thee.'" (*Wisdom of the Desert*)

> An old man had one faithful disciple. One night, in a fit of anger, he drove him from his cell. The disciple waited all night outside the door. In the morning, when the old man opened it, and, when he saw him, was struck with shame, he said, "You are my father now, because your humility and patience have conquered my sin. Come in again, and from henceforth be the elder and the father. I will be the disciple, for you have surpassed me, though I am aged." (*Wisdom of the Desert*)

OTHER COMMUNITIES, OTHER VOICES

The pull to encapsulate Jesus, to distill his teachings, has been around for centuries. Long before Thomas Jefferson created his own gospel by cutting and pasting, there were other attempts to harmonize the Gospels or, more specifically, to interpret the teachings and purpose of Jesus for a community. This became all the more prevalent as the church grew and, over the passing of centuries, found itself increasingly distanced from the original voices and communities that birthed the Jesus movement in Galilee and Judea.

The ecumenical councils and the creeds were one way of bringing unity to the church—to distill the essence of belief into a recitation based on a commonly held canon of scripture and liturgy. But there had always been alternative methods as well.

Before the advent of the desert communities someone—likely a Syrian convert to the faith—had attempted to harmonize the four (yet to be canonized) Gospels in writing. Early citations attribute this work to a man named Tatian, who was touted as a convert under the tutelage of Justin Martyr. Very likely written in the mid-to-late second century, the *Diatessaron* was certainly used by Syrian Christian communities and Gnostics alike, and later generations would translate this book into Arabic and many other tongues.

What makes the *Diatessaron* so fascinating is its scope. It contains little else but the words of the canonical Gospels ably woven into a chronological tapestry and thus providing a first effort to create one Gospel out of the four (Matthew, Mark, Luke, and John). It is an amazing work—but the history of it and its scope is far beyond a detailed study here.

However, the existence of this work from the second century does show how the church—or as some would later believe, a more Gnostic form of Christianity—was attempting to harmonize the life and teachings of Jesus into one rule of faith. But the fact that the *Diatessaron* is composed entirely of the four Gospels should also indicate that while the Gospels were by this time clearly delineated as the rule in the churches, there were also questions as to how one could form a coherent and unified vision of Jesus.

Later church fathers would caution the church against using the *Diatessaron*—as it was recommended that the four Gospels be allowed to stand on their own and offer their four unique—though sometimes *synoptic*—views of Jesus. But as the *Diatessaron* was used in Syria, it was an early form of biography, a harmonized Gospel of the birth, life, teachings, death, and resurrection of Jesus.

Also interesting is the way that this writer, or community, sought to harmonize the often troubling chronologies of the Gospels. While Matthew, Mark, and Luke seem to tell the story of Jesus making a single trip to Jerusalem near the end of his life, in John's Gospel Jesus moves back and forth between Galilee and Judea at least three times. The *Diatessaron* harmonizes the chronology by simply using words from John's Gospel at various places. Most common we find the phrases "and when Jesus entered Jerusalem" (section 32), "and they came to Jerusalem" (32:27), and "and they came again to Jerusalem" (section 34:26).

Likewise this work reveals an early attempt to make sense of the variety of resurrection appearances in the passion narratives. Sometimes Jesus appears to the disciples in Galilee. And in other Gospels these sightings occur in Jerusalem. The *Diatessaron* begins with the resurrection appearances in Judea/Jerusalem (again, verbatim from the Gospels) and then moves majestically and confidently back to Galilee, where Jesus again meets his friends, first at the Sea of Tiberias (Sea of Galilee) and later on an unnamed mountaintop. Noticeably missing are the longer endings to Mark's Gospel (see chapter 1), which may indicate that this community did not regard these longer endings as necessary to the Gospel or simply did not know of their existence in other manuscripts. At any rate, these longer versions of Mark were not regarded as essential gospel.

What the *Diatessaron* does is lead us further into an understanding of the early church and the various ways that these early communities and converts sought to imagine Jesus and offer his story to the world. This particular work would also enter, later, into the intersection of Christianity with Islam in the seventh century and became a source of Jesus (Isa) material for both Islam and Christianity, as we know this work was most commonly found in the Arabic tongue.

Further deepening our understanding of the early church—and the images that these communities used to spread the gospel—is the *Didache*. The *Didache* (or "teaching") predates the *Diatessaron* and may actually date to the late first century. This collection of teachings, therefore, offers an even earlier glimpse into a communal understanding of Jesus—and demonstrates how these images fanned out into other arenas and interpretations. The *Didache* likely impacted the latter movements to the desert, but it was also used by the learned to teach the faith and capture what were then regarded as the essential teachings of Jesus.

It is interesting to note that most scholars date the *Didache* (see the appendix) to a period earlier than many of the New Testament books, further demonstrating how images of Jesus—or at least what was regarded as his essential teachings—predate some of the biblical images, especially the Gospel of John and some of the pastoral letters attributed to Paul.

The *Didache* is a short work—very likely used originally as a rule for living and practice in an early Jewish/Christian community. While the work itself enjoyed a wide influence early on among the so-called apostolic fathers—and is fully translated as *The Teaching of the Twelve Apostles*—it was never fully accepted by the later church fathers, and certainly not by the time of the historian Eusebius, who lists it alongside books such as the *Acts of Paul, The Shepherd of Hermas, The Apocalypse of Peter, The Epistle of Barnabas*, and *The Apocalypse of John* as being of doubtful authorship or authority. But although later rejected by the bishops at Nicaea, we know that the *Didache* was known (and used) by such luminaries as Irenaeus, Clement of Alexandria, and Origen. In earlier times the *Didache* was certainly used as a devotional work if not regarded as scripture by many—and for the early Christian community that created the *Didache*, it was regarded as a rule of life.

As an early document alongside certain of Paul's letters and *The Gospel of Thomas*, the *Didache* does reveal one of the first expressions of a community attempting to live through the teachings of Jesus. Though Jesus is mentioned scarcely by name in the *Didache*, the bulk of the work is dedicated to understanding the meaning of his teachings as they pertain to a second- or third-generation community that was attempting to interpret word, sacrament, and order in a time where the original teachings of Christ did not explain enough or left behind additional questions. This has always been the case with the church, as the Gospels and Paul's writings do not answer all questions for subsequent generations of believers. The *Didache* reflects one of the earliest attempts to get at the core of Jesus's teachings while offering his authoritative answers to a new generation of believers who were, by now, far removed from their Jewish roots.

As such, the *Didache* reflects the idea that Jesus was not just a historic messiah but was a living Christ who could answer new questions posed by a community that was seeking his face. This work also shows how answers were forthcoming in the form and function of the community itself and how Jesus has always been used to verify the rules and disciplines of the church. Behind all of the rules there is an a priori assumption that Jesus would support the rules if he were here—and through the document itself there is an image of Jesus that is being espoused and offered.

The *Didache* is the earliest church order yet discovered, written in Syriac, and explains the various virtues and vices, rituals and prayers, and offices and functions found in this early church community. There is also an interesting apocalyptic section toward the end of the work that echoes Matthew 24—and may reveal an external source that was utilized by both the author of the *Didache* and the author of Matthew.

The Gospel of Matthew likewise holds a prominent place in the *Didache*, though it is often formulated as subtext or commentary on the various rules. These rules range from concepts and practices associated with baptism, fasting, and the Lord's Supper, or Eucharist. But underneath these one can find an idea about Jesus that was operative at the turn of the first century in these Jewish-Christian communes. The *Didache* is an attempt to capture the apostolic teaching—as it existed at that time—in a summarized and liturgical form.

But a few early images or suggestions about Jesus also occur.

For example, the *Didache* begins with "The Teaching of the Lord to the Gentiles according to the Twelve Apostles." But while an actual summary of these teachings would have been impossible to compile, the document makes the bold assertion that these are the teachings of Jesus as passed along to the original twelve. In reality, however, the document shows how one early community attempted to bridge gaps between Jew and Gentile and offer practices and virtues that would lead followers from "death to life."

Heavily dependent upon Matthew's version of the Sermon on the Mount (Matthew 5–7), the *Didache*'s introductory sections attempt to distill this long passage into nuggets of truth—and the guidance here is regarded as from the very mouth of the Lord. The way is clear: those who wish to be followers of Jesus will keep the rules, these commandments, and although the path is difficult, it will lead a person to life eternal.

(1) This is the way that leads to life: First, you will love the God who created you and you will love your neighbor as you love yourself. And then this: whatever you don't want done to you, don't do that to someone else. And there is another rule that flows from this. Namely—bless those who hate you, pray especially for your enemies, and even fast for those people who want to harm you. Really, what good does it do to simply love those who love you back? Even pagans can do that. But try loving those who hate you and soon you won't have an enemy. Don't succumb to lusts. If anyone hits you on one cheek, go ahead and offer the other one, too. You are called to live with perfection as a goal. Or if someone compels you against your will to

walk a mile, don't stop there, walk two miles. Or if someone steals your overcoat, give the shirt off your back also. Or if someone takes what belongs to you, don't worry about getting it back (you won't be able to anyway!). Anyone who asks something from you, go ahead and give it—you are just giving out of God's generosity anyway, and God gives to all. You'll be blessed if you give accordingly and will then be without guilt. But beware of receiving gifts. If you really have a need, then ask, that's fine—but if you ask for things when you don't have a need, you'll have to answer for this and give an accounting of why you wanted to hoard. You'll have to account for the very last penny you received when you weren't the needy one. But remember His words: Don't grip your money tightly, but learn how to open your hand and give generously.

(2) Now here's the second installment of commandment(s). Don't murder. Don't commit adultery. Don't use young men for sex. Don't have sexual relations outside of marriage. Don't steal. Don't dabble in magical practices or sorcery. Don't kill the unborn and don't kill a child at birth. Don't covet your neighbor's possessions. Don't lie and don't gossip about others. Don't speak evil and don't harbor a grudge. Don't say one thing and do another—that's a path to death. If you give your word, then fulfill it with action. Don't be vicious, or a hoarder, or a hypocrite, or difficult to work with, or proud. Just don't entertain anything evil against a neighbor. In fact, don't hate anybody, but try to teach through disagreement, pray for everyone, and love others more than you love yourself.[3]

It is noteworthy that contained in these first two sections of the *Didache*, one can pick out no less than a dozen selections lifted entirely or partially from the Sermon on the Mount (Matthew 5–7). Some commandments from Exodus are also found. But here the tone is much less playful than is found on the lips of Jesus (as in Matthew's Gospel). The *Didache* doesn't preserve any of the double metaphors that Jesus used (salt and light, eye and splinter, for example), nor the beatitudes or the subsequent explanations about almsgiving and prayer.

And so the message of the *Didache* is meant to be clearer. Jesus is the new Moses—the new lawgiver. Those who heed his words and live through them will pass through the waters of death into life.

The *Didache* also reveals one of the difficulties faced by these young Christian communities: namely, interpretation. When left to speak for themselves, the words of Jesus are more difficult to get at, especially the parables and the metaphors. And Jesus was frequently, if not predominantly, a metaphorical teacher. What does it mean to be salt? Or light? Or how is one to live through the metaphors of happiness as defined by "blessed are the peacemakers" or "blessed are those who mourn?" These, too, can be found in Matthew's Gospel—which the *Didache* most certainly reflects—but these metaphors leave interpretation open to the hearers, and their original meanings may have been lost on subsequent generations.

How a first-century Jewish peasant in Galilee would have heard these metaphors may have been vastly different from how a second- or third-century convert would have heard them in Egypt or Syria. And when we consider how these metaphors play to our hearing and understanding today, we begin to understand the reason why so many of the early Christian communities opted for specific moral teachings and codes ("don't murder," "don't lie," etc.) as opposed to the Jewish metaphor. One can't take risks with a Jesus who offers a story instead of an answer—especially when those in the community are asking questions.

It should be noted that the *Didache* does reflect these ideas about Jesus. For example, while Jesus said, "It is more blessed to give than to receive," the *Didache* more specifically defines the dangers of receiving gifts and then extrapolates further that those who ask for gifts have a lot of explaining to do. So underneath the surface of the *Didache*, or reading between the lines, we can understand that this early community was particularly troubled by those in need or by those who were willing to receive the generosity of the community. It may also reflect some tone that was meant for the leaders—or those who may have been receiving some form of remuneration for their work. Regardless, this image of Jesus is one who touted rigid responsibility. Most of the commandments are heightened by one or two other details so that those in the community can't miss the implications.

Further in the *Didache* we see that this community also recognized different levels of disciples. Some were more spiritually enlightened than others. In section 6, the shortest of the sixteen sections, we find these words:

> (6) Take care that no one leads you away from the path of righteousness, or teaches what is opposed to God. If you are able to bear up under the full yoke of the Lord, then live it complete. But if not, then live out the portion that you are able. Take food, for example: keep

the dietary restrictions if you can. But just one thing you need to do: don't eat food that has been sacrificed to idols, for that's akin to worshipping a dead god.[4]

This portion of the *Didache* is fascinating because it reveals one of the early debates between Jewish and Gentile converts—and may also reflect some of these disagreements inherent in this early Syrian community. In some of his letters to the churches, the apostle Paul takes on this issue of food sacrificed to idols with his usual practical theology, and at one point in his correspondence with the church at Corinth, he shows his frustration with this debate by announcing that it is based upon a silly notion. "Eat whatever is sold in the meat market," Paul writes (1 Corinthians 10:25–26, NRSV), "without raising any question on the ground of conscience, for the earth and its fullness is the Lord's."

Later in his letter, Paul hedges a bit by pointing out that weaker Christians may be offended by the practice of eating these meats, and so more mature Christians shouldn't eat the meats when in the company of weaker brothers and sisters (1 Corinthians 10:28–29). Still later in this same epistle Paul espouses love as the highest expression of the Christian life—which should be the basis of all decisions and practices, as love demonstrates the very nature of Jesus (1 Corinthians 13).

The *Didache* emerged from this same time period, when idol food and questions about the Jewish dietary laws were hotly debated and may have, by this time, led to further divisions between Jewish Christians and Gentile converts. But creating a community in the midst of such debate was not easily accomplished. And so there were rules.

The *Didache* eases toward its denouement and in section 12 takes up the question of hospitality. This was also a sticky wicket for these early communities, and here the *Didache* brings to bear some practical advice rather than looking to the teachings of Jesus. Specifically, the matters are described this way:

(12) If a traveler stops among you, assist as far as you are able. But be careful that you don't allow the traveler to stay more than two days—three at the most. Or, if the traveler desires to settle among you and be part of the community, make sure he has employment. No idle hands! Everyone must work for their sustenance. Or if the newcomer doesn't have a craft, then figure out among yourself what he can do to be a Christian among you. But again, no freeloaders. Folks like

this are just taking advantage of Christ and you should be aware of them.[5]

The *Didache* is most remarkable at those places where it shows how some of the teachings of Jesus ("give your coat as well as your tunic," "go two miles, not just one," "forgive seventy times seven") have lost their luster in the practical concerns of the world. Early Christian communities like the ones instructed through the *Didache* obviously felt that they were at a disadvantage when trying to live out the letter of Jesus's teachings around hospitality, acceptance, and forgiveness.

And so the idea of Jesus and his teachings are adapted to fit the community and the times. These were not alternative Christianities, but they were alternatives to living out the faith in a hostile environment or during those times when the communal faith was beginning to demonstrate the difficulties of Christians living together.

Extrapolated and compared, one can see how the communities informed by the *Didache* had a different experience of Jesus than, say, the desert father communities. They both speak of Jesus, have him at the center of their faith, but their images are different.

It has always been the case—and all Christian literature, from the Gospels and Pauline epistles to the *Didache* and the writing of the church fathers, demonstrates the disparity of these Jesus ideas.

But in the diversity is the richness.

We can see that the Jesus of the first four centuries was not a cardboard cutout. He could be, and was, many things to many people. He could lead a community with his teachings much like another Moses (the *Didache*). Or he could be that still, small voice of love and object of devotion (the desert fathers). It is not easy to ascertain what these images of Jesus actually meant to those who lived with them, but we can see how the images differed.

FROM THE ONE: MANY

Near the end of the fourth century, in Syria, there was yet another collection of Jesus material that demonstrates this proclivity. The *Liber Graduum*, or *Book of Steps*, is a document comprising thirty tracts. Written originally in Syriac, the document's history may well date back to a Christian community devoted to disciplined life. The *Liber Graduum* may have been the manual that communicants used to deepen their spiritual quest as they sought a deeper relationship with Jesus.

For our purposes here, the *Liber Graduum* is a fascinating collection of Jesus material that, while loosely based on certain portions of the Gospel teachings (again, Matthew in particular), also contains material that is independent of the canonical Gospels or Paul's Epistles. Portions of the *Liber Graduum* seem to reflect a movement defined by celibacy and singleness and by rules that are reflective of a closed and proud community. But other portions of this document contain challenging teachings of Jesus—not unlike those found in the Gospels—but which have a fresh spirit attached to them.

For example, one teaching has Jesus encouraging his followers to enter the houses of tax collectors and prostitutes and thus save them through his teachings. And another, much like the Gospels, has Jesus admonishing his followers to leave behind children and parents and brothers and sisters if they are to be worthy of him.

More austere teachings—bordering on the incredible and metaphorical—have Jesus telling his disciples that if they own anything, they are not worthy of him and, at another place, that they are required to go to all who need them or who request their presence.

The *Liber Graduum* has sometimes been described as a book of charity, but it is more than that. It also demonstrates the ways that a fourth-century community imagined Jesus and tried to order their lives around his call to charity. Whether a Christian document or one produced by an amalgam of Christian and philosophical thought, it nevertheless reflects yet another strand of Jesus material that emerged from canonical and noncanonical ideas.

Today we might see the *Liber Graduum* as a devotional work, a series of thirty reflective readings designed to instruct and enlighten. Or we could see it as wisdom. Or perhaps a guidebook to the Christian faith—or at least a faith associated with Christianity and knowledgeable of the teachings of Jesus.

Perhaps the most intriguing saying in the *Liber Graduum* attributed to Jesus is this one—reminiscent of the Gospels on several points—and yet combined to form a most powerful and articulate pericope of the crucial teachings of Jesus:

Be humble and holy, and separate from the world and from marriage, and love all people, and follow me. Do not be of the world, for
I was neither in it, nor worked in it. But follow me and be perfect.
(25:4)[6]

Here are several points of Gospel, including the call of the disciples
by the Sea of Galilee ("follow me"), the call to love others (1 John), and
at least three points found in the Sermon on the Mount in Matthew
("be perfect," "do not love the world," and "blessed are the meek"). Yet
here they are combined in a new form—a kind of superteaching—that
has Jesus announcing these as the mark of true discipleship.

Like the Shakers, however, this community was obviously not able to
propagate and gain new adherents. Once the call to singleness and
chastity is made mandatory for inclusion in the community, there is very
little hope of multiplying the community through children. The *Liber
Graduum*, then, may well reflect a solitary community that existed for a
short time and quickly died out in the interim between inception and
culmination, without having ever realized the goal of discipleship.

On a final note, the *Liber Graduum* is also an important document
in that it begins to reflect some of the ascetic tendencies that would
show up in certain strands of Islam a few centuries later. And, in fact,
some of the Jesus traditions found here may have influenced certain
Jesus traditions within Syrian Islam. But we can only surmise.

Taken as a whole, there is a great deal more to Jesus—and the development of the idea of Jesus—than these alternative communities offer to
this study. While the canonical Gospels (and perhaps *The Gospel of
Thomas*) offer those ideas of Jesus that became, in time, the tradition
and the creed, one can see that even during the first three centuries
there were other images afloat in and through the church. Some of
these ideas were countered by the Gospels themselves, or by Paul, or by
the church fathers up to and including Origen. But other ideas and
sayings and portions of noncanonical Jesus material were embraced,
even utilized, by the same.

What we are left with as we explore these other Christs is a mixture
of fascination and question. How did certain ideas about Jesus remain
at the center of the apostolic tradition (i.e., Messiah, atonement, resurrection.)? Why did other ideas about Jesus or certain strands of his

teaching get explained away, reduced, or even removed (i.e., self-sacrifice, peacemaking, radical hospitality)?

We can see in some of Paul's letters the earliest struggles with a few of these very questions (as some would maintain that the Jesus of Paul is quite different from, say, the Jesus of Luke). And we can see how the church fathers began to emphasize and extrapolate various teachings of Jesus to address the issues of their age. Then, layered between these, we have the many other documents and communities that reflect alternative voices and Jesus material—not all of it essentially noncanonical. It is just different.

It has been said that the winners write history. And in large part that is true. When it comes to concepts about Jesus, we see how those ideas have lived on that were declared victorious by the ecumenical councils, and thus canonized in both scripture and creed. That is not to say, however, that these noncanonical ideas were wrong or somehow corrupted. The very opposite may, in fact, be true. Or, in the canonized faith, we may simply operate with one strand of Christianity to the dismissal of others. One image of Jesus prevails to the exclusion of others.

But history can also teach that some ideas simply didn't have enough clout. It is not that they were corrupt, untruthful, or built of straw—but rather, they lived on in communities and in writings that were lost, were misunderstood, or simply perished into the dustbin of history.

If, in fact, the Gospels of Luke and John are accurate in their respective assertions that "more has been written" and "there are many other things that Jesus said and did that are not written here . . . and which the world cannot contain," then we have every reason to assume that some of these traditions and words may have lived on in some of the documents and some of the communities here described. Not all of the words of Jesus are found in the Gospels. Not all of the deeds. All of the Christology is not found in Paul's letters. The church fathers have a wide swath of theology that is not always, in all points, in agreement—and some quote from Jesus material not found in the biblical canon.

What we gain, then, from a study of these centuries of Christian thought is a deeper appreciation for the resiliency of the *idea of Jesus*—which is remarkable once we consider a first-century Jewish peasant, an itinerant preacher and healer, who could easily, like dozens of other touted messiahs, have died and faded to obscurity. How this same Jesus could appeal to so many communities and strands of thought in these early centuries borders on the incredible. But then, perhaps humanity has always been enamored of gods and goddesses, and people have always chosen their meaning.

Jesus, nevertheless, occupies a unique place in history—even if one regards only the amount of written material produced about him. Not all of this material is of Christian origin, as we shall see. And the images of Jesus over time have been written, even, into other faiths and cultures.

Moving beyond the fourth and fifth centuries there are more images and teachings of Jesus that emerge. Islam, in particular, would reserve a special place for Jesus (Isa), the prophet of love, and in faiths as diverse as Taoism and Buddhism, Jesus (or his teachings) would touch upon these cultures and communities in new and unexpected ways.

4

ISA AND MUHAMMAD

The Jesus of Islam

And when God said, "O Jesus, son of Mary, did you say to men, 'Take me and my mother as gods besides God?' he said, "Praise be to God! It is not fitting for me to say what is not mine by right. If I had said it thou wouldest have known it. I said to them only what thou commandest me, 'Worship God, my Lord and your Lord.'" —Qur'an 5. 116–118

Much has been written about the three great monotheistic religions—Judaism, Christianity, and Islam—in terms of each faith's distinctive history and traditions as well as their commonalities. Of the three religions—Islam emerged in due course as a "corrective" faith, with the Qur'an and subsequent Islamic teachings being understood as correcting the divergent or corrupted faiths of the former two. Muhammad—whom Muslims regard as the last and most important of the prophets—most certainly knew and interacted with both Jews and Christians. This interaction is not inconsequential when one begins to study the place and importance that Jesus occupies within the Muslim faith.

But a bit of background can help.

Muhammad was born in Mecca in the year 570 CE. This was the same year that a Christian army commander attacked Mecca, using elephants as heavy artillery. These were precarious times, and after centuries of various occupations and military conquests, the nomadic tribes of Arabia were looking for someone who could unite them and bring stability to this region—which was then inhabited by a loose confederacy of tribes who were encircled by other larger and more powerful nations. In no small way, Muhammad fulfilled these hopes.

Prior to Muhammad, the clans of the Arabian Peninsula each worshipped their respective gods. Judaism did have some influence (strictly monotheistic), as did Christianity, but for the most part the clans had no religious unity, and when people made pilgrimage to the Ka'bah in Mecca, they paid homage to their respective gods and thereby made peace with the other clans. But after Muhammad, whom the clans accepted as a prophet, the Ka'bah became strictly dedicated to God (Allah), and the clans were essentially unified as one people dedicated to the five pillars of Islam. These pillars are: The *Shahada* (or Islamic creed), daily prayers, almsgiving, fasting during the month of Ramadan, and making pilgrimage (*hajj*) to Mecca at least once in one's lifetime.

The *hajj*—or pilgrimage to Mecca—cannot be underemphasized as it relates to the unity of Islam. Pilgrims making this journey are, today, not exclusively Arabs—and dressed in the traditional pilgrim dress, all distinctions of nationality and ethnicity are eradicated. Pilgrims affirm in unison: "Here I am at your service, O Allah." In essence, God becomes the center of worship, and during the *hajj* all thoughts of violence (or even harm to animals and insects) are displaced to give way to the strict focus on prayer and offering oneself to the service of Allah. Peace and unity are the themes of the *hajj*.

Islam also affirms five pillars of belief—which are lived out in various traditions within the faith, but essential to the whole. Again, there are aspects of these beliefs which would be shared by Jews and Christians, but the creed also demonstrates the unique approach of Islam as it relates to both Muhammad and, as we shall see, Jesus. While Jesus is not mentioned specifically anywhere in the creed—there are aspects to the Muslim understanding of "revelation" which certainly have connecting influence, and some of these beliefs can be affirmed by Muslims and Christians alike.

Again, some of the connections to Jesus are noted thus—and the development of various Jesus traditions (*hadith*) that have certainly emerged from the high respect and honor afforded to this prophet of the Islamic faith.[1]

Like the other monotheistic faiths, some of these five pillars of belief are affirmed by both Judaism and Christianity, though perhaps in different nomenclature. But these beliefs of Islam may be described here as:

1. There is only one God.
2. Belief in the prophets of God (every group has had its prophets—Jewish and Christian alike—but Muhammad is the final seal of all the prophets).
3. Belief in the books of revelation, which include five: the *Suhuf* (pages) of the prophet Abraham, which have been lost, the Torah of Moses, the Psalms of David, the Gospel of Jesus, and the Qur'an.
4. Belief in angels.
5. Belief in a last day and final judgment of God.

Among these beliefs one can find the words and actions of Jesus sprinkled throughout—not only as they are found in the Qur'an but also in subsequent traditions. In fact, while the Qur'an gives expression to Jesus and his belief in the five pillars, the more sizable collection of teachings comes from the Hadith—the oral and written traditions/stories about Jesus that emerged later. The predominance of the Jesus traditions explored here do, indeed, come from the Hadith. And these various traditions—much like the Gospels themselves—emerged over a long period of time as people discussed Jesus and retold stories about him.

But the essence of Islam is a consistent message.

Although Jesus enters into the picture in Islam, he is no more central to the faith than Muhammad himself—as the message of all the prophets was to point the way to God. Jesus is important, and Muhammad absolutely essential—but even the greatest of the prophets did not ask for adoration for themselves but pointed to God.

Muhammad, in fact, insisted that he was not proclaiming a new religion. Rather, he taught that the true religion had been given to humanity from the beginning (with Adam also being a prophet) and that God's messengers had proclaimed a consistent word—namely, that people should submit to God and follow the whole of God's law. Muhammad did not see the prophets as a succession of revelation or as one prophet being superior to another but as a continuous stream of messengers who offered the same proclamation. Abraham, Moses, and Jesus—just to name a few prophets—were all regarded as having the same task. The proclamation was always the unity of God and a summons for people to worship God alone.

Muhammad's teachings and, later, the gift of the Qur'an brought a unified expression of faith to the Arabic region. This history and summary of belief cannot be understated if one is looking to understand the core of Islam.

But when seeking to understand the differences between Islam and Judaism or Islam and Christianity, one must also look deeper.

Like Judaism and Christianity, Islam is an Abrahamic faith—tracing its roots back to Abraham. But unlike Judaism and Christianity (and the Biblical account of Abraham's journey from Haran and Isaac's birth through Sarah), Islam traces its lineage through Abraham and Ishmael (born of Hagar). In many respects these differences were born of the book. Unlike Judaism and Christianity, which shared the same Hebrew scriptures, Islam originally had no holy book, and so, when Muhammad received the Qur'an and offered it to the people, it was received as a great miracle and a direct revelation from God. The Qur'an was also received and regarded as the final revelation and guidance of God for all humanity, correcting and summarizing all former scriptures (such as the Bible).

Any exploration of Jesus in Islam must begin here (with the Qur'an)—as the Qur'an contains much information about Jesus, who is known as Isa. Likewise, Islam gives Jesus a place of high honor and respect—he is regarded as the most important prophet prior to the arrival of Muhammad (the last prophet) and is sometimes referred to as the Prophet of Love, the Breath of God, the miracle of God's Word, or even the Seal of the Israelite Prophets.

Muslims and Christians also find much agreement about Jesus. For example, both faiths affirm that Jesus was born of the Virgin Mary, that Jesus taught and gave the Gospel message to his disciples, that he performed miracles such as healing and raising the dead, and that he is the Messiah. The latter has different meanings, however, to Muslim and Christian, as Islam differs with Christianity regarding Christ's death and resurrection. The Qur'an affirms that Jesus ascended to God and was a son of God—but not God's unique Son. However, as such, Jesus is also given a central role in eschatology—the end of human history—as in both Islamic and Christian understanding, Christ will return at the end of time to usher in the kingdom of God and the new era of peace. Both Islam and Christianity espouse Christ's return at the end of time to battle the Antichrist and usher in the final age of God.

In the Qur'an itself, the various references to Jesus could be said to occupy four larger strands: there are references to Christ's birth and infancy, his miracles, many discourses between Jesus and God (or Jesus and his people), and particular pronouncements issued by God (or by Jesus himself) that clear up misunderstandings about his relationship with God or his divine versus human nature. While some references to Jesus in the Qur'an—especially Jesus's teachings—are nearly verbatim to the Gospels, Jesus is also the only prophet mentioned in the Qur'an who intentionally distances himself from the teachings of his adherents—namely, the opinions that others hold of him, especially where they regard him as equal to God or as God's only son.

For example, while Muslims affirm that Jesus was born immaculately, here the understanding would be that this conception was no different than the power that gave Adam and Eve breath. In other words, God does not "birth" children (such as the Son of God) but rather gives life to all. We find this in the Qur'an: "Truly, the likeness of Jesus with God is as the likeness of Adam. He created him of dust, and then said to him, 'Be!' and he was" (3:59).

Likewise, in the Qur'an, we note that Jesus is also a miracle worker: "I have come to you with a sign from your Lord: I make for you out of clay, as it were, the figure of a bird, and breathe into it and it becomes a bird by God's leave. And I heal the blind, and the lepers, and I raise the dead by God's leave" (3:49).

Along this same Qur'anic strand, we can note that Jesus was neither Jewish nor Christian but Islamic, in that he came to proclaim not a self-adulation or worship, but the worship of God alone. This is a prevalent theme about Jesus in both Qur'anic thought and throughout the Hadith. Jesus is seen as correcting the false theologies of the Christian faith. Such as: "[I have come] to attest the law which was before me, and to make lawful to you part of what was forbidden you; I have come to you with a sign from your Lord, so fear God and obey me" (3:50).

As the Hadith affirms time and again—often through the words of the prophet Muhammad correcting the overzealous adoration of Jesus followers—Jesus himself came to proclaim the unity of God and did not ask for his own. These distinctions are paramount—and play a central note of theology within the hundreds of Jesus traditions recorded throughout the Hadith. God is not given allowance to partner with a Son, or to be divided into thirds, or to slip into the created world through incarnation or any doctrine that would remove God from inaccessible light.

Not all of these affirmations come through the Qur'an—or are even found on the lips of Muhammad—but they are there, nevertheless.

Muhammad is noted as saying, for example: "Whoever believes there is no God but Allah, alone without partner, that Muhammad is his messenger, that Jesus is a servant and messenger of God, his word breathed into Mary and a spirit emanating from Him, and that Paradise and Hell are true, shall be received by God into heaven."

One will note in this brief affirmation that there is much information meant to correct certain Christian emphases, namely, that Jesus should be regarded as a servant of God only, a messenger, and that he is a spirit come from God (but not born of God).

Additional Qur'anic references to Jesus provide a more pointed summary of his life and work—however brief. With regard to Christ's birth:

> Behold! the angels said, "Oh Mary! God gives you glad tidings of a Word from Him. His name will be Christ Jesus, the son of Mary, held in honor in this world and the Hereafter, and in (the company of) those nearest to God. He shall speak to the people in childhood and in maturity. He shall be (in the company) of the righteous. . . . And God will teach him the Book and Wisdom, the Law and the Gospel." (3:45–48)

> Christ, the son of Mary, was no more than a messenger; many were the messengers that passed away before him. His mother was a woman of truth. They had both to eat their (daily) food. See how God makes His signs clear to them; yet see in what ways they are deluded away from the truth! (5:75)

> He [Jesus] said: "I am indeed a servant of God. He has given me revelation and made me a prophet; He has made me blessed wheresoever I be; and He has enjoined on me prayer and charity as long as I live. He has made me kind to my mother, and not overbearing or miserable. So peace is on me the day I was born, the day that I die, and the day that I shall be raised up to life (again)!" Such was Jesus the son of Mary. It is a statement of truth, about which they (vainly)

dispute. It is not befitting to (the majesty of) God that He should beget a son. Glory be to Him! When He determines a matter, He only says to it, "Be," and it is. (19:30–35)

It can be noted that each of these references regards Jesus as a prophet—and an important one—while at the same time correcting certain emphases or ideas about Jesus. Messengers come and go—Jesus among them—but the central point of these Qur'anic texts is that Jesus took his place as a major prophet by proclaiming the truth of Islam and by correcting misunderstandings about being "begotten" or what it means to be God's son.

As we shall see in the later traditions, these themes come full circle and are explored more deeply—but often not as pointedly as we find them in the Qur'an—such as:

And behold! God will say [i.e., on the Day of Judgment]: "Oh Jesus, the son of Mary! Did you say unto men, worship me and my mother as gods in derogation of God?" He will say: "Glory to Thee! Never could I say what I had no right (to say). Had I said such a thing, You would indeed have known it. You know what is in my heart, though I know not what is in Yours. For You know in full all that is hidden. Never did I say to them anything except what You commanded me to say: 'Worship God, my Lord and your Lord.' And I was a witness over them while I lived among them. When You took me up, You were the Watcher over them, and You are a witness to all things." (5:116–117)

Perhaps the clearest distinction in the Qur'an with regard to Jesus has to do with the meaning of the Messiah. In Christian teaching and tradition (going back to the earlier Jewish), the word "messiah" means, literally, "the anointed one." In Jewish history, kings were often anointed, as were some prophets. This anointing with oil was meant to bestow special privileges and powers of the spirit upon the individual, setting the person aside for a special mission or work. The outward witness of the anointing was meant to demonstrate the power of God and clearly mark the individual for the tasks ahead.

As for kings, the notion of the anointed was to denote a sonship of God—an earthly representation of the heavenly. In time, this anointing of kings was deemed to be a witness of the Davidic lineage, a mark of progression in bloodline and the gifts of the spirit denoted by leadership of a people and the establishment of covenant. The kings were anointed as a representative of the divine—and many of the royal Psalms or coronation Psalms in the Bible reflect this idea. The second Psalm is perhaps most indicative of this arrangement and theology:

> Why do the nations conspire, and the peoples plot in vain? The kings of the earth set themselves, and the rulers take counsel together, against the Lord and his anointed, saying, "Let us burst their bonds asunder, and cast their cords from us." He who sits in the heavens laughs; the Lord has them in derision . . . I will tell of the decree of the Lord: He said to me, "You are my son; today I have begotten you. Ask of me, and I will make the nations your heritage, and the ends of the earth your possession." (Psalm 2:1–4, 7–8 NRSV)

Of course, the Jewish interpretation of this Psalm as it relates to "the anointed" is one perspective, the Christian, another. And Islam represents a third.

As for prophets, the Jewish and Christian idea was marked by the spirit's power, with messengers—those who appeared or were raised up to bring people back to covenant and faithfulness—as primary witnesses. This anointing was not always marked by oil itself but sometimes simply by the power of the spirit, a movement of voice in history that would call the people back to the law, or to works of righteousness, or to justice, or even to God's judgment.

It is no small insight to note that the arrival of the prophets (as anointed) coincided with the insatiable desire for a royal lineage (1 Samuel). Once the kings of Israel and Judah appear on the scene (as anointed ones), the prophets are not far behind—speaking truth to power and correcting the corruptions of the crown. These juxtapositions of power and spirit, of earthly and heavenly, became the centerpiece for much deeper expectations and traditions about the Messiah (the Anointed One) in both Jewish and Christian thought.

Most of these differences had already been birthed and broken apart by the time the prophet Muhammad appeared and the Qur'an was offered as yet a third, or corrective, teaching. In the Qur'an, Messiah holds neither the significance of the promise held by the Jew nor the descriptive, redemptive, and apocalyptic meaning denoted by the Christian. Messiah is a name, and neither Jew nor Christian should assign any particular weight to it or drag predetermined meaning into the text.

Consider here the various Qur'anic implications for Messiah—which are not descriptive, but again, serve as something of an apology for the Islamic path.

> When Jesus came with Clear Signs, he said: "Now I have come to you with Wisdom, and in order to make clear to you some of the (points) on which you dispute. Therefore, fear God and obey me. God, He is my Lord and your Lord, so worship Him—this is a Straight Way." But sects from among themselves fell into disagreement. So woe to the wrongdoers, from the penalty of a Grievous Day! (43:63–65)

> They said, "We killed the Messiah Jesus, son of Mary, the messenger of God." They did not kill him, nor did they crucify him, but the likeness of him was put on another man—and they killed that man. (4:157)

> Say, He is God, the One and Only, The Eternal, Absolute; He begets not, Nor is He begotten; And there is none like unto Him. (112:1–4)

These Qur'anic citations can also provide insights into some of the New Testament Gospel pericopes: in particular, those that offer a more prophetic or human perspective on Jesus and do not carry the weight of the glorious. Christian scholars have long noted these inclusions in the Gospel texts and the various interpretations that gave rise to the full-blown messianic theologies that would come later. Not all may be explained away, however, as later theologies or as subsequent teachings that were quite distant from the original. Nevertheless, the New Testament Gospels do offer insights into the type of conversations and theologies that would have been bantered about whenever Christian and Islamic communities came into contact with one another—or were in close proximity.

Some of these Gospel citations that seem to have influenced Islamic thought on the matter of Jesus as Messiah are:

> Then Jesus came from Galilee to John at the Jordan, to be baptized by him. John would have prevented him, saying, "I need to be baptized by you, and do you come to me?" But Jesus answered, "Let it

be so now; for it is proper for us in this way to fulfill all righteousness." Then he [John] consented. (Matthew 3:13–15, NRSV)

As he was setting out on a journey, a man ran up and knelt before
him [Jesus] and asked him, "Good Teacher, what must I do to inherit
eternal life?" Jesus said to him, "Why do you call me good? No one is
good but God alone." (Mark 10:17–18, NRSV)

The Jesus we find here has the same humility and grace noted in the
later Islamic traditions—especially the Sufi—and at the very least there
is an infusion of the Christian idea of Jesus (as servant, as humble
prophet, as teller of truth) into the Muslim ideal. We rarely find one
without the other. There is a kind of dichotomy of traditions that bleeds
through both the Muslim and the Christian.

What makes this so fascinating, of course, is that the Muslim is aware
of the Christian ideal (which was earlier), while the Christian is rarely
aware of the Muslim concept of Jesus. While there has always been a
kind of conversational kinship between Jew and Christian (though not
always healthy), there has not always been one between Christian and
Muslim. Many of these conversations seem born of misunderstanding
or just snippets of truth—while the full weight of the words has fallen
into the cracks of history.

The Qur'an, as already noted, holds Jesus (Isa) in ample portions—
but a Jesus who can best be understood as a prophet (anointed) who
came to give witness to the unity of God. Other ideas about Jesus, as we
shall see, blossomed post-Qur'an, but none are inconsistent with the
first witness of the text. A composite summary of the Jesus of the
Qur'an may be described (with Qur'an citations listed) as follows:

- Jesus is the Messiah who came into the world as good news (3:45).
- Jesus proclaimed and established the Gospel (5:49; 19:30).
- Jesus's birth was announced to Mary by an angel (19:16–20).
- Jesus was born of the Virgin Mary (19:16–35).
- Jesus was without sin (19:19).
- Jesus is described as the word of God (4:171).
- Jesus is often described as the spirit of God (4:171).
- Jesus is only a prophet or apostle of God (19:34–35; 9:30; 4:171).
- Jesus was submissive to God (19:30).
- Jesus performed miracles (3:49).

- Jesus provided former scriptures—gospels (5:49).
- Jesus had a mission to the Jewish people for a period of time (3:49–50; 13:38).
- Jesus did not die on the cross, but was rescued (4:157).
- Like Elijah the prophet, Jesus was taken up into heaven and did not die (3:55–58).
- Jesus—not Elijah—will return at the end of human history to prepare people for God's final rule (43:61).
- Jesus prophesied about the coming of Muhammad (61:6).

The Qur'an, in total, has many references to Jesus.

Beyond these similarities and differences with the Christian faith, however, there is no doubt that Jesus has always occupied a place of honor within the Muslim faith. Many Islamic traditions did develop with regard to Jesus, and outside of the early Christian community itself, Islam is rich in Jesus story. With regard to the Qur'an, Muhammad is noted by name but four times in the scriptures, while Jesus (Isa) is noted by name some twenty-five times. The place and prominence of Jesus in the Qur'an no doubt gave rise to hundreds of stories about Jesus in later tradition, as sages and leaders retold and shared these across the centuries. Sometimes these stories may have been polemic, at other junctures instructive, and, as we shall see in the Sufi stories of the next chapter, often humorous.

UNDERSTANDING HADITH

Any exploration of the Jesus of Islam must begin with an understanding of the past—and then finger out into the questions that emerge from the various faces of Jesus that are portrayed in the diversity of the faith itself. The Islamic Jesus is rich in tone, intent, and teaching—with many of these Jesus stories containing similar composites in the Gospels or early Christian tradition, while others are wholly unique and born of the internal discourses of Islam.

These discourses, again, which are known as Hadith, can mean a *report*, an *account*, a *tale*, or even a *tradition* affirmed by a particular community. And Islam is rich in Hadith. These stories would have been passed along orally originally, or they could have been written in some instances, but most Hadith in relation to Jesus are brief interludes or shorter descriptions of larger conversations. One might even regard the Hadith as oral tradition—similar, in fact, to the development of the Talmud in Jewish thought or the plethora of gospels and writings and oral traditions that were so prevalent in the first two centuries of the church.

The Hadith in Islam may also be regarded as early forms of guidance. After all, once a faith is established and the scriptures known, there are soon questions which develop about "how to live" or "how to interpret" or "how to fulfill" the various nuances of the faith. The Talmud represents centuries of these questions and answers in the Jewish faith, and to some extent one might understand the apostle Paul's epistles in this vein or, later, the writings of the early church fathers from their various vantage points in the church and the world.

Hadith is conversation attributed to Muhammad. And many of the stories about Jesus also provide a peek into the past as well as deepening our understanding of these early points of conflict—both with the Jewish and Christian communities on the outside as well as from within the Islamic community. The context of many of these stories may seem wholly religious, but if we look and listen closely, we can also note some of the social dimensions at play and how Jesus was looked to as a prophet of love and reconciliation.

Likewise, in many of the Hadith—as we shall see—Jesus is brought alongside other prophets and sages to give some continuity with the past. Frequently we encounter Moses or David or Solomon or Job. John the Baptizer also appears. And Jesus has fascinating discourses with both living and dead. But the thread that runs through these later Hadith frequently has a reference point to the Qur'an or to the understanding of Christ that we encounter there. Other Hadith seem to have parallels in the Gospels or may have emerged alongside some earlier Christian communities when lines were more loosely drawn and peaceable conversation was the gift of the day.

Again, it should also be noted that while Jesus preceded Muhammad as a prophet, all who came before the Prophet Muhammad were said to have pointed *to him*: God's final messenger. Thus, the Jesus we encounter in Hadith is often pointing beyond himself, or denying his importance, or even walking in such humility that he can in no way be represented as having any final authority. If anything, the Jesus we encounter in Islamic Hadith is meant to be a prophet of miracle and love. He can be harsh, too—speaking the truth—but the Islamic Messiah is looking forward to the arrival of Muhammad and affirms that there is no God but Allah.

Islamic scholars and teachers have often noted that the Qur'an, at least where Jesus is concerned, is principally about rectifying certain doctrinal images of Jesus and has little concern for his teachings and miracles. The Messiah teaches sparingly in the Qur'an. However, in Hadith we discover a Jesus who loves to teach and who makes a point of clarifying misconceptions and offering opportunities to love and serve.

In short, the Hadith—or what some may call the Islamic gospel as it relates to Jesus—contains many traditions about Jesus that may have been a part of earlier conversations between Muslim and Christian, especially those times when Christians and Muslims lived in close proximity or Christians had questions about the Muslim faith, or vice versa.

For these reasons and more, it is not surprising that Jesus occupies such a large place in both the Qur'an and the Hadith—some of which may have originated during or soon after the time of Muhammad. In the year 622 CE, when Muhammad journeyed to Medina in his flight from Mecca and the Muslim calendar begins, Arabia was a hodgepodge of various beliefs. Paganism was abundant, since Arabia was a Hellenized area. But since it was far from the busier centers of civilization, there was no dominant religion.

In those early days of Islam, Christians were regarded as "people of the book," and in time the central figures of the Jewish faith (Abraham and Moses) and the Christian faith (Jesus) were considered prophets of the new faith—Islam. The Qur'an was central to the faith, but in time other great literature developed, particularly among the Sufi writers—and many traditions about Jesus were given voice and new characterization. Jesus in the Hadith is often referred to as "spirit of God," for example, or less frequently, "word of God."

By the second generation following Muhammad's death in 632 CE, the Muslim faith had expanded as far west as Spain, to Afghanistan, and into the various Jewish and Christian areas of northern Africa and the Near East, including Iran and Iraq. And while the Qur'an no doubt existed in a complete form during Muhammad's lifetime, the Qur'an was not necessarily read or regarded with the same stature among Muslims then as it is today. Rather, like early Jewish and Christian communities, much of the faith was passed along through the oral traditions and stories—the Hadith of Islam.

As we shall see, many of these traditions and stories had revelatory status—and some would have been formative for certain communities, perhaps no less so than the Qur'an, especially as illiteracy may have been higher among new converts. Some of the Hadith can be understood in the context of telling stories about the great prophets of the past—recounting words and actions that would inform and shape the communities in which they originated. All of these stories would have been closely associated with the day-to-day piety, prayer, devotion, and social matters of those communities.

As for Jesus, we can see that the early Muslim community would have been receptive to stories about him. In time, the Messiah was not regarded as a Christian personage but an Islamic one—the most important prophet before the arrival of Muhammad himself. And, like the early Christian communities which disseminated a surprising number of gospels and pseudogospels (such as the infancy gospel of Thomas), we see Jesus in the Qur'an being born of a virgin under a palm tree and creating birds out of clay. That Christian writings and traditions were known among the early Muslim communities there can be no doubt. The only divergence of opinion would simply be in how they originated or why.

The Qur'an, however, rarely quotes from other holy books (Torah, Psalms, or Gospels). There is some crossover in the Qur'an with these texts, but it is very rare. But not so in the Hadith. Here we frequently find Jesus quoting (or at least grazing in words very similar to) the Gospels, and there are stories and episodes that relate back to the Gospels in many instances.

In most respects, Hadith supplied for the needs of the early Muslim communities whenever questions arose regarding ethics, legalities, or even some theology. Though rarely longer than two to three sentences, the basic form of Hadith offered guidance in a broad range of social and religious concerns. The Hadith also serves as a type of storehouse—preserving the mood, the doctrines, and the opinions of the various Muslim sects centuries ago.

Like the Jewish citations of the Talmud, the Hadith normally cite a sage in respect to each tradition. Few are anonymous. These citations also provide a hint as to the time frame or origin of each Hadith—or perhaps even the community or group that preserved it. These particular Hadith, in reference to Jesus, may also be indicative of how the communities came to be—and how closely they may have been associated with or in conflict with those early Christian communities.

As far as Hadith themes go, Jesus often appears as a commentator on the end times—the apocalyptic vision of the final culmination of God. And it has been noted earlier that both Muslims and Christians see Jesus as instrumental in drawing human history to a close. The other common theme that Jesus visits is biblical commentary—usually from the Gospels, but with corrective or expository overtones. But this Jesus is more of a pious figure—and his expressions are likely indicative of the variations of opinion that were soon cropping up in the Muslim communities, with Jesus providing the correct answer or proving the superiority of one view over another.

Jesus, as we find him in the Hadith, is often characterized as an ascetic. But he is not always austere or aloof. Primarily he is humble—while also being quite to the point, or proving his point—that one should have no attachment to the world or the allure of it. Here Jesus is usually attached to the poor. Poverty and humility are regarded as the highest of virtues—according to the Hadith Jesus—and the stranger, the guest, and the foreigner are always shown abundant hospitality. Jesus also shuns worldly goods, and his thoughts and actions continually return to care for the least of humanity. Such tales may also quicken the tensions that existed, almost from the beginning, between early Muslim and Christian communities—as many in the Islamic communities could not find the connections between the poor Christ and the Christians who espoused to be his followers.

There are many tales of the prophets amid the corpus of the Hadith, but Jesus most certainly has a prominent place among them. While we do find stories about Adam, or Moses, or even David or Job—Jesus seems to tower above them, though certainly not theologically or via special privilege or status. Rather, he simply appears more frequently.

At some point in the development of the Hadith traditions, there would have been an awareness of certain phrases from the New Testament Gospels. Perhaps these sayings came from a knowledge of the Gospels themselves (also regarded as a holy book among Muslims) or could have derived from a kind of lectionary or dictionary of renderings. As most Christian scholars accept the existence of a Q document—a first- or second-century collection of Jesus sayings that the Gospel writers used—so the Hadith traditions may have emerged from their own Muslim collection: sayings, acts, and expressions attributed to Jesus.

Among the common Jesus teachings that one can find in the Hadith but which carry back to the Christian Gospels themselves, are phrases like:

> You are the salt of the earth (Matthew 5:13).
> Your left hand must not know what your right hand is doing (Matthew 6:3).
> Store up for yourselves treasures in heaven (Matthew 6:19).
> Look at the birds of the sky (Matthew 6:26).
> When you fast, put oil on your head (Matthew 6:17).

Christians will note that most of these sayings originate from the Gospel of Matthew, from a long discourse of Jesus commonly called the Sermon on the Mount (Matthew 5–8). This insight may also be indicative of the existence of other "sayings" documents—perhaps loosely associated teachings that were, in the final form of Matthew, woven together to form one complete message. But as far as the Muslim community is concerned—and the various Hadith associated with these sayings and Jesus—we can see that Jesus held a place of honor and his words were given weight to address those conversations in the Muslim communities. The Hadith didn't necessarily hark back to the New Testament Gospels themselves, and there could have existed within the Muslim literature a type of Jesus tradition in and of itself—free of Christian interference or inference.

One such example of this would exist in the Hadith which has Jesus saying:

> Blessed is he who reads the Qur'an and does what is in it.

A Christian would recognize these words in their pace and structure, almost hearing them as poetry—but would recognize them as:

> Blessed are those who hear the word of God and keep it.

Notable among the Hadith traditions is the absence of parables. While the parables of Jesus play a large—if not central—method of teaching in the synoptic Gospels of the New Testament (Matthew,

Mark, and Luke), there are few parables to be found in Hadith. Sayings and deeds, answers to questions, these are the prominent methodologies that Jesus uses in the Hadith—an observation which may hark back to the Qur'an itself, which is devoid of parables.

As the Hadith expanded over time, we can also see how certain earlier stories were expanded or extra commentary added. Like the Talmud—which is layered with commentary upon other commentary, from one generation to the next—the Islamic Hadith begins to take on a life of its own as the Muslim faith expands and takes on various expressions. A Shi'ite Hadith, for example, might differ from a Sunni Hadith in ways that could reflect the Shi'ite regard for and veneration of various imams and holy sites. The history of these differences is far too complex to relate for our purposes here—but as far as the Jesus traditions are concerned and how they developed among the Islamic sects, one can see how interpretation and history play a much larger role in the formation of the Hadith.

In general, these later Hadith related to Jesus often have associations that were not present or perhaps accepted in earlier forms. We can be certain, for example, that a Hadith is of later variety if we find Jesus more at home in the world—noting the beauty of mountains, or stones, or even skulls.

In one famous Hadith, no doubt of a later origin—and perhaps even influenced by Buddhist thought—we find Jesus and his disciples thus:

> One day Jesus and his disciples walked past the carcass of a dead dog. The disciples said, "The stench is horrendous." To which Jesus replied: "But note how white the teeth are!" (author paraphrase)

While this Hadith is concise, it does have a slight parable form (with Jesus a principal character) predicating that it is probably of later origin, but also because it does exist in forms beyond Muslim Hadith as well. Likewise, the tale would have been distasteful to early Muslim sensibilities, and we find few early Hadith depicting Jesus noting beauty in odd places or calling forth observations about mundane details that would have to be interpreted through introspection or with such philosophical panache.

Another Hadith, likely of later origin, depicts Jesus talking to a pig (an unclean animal). Again, this is a well-known Hadith, perhaps even circulated beyond Muslim communities. It demonstrates also the later use of an earlier Jesus form, setting the situation as a kind of morality lesson, with Jesus providing the punchline.

> One day, a pig approached Jesus on the road and Jesus said to it, "Pass in peace." The pig asked, "Spirit of God, why would you say such a thing to me?" Jesus replied, "I cannot bring my tongue to speak evil of anyone." (author paraphrase)

As we encounter the richness of the Muslim Jesus, we find ourselves asking many questions. Some of these involve questions of history or even the transference of information and sacred text from one generation to the next. How was this accomplished? Toward what ends?

We may also ask questions about the Muslim Jesus in much the same way scholars have explored the New Testament presentation of Jesus. Where does the historical Jesus end and the Jesus of faith begin? How can we sift the various traditions about Jesus and discover the center of his life and teaching? Why did the Muslim community continue to use Jesus so predominantly in the Hadith, and why is he featured so often in later discourses that were generations removed from the Qur'an?

The existence of this huge corpus of Jesus traditions also provokes questions about the association and coexistence of early Muslim and Christian communities. Why were some Jesus stories shared so willingly between Muslims and Christians? What were the harmonies that existed then—a culture that allowed for a free association of creed and witness? Can these Jesus traditions help to illuminate the need for Christians and Muslims to have deeper dialogue and understanding today?

HADITH AND THE MUSLIM SECTS

The history of Islam following Muhammad's death is important to understanding the Hadith. Beginning in the year 610, Muhammad preached in Mecca for a dozen years. During this time he and his followers experienced severe opposition, but in 622 he and his group migrated to Medina, a city some 250 miles to the north. This migration, or *hijrah*, is actually the beginning of the Muslim era.

In Medina, Muhammad was able to preach without persecution, and he began to develop a structure to the Muslim movement—forming a community around him that became known as the *ummah*. The *ummah* was, in many respects, a style of government that established the Muslim movement as a political, economic, and military force. From the Medina capital, the *ummah* successfully conquered neighboring regions of the peninsula, including Mecca, and in less than a decade after his move north, Muhammad had essentially become the leader of a Muslim nation.

Muhammad's vision, however, did not stop with the Arabian Peninsula. He also sent envoys into the regions of Persia and Byzantium—then powerful Christian strongholds—and within the years preceding Muhammad's death, these armies had successfully overpowered other governments along the periphery of the Muslim nation.

Portions of the Qur'an reflect the theology of this *jihad*, or holy war—but the essence of these wars was deemed to be in self-defense. In fact, the Qur'an states as much:

> Fight in the way of Allah against those who fight against you, but begin not hostilities. Lo! Allah loveth not aggressors. And slay them wherever you find them, and drive them out of the places whence they drove you out, for persecution is worse than slaughter . . . and fight them until persecution is no more, and religion is for Allah. But if they desist, then let there be no hostility except against wrong-doers. (2:190–193)

Despite the many successful military campaigns in the region, there were mounting hostilities inside the Muslim nation following Muhammad's death. Some of these tensions were indicative of any new movement or government—as various voices struggled to be heard or thrust to the front of leadership—while other tensions were born of differences of opinion about how to live out the Muslim creed following the Prophet's death.

For nearly thirty years following Muhammad's death there were four "caliphs"—or leaders—who succeeded one another as leader of the Muslim people. But the last two leaders, Uthman and Ali, were murdered.

This period of dissension and civil unrest gave birth to the two major sects within Islam—the Sunni and the Shi'ites. The reasons for the division are numerous and complex—and are still evident within Islam today.

In Sunni understanding, Islam is practiced and interpreted strictly in accordance with the Qur'an and Muhammad's teachings. The Hadith (words or stories) and the *sunna* (practices) attributed to Muhammad became sacrosanct. The Sunnis, then, are those who sought to teach and practice only what Muhammad prescribed. There was an aversion early on toward relying upon successors or their various interpretations of the practices of Islam.

Over time, there were internal debates about the nature of the Hadith and the *sunna*—but it is important to note the Hadith continued to expand well beyond the age of the caliphs. Some of the Hadith took on near-Qur'anic authority, with their weight being attributed to actual words that God spoke to Muhammad. But the question of God's immanence, or presence with the believer, also became of paramount importance to many. God's complete transcendence became more difficult for the *sunna* of Islam. Eventually, some of the Hadith began to reflect theological aspects of Judaism and Christianity, with more weight being given to the presence of God with the believer.

One famous Hadith reflects as much:

> My servant draws near to me by means of nothing dearer to me than that which I have established as a duty to him. And my servant continues drawing nearer to me through supererogatory acts until I love him, I become his ear through which he hears, his eye through which he sees, his hand with which he grasps and his foot whereon he walks.

There were Muslims who believed in this type of presence of God—as practiced by Muhammad—and those who did not. These traditionalists believed that the caliph leaders did not need any exceptional spiritual qualities—but were egalitarian in approach. A caliph was basically a leader. These Sunni practitioners also rejected the opposition group—the Shi'a—who placed greater importance on the succession of Muhammad and his leadership, and thus began to revere the various holy sites and shrines where the caliph had spoken or prayed or even died. The Shi'a likewise placed greater importance on the Hadith, while the Sunni traditionalists eventually developed the concept of the uncreated

Qur'an—a book that existed from the beginning of creation and was, literally, handed to Muhammad by the hand of God.

These variations within Islam should not go unnoted, as there are certain Jewish and Christian beliefs of a similar ring.

For instance, with regard to Jesus, Christians speak of him as the eternal Word which existed with God before the creation of the universe (John 1:1–18). For the Muslim, the Qur'an is the eternally existing Word. For the Christian, Christ is the eternal Word. Likewise, God's eternality is juxtaposed with the concept of God's intervention in human history—namely, through covenant with Abraham, Moses, and subsequently in the presence and message of the prophets.

In time the Shi'a gravitated toward ideas that appeared to be even closer to the Christian doctrine of incarnation. For example, after the death of Husayn, the Shi'is maintained that only the descendants of Ali (Muhammad's closest relative) could lead the *ummah*. They were convinced that a strict bloodline leading back to Muhammad must be maintained and that there was a spiritual ancestry that would ensure the blessing of Islam. Over time, some of the descendants of Ali were elevated to almost divine status, and shrines were erected to remember the various leaders.

As Christians regard Jesus as the way to God (or the gate of the sheepfold), many strict Shi'is began to speak of their revered imams as a gateway to God, or a path, which would guide the faithful to Allah. Again, these distinctions within Islam are important as one begins to understand the Hadith and the various traditions of the Muslim Jesus. The Hadith offer a variety of approaches to Jesus, and one can often see parallels between certain Hadith and the Gospels, for instance, or to other Jewish and Christian scriptural references.

The fact that the Hadith exist in great numbers also attests to the history and progression of the Jesus narrative within Islam. The Hadith can even be studied now for their origins, and some may reflect a Sunni understanding, while others show a Shi'a or Sufi approach to Jesus.

The theological variations within Islam are beyond the scope of this book, but for our purposes as they relate to the Muslim Jesus, we can see how the Hadith create a kind of panorama or lens through which Jesus is viewed. The Muslim Jesus is many—or could perhaps be understood in much the same way as a Christian would read the four Gospels of the New Testament. There are similarities among the four—

but each is also distinct in style and voice and certainly in its respective view of Jesus. Some of these views can be understood out of a historical context—with Jesus broadly painted against the first-century Jewish community, or the destruction of the Second Temple, or the Roman occupation, or even as a counter to the predominant teachings of the Pharisees or Sadducees, the religious leaders of the time. Likewise, the Jesus of the Gospels may also be seen through theological lenses, with Mark, for example, possessing a more Roman interest while Luke's Jesus is more largely concerned with the marginalized Jews and the inclusion of the Gentiles.

The Muslim Jesus embodies some of these same concerns for the Islamic community, and the Hadith form, overall, is a type of narrative at best, or a kind of patchwork quilt of Jesus sayings and events. The Hadith can be understood not always as going back to Muhammad but in many instances as later reflections about Jesus that would have spoken to and for the Islamic communities of their times.

It would also be important to understand the Hadith as an attempt to couple earlier religious experiences with God to ordinary practice of the faith. Without guiding principles or narrative, believers can often get lost in the structure of faith or in the concepts of God's transcendence that do not lend themselves well to the daily practices of devotion. It is significant that there are many Hadith related to Jesus—and Jesus is often considered the Prophet of Love, of humility, and of complete dedication to God. The Jesus Hadith would have offered Muslims in earlier eras a lens through which to understand, for example, poverty—or perhaps an approach toward understanding the very nature of Allah.

And so the Hadith is where we predominantly encounter the Muslim Jesus. We might say that, in the Qur'an, Jesus is something of an abstraction or is referenced in large part to give corrective measure to Christianity. But in the Hadith we encounter a more philosophical Jesus who embodies personality and, at times, charisma and charm.

The Muslim Jesus seems to take on a life of his own.

THE TEXTS

There are many texts (accounts, stories) regarding the Muslim Jesus. And there is much to consider. First, it should be noted that to Muslims the Qur'an is regarded as the Word of God—and as such is not regarded as Word of God in any language other than Arabic. So while the Qur'an has been translated into hundreds of tongues, it is Qur'an only in the original. Translations are abundant—and in this book thus far I have used several translations to give a varied pace and voice. But only the meaning of the Qur'an can be translated, according to Islamic teaching.

As a seminary student some thirty years ago at Duke University, I first became aware of the Muslim Jesus when I encountered him through friendship with other graduate students from Iraq and Syria. My studies in those days also took me into the Semitic tongues—namely Hebrew, Aramaic, and Syriac—but also Arabic. And I recall as a twenty-two-year-old graduate student attempting to read portions of the Qur'an to gain a better understanding of both the Arabic language and the Muslim faith.

I also became aware of the Muslim Jesus in the bowels of the library, where I first discovered books written by the famed English scholar David Margoliouth—who from 1896 to 1912 published a number of books about Islam and, in particular, the various Hadith stories about Jesus. Margoliouth was fresh and his renditions often difficult to read, but his were the first Christ sayings and episodes that I encountered outside of the Gospels, and they were exciting.

Later followed my discovery of James Robson and his still-in-print book—*Christ in Islam*—which contains what was, up to that juncture in 1929, the most comprehensive collection of Jesus Hadith. Robson's collection was in no small way dependent upon a compilation, *Revival of the Religious Sciences*, by al-Ghazali, and his sources are still important for any study of the Jesus Hadith yet today. For the writing of this book I also cite Tarif Khalidi's quintessential offering—*The Muslim Jesus: Sayings and Stories in Islamic Literature* (Harvard University Press, 2003). Anyone reading Khalidi's book will certainly gain a deeper insight into the Muslim Jesus and will find here the richest single source of the Hadith material in English. Likewise, his commentary throughout is insightful—and Khalidi has performed a rich service by noting points of crossover and familiar themes within the Gospels. He, too, uses Robson and al-Ghazali and even Margoliouth—but Khalidi has also gathered unique material . . . much of it found only in Arabic publications or oral history.

It should be noted that in most instances here, I use the Robson text (*Christ in Islam*, 1920), with other Hadith from Margoliouth's varied sources (including *Mohammed and the Rise of Islam*, *The Early Development of Mohammedanism*, *Mohammedanism*, and Margoliouth's lectures at the University of London, with certain paraphrases of my own sprinkled in for clarity). For ease of reading, I have included commentary on some of the Hadith inside the paragraphs immediately following, including source at the end. Where not noted, the texts are from Robson. Other notes and the bibliography at the end of the book will provide further insights and commentary to the ones I offer here.

THE HADITH OF JESUS: SAYINGS AND STORIES

With the exception of the quotes from the Qur'an, all of the stories in this section are taken from the vast collection of Hadith tales. I have attempted to categorize the Hadith by theme wherever possible.

> And when God said, "O Jesus, son of Mary, did you say to men, 'Take me and my mother as gods beside God?'" he said, "Praise be to God! It is not fitting for me to say what is not mine by right. If I had said it thou wouldest have known it; thou knowest what is in my soul, but I do not know what is in thy soul; verily thou art the knower of hidden things. I said to them only what thou commandest me, 'Worship God, my Lord and your Lord,' and I was a witness against them as long as I was among them. If thou punishes them, they are thy servants; and if thou forgives them, thou art the mighty and the wise one." (Qur'an 5:116–118)
>
> His prayer by which he was curing the sick and bringing the life to dead was, "O God, Thou art the God of those who are in heaven and of those who are on earth; there is no god in them other than thee. And thou art the almighty one of those who are in the heavens and the almighty one of those who are on the earth; there is no almighty in them other than thee. And thou are the king of those who are in the heavens and the king of those who are on the earth; there is no king in them other than thee. And thou are the judge of

those who are in the heavens and of those who are on the earth; there is no judge in them other than thee. Thy power on earth is like thy power in heaven, and thy authority on earth is like thy authority in heaven. I ask thee by thy noble names. Verily thou art omnipotent.

(There is a phrase one finds frequently in the Hadith in reference to Jesus raising the dead, and that is "by God's permission," or sometimes, "with the permission of God." This is an important distinction, making clear that Jesus did not raise the dead of his own power, but by the word and permission of God. Later in this chapter we will see how this strand of Hadith forms one of the predominant themes of the Islamic Jesus. — Robson)

> In a tradition is it said that Jesus, son of Mary (Peace be upon him!) met a man and said to him, "What are you doing?" He replied, "I am devoting myself to God." Jesus said, "Who is giving you what you need?" The man said, "My brother." Jesus replied, "Your brother is more devoted to God than you."

(An insightful story—likely Sufi in origin, and certainly in spirit. The intent here seems to point out the distinction between self-interest—cloaked in a façade of devotion—and true devotion, which is service to humanity in the spirit of Jesus. —Robson)

> The Messiah (God bless him and grant him peace!) passed by some people of the children of Israel who were weeping and said to them, "What makes you weep?" They replied, "We are weeping for our sins." He said, "Leave them alone. They are forgiven."

(Overtones of gospel. Compare Mark 4:12, Luke 7:47, John 20:23. —Robson)

> Jesus, son of Mary (Peace be upon him!), in what Ibn al Hamal the Christian scribe told us said to his disciples, "The sign by which you are known as being from me is that you love one another." And Jesus said also to his disciple, Joshua, "As regards the Lord, you must love him with all your heart, then love your neighbor as you love your-self." They said to him, "Explain to us, O Spirit of God, what is the difference between these two loves, so that we may prepare for them with discernment and clearness." He said, "You love your friend for yourself, and you love yourself for your Lord; so when you guard

your friend you do it for yourself, and when you are bountiful yourself you are so towards your Lord."

(Deuteronomy 6:5, Leviticus 19:18, Matthew 22:37–39. —Robson)

When Jesus was asked, "How are you this morning?" he would answer, "Unable to forestall what I hope, or to put off what I fear,
bound by my works, with all my good in another's hand. There is no
poor man poorer than I."

(Another Sufi theme celebrating the poverty and humility of Jesus.
One can find overtones of gospel here as well. Compare with Luke
9:58. —Margoliouth)

Jesus (God bless him and grant him peace!) said, "He who knows and
works and teaches, that man shall be called great in the kingdom of
heaven."

(A bit of rabbinical affirmation, much in the spirit of the Talmud—
celebrating the work of the religious teacher who takes no money for
hire. —Margoliouth)

Jesus (Peace be upon him!) said, "How many trees are there, but not
all of them bear fruit; and how many fruits are there, yet not all of
them are good; and how many sciences are there, yet not all of them
are useful."

(Compare with Matthew 7:17–19, 12:33, 13:1–26. —Margoliouth)

Jesus (Peace be upon him!) said, "Do not entrust wisdom to those
who are unworthy of it, for you wrong it. And do not withhold it from
those who are worthy of it, for you wrong them. Be like a kindly
doctor who applies the medicine to the diseased spot. He who en-
trusts wisdom to those who are unworthy of it is foolish, and he who
withholds it from those who are worthy of it does wrong. Verily
wisdom has a right and it has people who are worthy of it; so give his
right to everyone who possesses a right."

(A wisdom saying, again with Jewish flavor. Perhaps echoes of Matthew 7:6—where Jesus uses a derogatory term when speaking to a
Canaanite woman, or Luke 5:31. —Margoliouth)

It is related that one day the rain and the thunder and the lightning were fierce about Jesus (Peace be upon him!), so he began to seek something under which he might find shelter. His eye fell on a tent far off, so he came to it, but behold there was a woman in it, so he turned away from it. Then he saw a cave in a hill and came to it, but behold there was a lion in it. Then he put his hand on it and said, "My God, thou hast given everything an abode, and thou hast not given me an abode." Then God (Exalted is He!) revealed to him, "Your abode is in the dwelling of my mercy. Verily I will give to you in marriage on the Day of Resurrection a hundred virgins whom I have created with my hand, and I will give a feast at your wedding for four thousand years, each day of which is like the duration of the present world, and I will command one to proclaim, 'Where are those who were ascetics in this world? Visit the marriage of the ascetic, Jesus, son of Mary.'"

(One of many ascetic Hadith attributed to Jesus and reflecting Arabic desert life. The subsequent ascetic section and Sufi teachings will shed further light on this familiar portion of Jesus. —Margoliouth)

If you wish you may follow him who was the Spirit and the Word, Jesus, son of Mary (Peace be upon him!), for he used to say, "My seasoning is hunger, my under-garment is fear of God, my outer garment is wool, my fire in winter is the rays of the sun, my lamp is the moon, my riding-beast is my feet, and my food and fruit are what the earth bring forth. At night I have nothing and in the morning I have nothing, yet there is no one on earth richer than I."

(A good example of a Hadith noting the ascetic Jesus as God's Spirit and Word. —Margoliouth)

The Messiah (God's blessing and peace be upon him!), said, "Verily I love poverty and hate comfort." And the dearest name to him (peace be upon him!) was that he should be called, "O Poor One."

(—Margoliouth)

Someone said to Jesus (Peace be upon him!), "Why do you not buy an ass to ride?" Then he replied, "I am too dear to God (Exalted is He!) for Him to allow me to be occupied with an ass to the neglect of Himself."

(—Margoliouth)

The disciples said, "O Spirit of God, we pray as you pray, and we fast
as you fast, and we glorify God (Exalted is He!) as you have ordered
us, yet we are unable to walk on the water as you do." Then he said,
"Tell me how your love of the world is." They replied, "We love it."
So he said, "Truly the love of it spoils religion, but in my opinion it is
merely like stone and mud." And in another story it is said that he
lifted up a stone and asked, "Which of the two is dearer to you? This,
or a dinar or dirham?" They replied, "A dinar!" He said, "They are
both alike to me."

(Compare with Matthew 14:28–29. —Margoliouth)

There was a robber who had been committing highway robbery for
forty years. One day Jesus and one of his disciples passed by. The
robber said to himself, "This is the prophet of God and one of his
disciples. If I joined them, I would make a third." And so he left
behind his old life and followed. But he thought to himself, "I am not
worthy to walk with them." And thus he despised himself. The disciple of Jesus noticed the robber, and so he walked ahead and said to
Jesus (Peace be upon him!), "He is not worthy to walk with us." God
(Exalted is He!) then revealed to Jesus (blessing and peace be upon
him!), "Let the two men begin their work afresh, for I have nullified
their past work. As for the disciple, I have nullified his good deeds
because of his self-conceit. And as for the other man, I have nullified
his evil deeds because he despised himself." And so Jesus joined the
robber to himself, and made him one of his disciples.

(Author paraphrase, based on Margoliouth. Here the central goal of
Islam—"surrender" or "submission"—is exercised by Jesus at the expense of his followers. This Hadith would speak, also, to the *hajj*, perhaps enlisting the spirit of the journey and true worship. There are also
interesting Talmudic overtones here—as humility pertains to learning—and perhaps some Gospel, such as Matthew 18:1–4, 23:11ff.; Luke
9:46, 22:24–26.)

There are many Hadith which have more striking parallels in the
New Testament Gospels. These include, especially, those passages
which reveal the love or generosity of Jesus. The disciples are sometimes noted—though rarely by name—and the bulk of these passages

seem to point to a source that would have contained, primarily, the teachings. Where not noted specifically, the sources are either Robson or Margoliouth.

> It is related that Jesus (Peace be upon him!) passed a monastery in which were two blind men and said, "What are these?" Someone replied, "These are people who sought death and blinded themselves with their hands." So Jesus replied, "What compelled you to do this?" They said, "We feared the punishment of death, so we did what you see to ourselves." Then he said, "You are the learned and the wise and the monks and the excellent ones. Rub your eyes with your hands and say, 'In the name of God.'" So they did, and lo!, they received their sight.

(See Matthew 20:33–35. —Thalabi, *Stories of the Prophets*)

> The disciples said to the Messiah (Peace be upon him!), "Look at this mosque, how beautiful it is." Then he said, "My people, my people, truly I say to you, God will not leave one stone of this mosque standing upon another, but will destroy it for the sins of the people. Truly, God does not pay any heed to gold or silver or these stones which charm you. The things dearest to God (Exalted is He!) are pure hearts."

(An injunction against idol worship or associating materialism with the things of God. See Luke 21:6. —Robson)

> Jesus (Peace be upon him!) was asked about the best work. He said, "Resignation to God (Exalted is He!) and love for Him."

(Compare with Matthew 22:37ff.)

> They saw him coming out of a prostitute's house and asked him, "O Spirit of God, what are you doing with this woman?" He answered, "The doctor visits only the sick."

(Compare with Luke 5:31.)

> We are told concerning the Messiah (God bless him and grant him peace!) that he said, "If God shows generosity to one of his worshippers, His generosity is necessary for all His creatures."

(Compare with Matthew 5:45.)

> Jesus, son of Mary (Peace be upon him!) said to his disciples, "The sign by which you are known as being with me is that you love one another."

(Compare with John 15:17.)

> There was handed down to Jesus (Peace be upon him!): "He who has not been born twice shall not enter the kingdom of heaven."

(Compare with John 3:7.)

> Some people asked Jesus (Peace be upon him!), "Teach us one piece of knowledge for which God will love us." He replied, "Hate the world, and God (Exalted is He!) will love you."

(This interesting Hadith strikes at the heart of the tension in all faiths—namely, a desire to live well in the world while also not being a part of it. One can note, for example, the contrast between John 3:16—and God's love for the world—and John 15:19ff, where Jesus speaks to the goal of being not of the world and its allures. In 1 John 2:15–17 and many of the apostle Paul's epistles, we see this tension heightened further. "World" in Gospel and Epistle has metaphorical meaning—and much like Paul's references to the "flesh" versus the "spirit," we encounter a later understanding that might not have been a part of the original intent. The Jesus of Islam, on the other hand, has completely eschewed the "world" and all things associated with it—except life itself. The "world" in the Jesus Hadith are often references to these attachments—even the smallest of comforts.)

> The Messiah (God's blessings and peace be upon him!) said, "With difficulty does a rich man enter heaven."

(Compare with Mark 10:25.)

> God (Exalted is He!) revealed this to Jesus (Peace be upon him!): "A prophet does not lack respect except in his own country."

(Compare with Matthew 13:57.)

The Messiah (Peace be upon him!) said to his disciples, "If you do what I have commanded you, you will be with me tomorrow in the kingdom of heaven."

(Compare with Luke 23:43.)

THE HADITH AS "SERMON ON THE MOUNT"

Throughout the Hadith one encounters a number of similarities—in both style and structure—to the Jewish Torah and the New Testament teachings of Jesus, particularly as related in the Gospel of Matthew (5–7). These comparisons, to my knowledge, have not been noted in narrative form, with the Hadith interspersed with the New Testament Gospel and Torah references. Such a comparison is both helpful and elucidating, as it shows that the Jesus of Islam is regarded as both a prophet and a sage (though a Muslim one) who taught with a rabbinic style to his disciples—followers who are sometimes referred to as "children of Israel" or, simply, "disciples."

A close reading of the Hadith demonstrates how Jesus is able to ebb and flow in and out of Judaism, Christianity, and Islam at once—with teachings that, whether regarded as "corrective," "historical," or "borrowed" produce a similar effect of the spirit. Certainly, within these teachings, one can hear echoes of the Jewish prophets along with a Christian ethic—but all the while offered through the voice of a Muslim Jesus.

Presented in this way, the similarities are startling—and one can then move on to the ascetic Jesus, the poor Jesus, and the miracle-worker Jesus wholly confident of discovering truths from the Muslim Messiah. One might even say that these Hadith could add to the pursuit of the historical Jesus. In just a few words we obtain a deeper sense of the voice and mind behind the teachings, and the particular adds to the whole.

The reader will note that I have taken these Hadith from Margoliouth or Robson (and that most can be found in both)—with the Hadith in boldface for ease of distinction. The Matthew text is from the King James Version (KJV) of the Bible, and the citations in parentheses are references to the Hebrew Bible (the Torah).

And seeing the multitudes, he went up into a mountain: and when he was set, his disciples came unto him. And he opened his mouth, and taught them, saying,

Blessed are the poor in spirit: for theirs is the kingdom of heaven.

Blessed are they that mourn: for they shall be comforted.

Blessed are the meek: for they shall inherit the earth.

Blessed are they which do hunger and thirst after righteousness: for they shall be filled.

Blessed are the merciful: for they shall obtain mercy.

Blessed are the pure in heart: for they shall see God.

Blessed are the peacemakers: for they shall be called the children of God.

Blessed are they which are persecuted for righteousness' sake: for theirs is the kingdom of heaven.

Jesus (Peace be upon him!) said, "Make your livers hungry and your bodies naked; perhaps your hearts may see God (Great and Glorious is He!).

God revealed unto Jesus: Command the children of Israel that they may not enter my house save with pure hearts, and humble eyes, and clean hands; for I will not answer any of them against whom any has a complaint.

It is mentioned to us that the following is written in the gospel: "O son of man, as you show pity so will you be pitied; for how can you hope that God will pity you if you do not show pity to his servants?"

A man asked Jesus (Peace be upon him!) "Who is the best of men?" Then he took two handfuls of earth and said, "Which of these two is the better? Men were created from the earth, so the most honorable of them is the most God-fearing of them."

Blessed are ye, when men shall revile you, and persecute you, and shall say all manner of evil against you falsely, for my sake.

Rejoice, and be exceeding glad: for great is your reward in heaven: for so persecuted they the prophets which were before you.

The Messiah (Peace be upon him!) said, "Blessed are the humble in this world; they will be set on high on the Day of Resurrection. Blessed are they who make peace between men in this world; they are those who will inherit Paradise on the Day of Resurrection. Blessed are they whose hearts are purified in

this world; they are those who will see God (Exalted is He!) on the Day of Resurrection."

Ye are the salt of the earth: but if the salt have lost his savour, wherewith shall it be salted? it is thenceforth good for nothing, but to be cast out, and to be trodden under foot of men.

Ye are the light of the world. A city that is set on an hill cannot be hid.

Neither do men light a candle, and put it under a bushel, but on a candlestick; and it giveth light unto all that are in the house.

Let your light so shine before men, that they may see your good works, and glorify your Father which is in heaven.

Jesus son of Mary (God's blessings be upon him!) said to the disciples, "O salt of the earth, do not become bad, for when things become bad they can be treated only with salt, but when salt becomes bad it cannot be treated with anything. O company of the disciples, do not take remuneration from those whom you teach, except like what you have given me. And I know that there are two characteristics of ignorance in you: laughter without anything extraordinary, and sleeping in the morning without vigil."

Think not that I am come to destroy the law, or the prophets: I am not come to destroy, but to fulfill.

For verily I say unto you, Till heaven and earth pass, one jot or one tittle shall in no wise pass from the law, till all be fulfilled.

Whosoever therefore shall break one of these least commandments, and shall teach men so, he shall be called the least in the kingdom of heaven: but whosoever shall do and teach them, the same shall be called great in the kingdom of heaven.

For I say unto you, That except your righteousness shall exceed the righteousness of the scribes and Pharisees, ye shall in no case enter into the kingdom of heaven.

Ye have heard that it was said by them of old time, Thou shalt not kill; and whosoever shall kill shall be in danger of the judgment:

But I say unto you, That whosoever is angry with his brother without a cause shall be in danger of the judgment: and whosoever shall say to his brother, Raca, shall be in danger of the council: but whosoever shall say, Thou fool, shall be in danger of hell fire.

John (the Baptist) said to Jesus (Peace be upon them!), "What is the fiercest thing?" Jesus replied, "God's anger." He said, "Then what comes next to God's anger?" He replied, "That you should be angry." He said, "Then what makes anger begin, and what makes it increase?" Jesus said, "Pride and boasting and arrogance and indignation."

Therefore if thou bring thy gift to the altar, and there rememberest that thy brother hath ought against thee;

Leave there thy gift before the altar, and go thy way; first be reconciled to thy brother, and then come and offer thy gift.

Agree with thine adversary quickly, whiles thou art in the way with him; lest at any time the adversary deliver thee to the judge, and the judge deliver thee to the officer, and thou be cast into prison.

Jesus (Peace be upon him!) said, "Seek a great amount of what fire cannot consume." Someone said, "And what is that?" He answered, "Kindness."

Verily I say unto thee, Thou shalt by no means come out thence, till thou hast paid the uttermost farthing.

Ye have heard that it was said by them of old time, Thou shalt not commit adultery:

But I say unto you, That whosoever looketh on a woman to lust after her hath committed adultery with her already in his heart.

And if thy right eye offend thee, pluck it out, and cast it from thee: for it is profitable for thee that one of thy members should perish, and not that thy whole body should be cast into hell.

Jesus (Peace be upon him!) said, "Blessed is the eye which sleeps and does not think of disobedience, and awakes to sinfulness."

And if thy right hand offend thee, cut if off, and cast it from thee: for it is profitable for thee that one of thy members should perish, and not that thy whole body should be cast into hell.

It hath been said, Whosoever shall put away his wife, let him give her a writing of divorcement:

But I say unto you, That whosoever shall put away his wife, saving for the cause of fornication, causeth her to commit adultery: and whosoever shall marry her that is divorced committeth adultery.

It is related concerning the Messiah (Blessing and peace be upon him!) that he said, "O company of the disciples, you fear acts of disobedience, but we, the companies of the prophets, fear infidelity."

Again, ye have heard that it hath been said by them of old time, Thou shalt not forswear thyself, but shalt perform unto the Lord thine oaths:

It is related concerning Jesus, son of Mary (Peace be upon him!) that he said, "Every word which is not accompanied by mention of God is vanity; and every silence which is not accompanied by meditation is negligence; and every speculation which is not accompanied by a tear is folly. So blessed is he whose speech is mention of God, whose silence is meditation, and whose speculation is a tear."

But I say unto you, Swear not at all; neither by heaven; for it is God's throne:

Nor by the earth; for it is his footstool: neither by Jerusalem; for it is the city of the great King.

Neither shalt thou swear by thy head, because thou canst not make one hair white or black.

But let your communication be, Yea, yea; Nay, nay: for whatsoever is more than these cometh of evil.

Jesus (Peace be upon him!) said, "If one tells many lies, his beauty departs. And if one quarrels with men, his manliness falls to the ground. And if one has many cares, his body becomes ill. And if one has bad manners, he punishes himself."

Ye have heard that it hath been said, An eye for an eye, and a tooth for a tooth:

But I say unto you, That ye resist not evil: but whosoever shall smite thee on thy right cheek, turn to him the other also.

And if any man will sue thee at the law, and take away thy coat, let him have thy cloke also.

And whosoever shall compel thee to go a mile, go with him twain.

Give to him that asketh thee, and from him that would borrow of thee turn not thou away.

I saw in the gospel that Jesus, son of Mary (Peace be upon him!) said, "It has been said to you formerly, 'Tooth for tooth and nose for nose; but I say to you, do not resist evil with evil. On the contrary, if someone strikes your right cheek, turn to him the left cheek; and if one takes your cloak, give him your mantle; and if one compels you to go a mile with him go with him two miles."

Jesus said to the children of Israel, "Do not reward an evil-doer with evil, for your favor will go for nothing with the Lord."

Ye have heard that it hath been said, Thou shalt love thy neighbour, and hate thine enemy.

But I say unto you, Love your enemies, bless them that curse you, do good to them that hate you, and pray for them which despitefully use you, and persecute you;

That ye may be the children of your Father which is in heaven: for he maketh his sun to rise on the evil and on the good, and sendeth rain on the just and on the unjust.

We are told concerning the Messiah (God bless him and grant him peace!) that he said, "If God shows generosity to One of his worshippers, his generosity is necessary for all His creatures."

For if ye love them which love you, what reward have ye? do not even the publicans the same?

And if ye salute your brethren only, what do ye more than others? do not even the publicans so?

Be ye therefore perfect, even as your Father which is in heaven is perfect.

Take heed that ye do not your alms before men, to be seen of them: otherwise ye have no reward of your Father which is in heaven.

Therefore when thou doest thine alms, do not sound a trumpet before thee, as the hypocrites do in the synagogues and in the streets, that they may have glory of men. Verily I say unto you, They have their reward.

The disciples said to Jesus (Peace be upon him!), "What is the purest of deeds?" He replied, "The one who works for God (Exalted is He!) not wishing for anyone to praise him for it."

But when thou doest alms, let not thy left hand know what thy right hand doeth:

That thine alms may be in secret: and thy Father which seeth in secret himself shall reward thee openly.

It is handed down in the Gospel, "When you give alms, do it so your left hand does not know what your right hand has done; then he who sees the hidden things will reward you openly. And when you fast, wash your face and anoint your head, that no one other than your Lord may know if it."

And when thou prayest, thou shalt not be as the hypocrites are: for they love to pray standing in the synagogues and in the corners of the streets, that they may be seen of men. Verily I say unto you, They have their reward.

But thou, when thou prayest, enter into thy closet, and when thou hast shut thy door, pray to thy Father which is in secret; and thy Father which seeth in secret shall reward thee openly.

Jesus, son of Mary (Peace be upon him!) said, "Be ashamed before God (Great and glorious is He!) in your secret affairs, as you are ashamed before Him in your public affairs."

But when ye pray, use not vain repetitions, as the heathen do: for they think that they shall be heard for their much speaking.

Be not ye therefore like unto them: for your Father knoweth what things ye have need of, before ye ask him.

Jesus said, "Speak much to God and speak little to men." They said, "How shall we speak much to God?" Jesus said, "Be apart in intercourse with Him; be in prayer to Him."

After this manner therefore pray ye: Our Father which art in heaven, Hallowed be thy name.

Thy kingdom come. Thy will be done in earth, as it is in heaven.

Give us this day our daily bread.

And forgive us our debts, as we forgive our debtors.

And lead us not into temptation, but deliver us from evil: For thine is the kingdom, and the power, and the glory, for ever. Amen.

For if ye forgive men their trespasses, your heavenly Father will also forgive you:

But if ye forgive not men their trespasses, neither will your Father forgive your trespasses.

It is said that it is written in the Gospel, "He who asks forgiveness for one who has wronged him routs the devil."

Moreover when ye fast, be not, as the hypocrites, of a sad countenance: for they disfigure their faces, that they may appear unto men to fast. Verily I say unto you, They have their reward.

But thou, when thou fastest, anoint thine head, and wash thy face;

That thou appear not unto men to fast, but unto thy Father which is in secret: and thy Father, which seeth in secret, shall reward thee openly.

Jesus (Blessing and peace be upon him!) gave the following instructions to one of his companions: "Fast from the world, and do not cease from your fast until you die, and be like him who treats his sore with medicine out of fear that it may become worse to him. And occupy yourself much with the thought of death; for death brings good to the believer with no evil after it, but evil to the wicked with no good after it."

Jesus the Messiah (God bless him and grant him peace!) said, "When a day comes in which one of you fasts, let him anoint his head and his beard and wipe his lips, that men may not see that he is fasting. And when he gives with his right hand let him hide it from his left hand, and when he prays let him lower the screen of his door, for God will apportion praise as he apportions provision."

Lay not up for yourselves treasures upon earth, where moth and rust doth corrupt, and where thieves break through and steal:

Jesus (Peace be upon him!) said, "Do not take the world as a master, for it will take you as slaves. Lay up your treasure with him who will not lose it, for he who possesses treasure in this world fears lest some calamity may come upon it, but he who

possesses God's treasure has no fear of calamity coming upon it."

But lay up for yourselves treasures in heaven, where neither moth nor rust doth corrupt, and where thieves do not break through nor steal:

For where your treasure is, there will your heart be also.

And Jesus said (the richest blessing and peace be upon him!), "O company of the disciples, I have overturned the world on its face, so do not raise it up after me. For part of the wickedness of the world is that disobedience to God is in it; and part of the wickedness of the world is that the next world is attained only by abandoning it. Is it not so? Therefore pass through the world, but do not stay in it; and know that the root of all sin is the love of the world. And the desire of an hour often leaves those who indulge in it an inheritance of grief which lasts for long."

The upright Jesus (Peace be upon him!) said, "Every man's heart is where his wealth is; so place your wealth in heaven that your hearts may be in heaven."

The light of the body is the eye: if therefore thine eye be single, thy whole body shall be full of light.

Jesus (Peace be upon him!) said: "Beware of looking, for it sows desire in the heart, and it is sufficient for seduction."

But if thine eye be evil, thy whole body shall be full of darkness. If therefore the light that is in thee be darkness, how great is that darkness!

No man can serve two masters: for either he will hate the one, and love the other; or else he will hold to the one, and despise the other. Ye cannot serve God and mammon.

Jesus (Blessing and Peace be upon him!) said, "In wealth there are calamities; that one should get it unlawfully." Someone interrupted: "Suppose one gets it lawfully." Then he said, "He may apply it unlawfully." The other said, "But suppose he applies it lawfully?" He answered, "Its management occupies him to the neglect of God (Exalted is He!)."

Jesus (Peace be upon him!) said, "The love of this world and the love of the next [cannot reside simultaneously] in the heart of the believer, just as water and fire cannot stay in one vessel."

Jesus (Peace be upon him!) said, "This world in relation to the next is like a man who has two wives. If he is pleased with one of them, he is displeased with the other."

Therefore I say unto you, Take no thought for your life, what ye shall eat, or what ye shall drink; nor yet for your body, what ye shall put on. Is not the life more than meat, and the body than raiment?

Jesus (Peace be upon him!) said, "Fine clothing is vanity of heart."

Behold the fowls of the air: for they sow not, neither do they reap, nor gather into barns; yet your heavenly Father feedeth them. Are ye not much better than they?

Jesus (Peace be upon him!) said, "Look at the birds; they do not sow, or harvest, or store up, yet God (Exalted is He!) feeds them day by day." But if you say, "We have larger bellies, look at the cattle, how God (Exalted is He!) has provided for them this creation as provision."

Muhammad, son of Fadl, told us of the authority of Salim, son of Abu al Jad (God be pleased with him!) that Jesus son of Mary (God's blessing and peace be upon him!) said, "Do not store food for the morrow, for the morrow comes bringing along with it its provision. And look at the ants and who gives them provision. And if some say, The ants' bellies are small, look at the bird. And if you say, The bird has wings, look at the wild beasts, how corpulent and fat they are."

Which of you by taking thought can add one cubit unto his stature?

And why take ye thought for raiment? Consider the lilies of the field, how they grow; they toil not, neither do they spin:

The Messiah (Peace be upon him!) said, "Do not look at the wealth of the people of this world, for the splendor of their wealth takes away the light of your faith."

And yet I say unto you, That even Solomon in all his glory was not arrayed like one of these.

Wherefore, if God so clothe the grass of the field, which to day is, and to morrow is cast into the oven, shall he not much more clothe you, O ye of little faith?

Therefore take no thought, saying, What shall we eat? or, What shall we drink? or, Wherewithal shall we be clothed?

(For after all these things do the Gentiles seek:) for your heavenly Father knoweth that ye have need of all these things.

But seek ye first the kingdom of God, and his righteousness; and all these things shall be added unto you.

Take therefore no thought for the morrow: for the morrow shall take thought for the things of itself. Sufficient unto the day is the evil thereof.

Jesus (Peace be upon him!) said, "Do not worry about tomorrow's food, for if tomorrow is one of your periods your provisions will come in it along with your periods; and if it is not one of your periods, do not worry about other people's periods."

Jesus, son of Mary (Peace be upon him!) said, "The world consists of three days: yesterday which has passed, from which you have nothing in your hand; tomorrow, of which you do not know whether you will reach it or not; and today in which you are, so avail yourself of it."

Judge not, that ye be not judged.

For with what judgment ye judge, ye shall be judged: and with what measure ye mete, it shall be measured to you again.

And why beholdest thou the mote that is in thy brother's eye, but considerest not the beam that is in thine own eye?

Or how wilt thou say to thy brother, Let me pull out the mote out of thine eye; and, behold, a beam is in thine own eye?

Thou hypocrite, first cast out the beam out of thine own eye; and then shalt thou see clearly to cast out the mote out of thy brother's eye.

Jesus (Peace be upon him!) said to the disciples, "Do not consider men's works as though you were lords, but consider your own works as though you were servants; for people are only of two kinds, tried and preserved. So have pity on those who have tried, and praise God for health."

Give not that which is holy unto the dogs, neither cast ye your pearls
before swine, lest they trample them under their feet, and turn again
and rend you.

**It is related that a pig passed by Jesus (Peace be upon him!)
and he said, "Pass in peace." Then someone said, "O Spirit of
God, do you say this to a pig?" Jesus answered, "I dislike ac-
customing my tongue to evil."**

Ask, and it shall be given you; seek, and ye shall find; knock, and it
shall be opened unto you:
    For every one that asketh receiveth; and he that seeketh findeth;
and to him that knocketh it shall be opened.
    Or what man is there of you, whom if his son ask bread, will he
give him a stone?
    Or if he ask a fish, will he give him a serpent?
    If ye then, being evil, know how to give good gifts unto your
children, how much more shall your Father which is in heaven give
good things to them that ask him?
    Therefore all things whatsoever ye would that men should do to
you, do ye even so to them: for this is the law and the prophets.
    Enter ye in at the strait gate: for wide is the gate, and broad is the
way, that leadeth to destruction, and many there be which go in
thereat:
    Because strait is the gate, and narrow is the way, which leadeth
unto life, and few there be that find it.

**It is related concerning Jesus, son of Mary (Blessings and
peace be upon him!) that he said, "There is nothing wonderful
about one perishing in the way he perishes, but there is something wonderful about one being saved in the way he is
saved."**

Beware of false prophets, which come to you in sheep's clothing, but
inwardly they are ravening wolves.
    Ye shall know them by their fruits. Do men gather grapes of
thorns, or figs of thistles?
    Even so every good tree bringeth forth good fruit; but a corrupt
tree bringeth forth evil fruit.

A good tree cannot bring forth evil fruit, neither can a corrupt tree bring forth good fruit.

Every tree that bringeth not forth good fruit is hewn down, and cast into the fire.

Wherefore by their fruits ye shall know them.

Not every one that saith unto me, Lord, Lord, shall enter into the kingdom of heaven; but he that doeth the will of my Father which is in heaven.

Many will say to me in that day, Lord, Lord, have we not prophesied in thy name? and in thy name have cast out devils? and in thy name done many wonderful works?

And then will I profess unto them, I never knew you: depart from me, ye that work iniquity.

Therefore whosoever heareth these sayings of mine, and doeth them, I will liken him unto a wise man, which built his house upon a rock:

And the rain descended, and the floods came, and the winds blew, and beat upon that house; and it fell not: for it was founded upon a rock.

Jesus (Peace be upon him!) said, "Who is he who builds a house on the wave of the sea? The world is like that, so do not take it as an abiding place."

The Messiah (God bless him and grant him peace!) said, "The world is a bridge, so pass over it and do not inhabit it." And some people said to him, "O prophet of God, if you would only order us to build a house in which we might worship God!" He replied, "Go and build a house on water." They said, "How will a building stand on water?" He replied, "And how will worship stand along with love of this world?"

And every one that heareth these sayings of mine, and doeth them not, shall be likened unto a foolish man, which built his house upon the sand:

And the rain descended, and the floods came, and the winds blew, and beat upon that house; and it fell: and great was the fall of it.

And it came to pass, when Jesus had ended these sayings, the people were astonished at his doctrine:

For he taught them as one having authority, and not as the scribes.

HADITH: JESUS THE ASCETIC

One predominant view of Jesus within the Hadith is that of an ascetic—a prophet devoted to prayer and fasting. Jesus renounces the world and lives apart from it even while in it. Many Hadith echo the words of Jesus in the gospels, "The son of man has no place to lay his head." But the Hadith flesh out these ascetic nuances to a much greater degree than we discover in the Gospels, and there are numerous examples of Jesus renouncing even the smallest possessions or comforts. Here, Jesus is both content and suffering at once—and he seems intent on giving to others what he deems too frivolous for himself.

Whether a cup or comb, or even a brick or stone pillow—these possessions are too worldly for the Muslim Jesus. And through this strand of Hadith one can see why Jesus is often referred to as the Prophet of Love or "Spirit of God." The embodiment of simplicity is a virtue.

In should be noted that some Hadith serve dual functions and are also attributed to Muhammad. The ascetic Jesus is not so much a prophet as he is a witness. He embodies what others can only yearn to achieve.

> Jesus (Peace be upon him!) once passed by a man who was leprous, lame, paralyzed on both sides, and whose flesh was plagued with elephantiasis. The man was praying, "Praise be to God, who has kept me free from that which has afflicted most of his creatures." Jesus asked him, "What was the affliction that has been removed from you?" The man answered, "O Spirit of God, I am better off than the one who does not know God." Jesus said, "Surely, you have spoken the truth. Give me your hand." The man stretched out his hand, Jesus touched him, and immediately he became a most handsome man, free of all of his diseases. And from that day the man accompanied Jesus (Peace be upon him!) and worshipped with him.

(My paraphrase, based on Margoliouth. Compare with Matthew 8:2, regarding healing. Here Jesus the ascetic restores the man to God and the religious community—realities which could not be accomplished under Judaic or Islamic law. A fascinating piece of this Hadith is to note that the man follows Jesus and worships him—a prohibition, as Jesus would not have asked for this place of adoration. One of the few Hadith where Jesus becomes the center of adoration—but here we should probably take "worship" in the spirit of gratitude.)

> The Messiah (God's blessings and peace be upon him!) said, "Truly I love poverty and hate comfort." And the dearest of names given to him was, "O Poor One."

(Jesus pictured among the poor—but not for poverty's sake, perhaps, but rather, again, as a revolutionary prophet who sought to turn the world on its head, producing devotion from decrying the comforts of existence at the expense of others. —Robson)

> The Messiah (God's blessings and peace be upon him!) said, "Do not look at the wealth of the people in this world, lest the splendor of their wealth remove the light of your faith."

(Overtones of the gospel "you are the light of the world," but with a deeper association and warning against pining after wealth. —Robson)

> The Messiah (God's blessings and peace be upon him!) used to say, "O children of Israel, use pure water and wild vegetables and barley bread, and avoid wheat bread, lest you be ungrateful to God."

(There are several strictures in Islam against eating impure foods—and this early Hadith notes the significance of a clean diet as setting apart the Muslim from society. Of course, Jesus, being a teacher of the law, would have insisted upon the Jewish dietary restrictions. Here is an Islamic counterpart.)

HADITH: JESUS, WHO RAISES THE DEAD BY GOD'S PERMISSION

While the Jesus of Islam was not raised from the dead—but, rather, ascended into heaven—he does have the authority and power to raise others. There are many Hadith referencing the Messiah of resurrection.

> One day Jesus (Peace be upon him!) passed by a man who was standing between two graves. The man was bowing and worshipping. Jesus greeted him and said, "I see that you are between two graves

bowing and worshipping." The man replied, "They are my parents, who were kind and gentle to me. After they died I took an oath that I would stand between their graves and worship until I died." Jesus asked, "And how long have you been doing this?" "Three hundred years," the man said. Jesus asked, "Has any news come from God, that your sins are forgiven, that God has granted a request, or perhaps you have asked God for something?" The man said, "No news has come to me. But I have prayed that I might meet Jesus. But I do not know if He has heard my prayer or not." Jesus said to him, "Be of good cheer. God has granted your request. I am Jesus." The man answered, "O Jesus, by Him who has accepted my prayer, would you not stretch out your leg that I may rest my head upon it for an hour?" So Jesus stretched out his leg, and the man put his head on Jesus' leg and closed his eyes and prayed, "O God, by the honor of this prophet you have answered my prayer and allowed me to meet him. And now I request that you receive my spirit while I am resting here in his bosom." The man had not come to the end of his prayer before he died while sleeping in the lap of Jesus (Peace be upon him!). Then Jesus looked for something in which to wrap the man, but he found nothing except a worn cloak and a brick, upon which Jesus would lay his head. So Jesus prayed, "O Lord, when Thou has gathered the first and the last and asked them what they have gained, what will you ask your servant?" Then God revealed to him, "O Jesus, by my greatness and my majesty I will ask him about this cloak—where he acquired it—and about this brick—from what ground he made it or from what wall he took it. Truly I have sworn by Myself that if an oppressor comes near Me I will be an oppressor. By My greatness and My majesty I will make him who mixes water with bricks separate the water from the bricks." Then Jesus prayed, "O God, forgive us by Thy mercy, and favor us with Thy kindness and Thy paradise; and pardon us all and make us die Muslims and join us to the upright. And praise be to God, the Lord of the worlds!"

(One of many Hadith attributed to Jesus, who raises the dead. In Islamic tradition, Jesus—like Elijah in the early Jewish paradigm—will return at the end of time to usher in the final kingdom and judgment of God. —Margoliouth)

It is mentioned that Jesus (Peace be upon him!) used to raise the dead to live by permission of God (Exalted is He!). Some unbelievers once said to him, "You have raised people who have died recently;

perhaps they were not really dead. Raise for us someone who died in the earlier times." He said to them, "Choose whom you will." They said, "Raise for us Shem, son of Noah." Then he came to his grave and prayed two rek'as and called on God (Exalted is He!), and God raised Shem, son of Noah, and lo!, his head and beard had become white. But someone said, "What is this? There were no white hairs in your day." He replied, "I heard the summons, and I thought the Resurrection had come, so the hair of my head and beard became white from terror." Someone asked him, "How long have you been dead?" He replied, "For four thousand years. But the agony of death has not left me."

(A humorous example—perhaps Sufi?—of Jesus as the unity of religion rather than exclusively an Islamic prophet. —Robson)

Jesus, son of Mary (Peace be upon him!), passed a graveyard and called to a man in it. Then God (Exalted is He!) brought him to life and Jesus said, "Who are you?" He replied, "I was a carrier, carrying things for people. One day I carried some firewood for a man and broke off a piece of it with which I was pierced; and I am being sued for it since my death."

(An interesting pericope shot with humor and legal tension—where Jesus raises to the life old animosities and troubles. For a longer version, see below. —Robson)

It is related that Jesus (Blessings and peace be upon him!) passed a grave and kicked it with his foot, saying, "O you who are in the grave, arise by the permission of God (Exalted is He!)." Then a man arose from the grave and said, "O Spirit of God, what do you want with me? For I have been standing in the judgment for seventy years when I heard the shout: 'Answer the Spirit of God.'" Jesus said, "O you, you have committed many faults and sins, so what do you do?" He replied, "O Spirit of God, I was a seller of fuel who carried firewood on my head and ate what was allowable and gave alms." Jesus said, "Praise be to God! A seller of fuel who carried firewood on his head and ate what was allowable and gave alms, and he has been standing in the judgment for seventy years." Then Jesus asked him about what his Lord said to him in the judgment, and he said, "O Spirit of God, one of the rebukes of my Lord was that he said, 'Do you remember the day my servant, so and so, hired you to carry a load of firewood for him, and you took a piece of wood from it and were pierced with it and threw it away from its place in the bundle out of your despite for Me, although you knew that I am God who looks at your work and your intention?"

(As prescribed by all three of the great monotheistic faiths, the Creator sees and knows all. All three faiths eventually became more than movements and were forced to prescribe rules for proper living—not just a desire for the life to come. This Hadith offers some legal advice couched in religious dress. Jesus is not central to the teaching here but provides a methodology for discussing the rather mundane realities of living in society and making proper judgments. —Robson)

> Malik, son of Anas, said: It reached me that two women came to Jesus (Peace be upon him!) and said, "O Spirit of God, pray for God to us to bring forth our father for us, for he perished and we are absent from him." He said, "Do you know his grave?" They replied, "Yes." So he went with them and they came to a grave and said, "This is it." Then he prayed to God and one was brought forth to them, and lo!, it was he. They clung to him and saluted him and said, "O prophet of God, O teacher of good, pray to God to make him stay with us." He said, "How can I pray for him when no provision by which he may live has been left for him." Then he sent him back and departed.

(Again, a practical Hadith with Jesus as foil. Though poverty is celebrated as the portion of the Messiah in Islamic tradition, it is nevertheless rebuked as a way of life, especially if one is reduced to beggary at the expense of others, even family. —Robson)

> There is a story related from the time of Jesus (Peace be upon him!) about a man named Isaac who was deeply devoted to his cousin— one of the most beautiful women of her time. After she died, Isaac visited her grave day and night. One day Jesus (Peace be upon hime!) passed by the grave and noticed him weeping. "What is making you weep, Isaac?" he asked.
>
> Isaac answered, "O Spirit of God, I had a cousin, who was also my wife, and this is her grave. I am unable to live without her and the separation is killing me."
>
> Jesus said, "Would you like for me to bring her to life again, by God's permission?"
>
> He said, "Yes, O Spirit of God."

So Jesus stood over the grave and said, "Arise, you who in this grave by God's permission."

Then the grave burst open and a black slave came out of it, fire issuing from his nostrils, eyes, and other openings in his face. And he was saying, "There is no God but God. Jesus is God's Spirit and Word, His servant and His apostle."

Isaac said, "O Spirit of God, this is not my wife's grave. It is here!" And he pointed to another grave.

So Jesus said to the slave, "Return to your former condition." The slave fell down dead and he buried him again.

He then stood over the other grave and said, "Arise, you who are dwelling in this grave, by God's permission." Then a woman arose, and she was scattering the dust from her face. Jesus asked, "Is this your wife?"

The man replied, "Yes, O Spirit of God."

He said, "Take her by the hand and go away."

So Isaac took her by the hand and they walked away. Soon, however, Isaac said to his wife, "Watching over your grave has nearly killed me. I need to rest."

His wife told him to take a nap. And so he put his head in her lap and slept.

While he was sleeping, the king's son happened to be riding by on his horse. He looked at the woman, who was very beautiful. And the woman noticed the prince, who was very handsome. Immediately they fell in love, and when the prince asked her to join him, she left her sleeping husband and rode away with the prince.

When Isaac emerged from his sleep, he was confounded by his wife's absence. He began to follow the trail left by the horses' hooves and he soon overtook them. He said to the prince, "Give me back my wife, who is also my cousin."

But she said, "I don't know you. I am only a slave to the prince."

While they were disputing, Jesus (Peace be upon him!) happened to walk by again and Isaac said, "O Spirit of God, is this not my wife and my cousin whom you brought back to life by God's permission?"

Jesus replied, "Yes."

But she denied it, saying, "I am just a slave to the prince."

Jesus said, "Are you not the wife I brought back from the dead by God's permission?"

She said, "No by God, O Spirit of God."

So Jesus said, "Then restore to us what we gave you."

Immediately she fell down dead.

And Jesus said, "Whoever wishes to look at a man whom God caused to die while he was an unbeliever, then brought back to life and allowed him to die a Muslim, let him look at the slave. And whoever wishes to look at a woman whom God caused to die while she was a believer, then brought her to life and caused her to die an unbeliever, let him look at this woman."

After this, Isaac made a covenant with God (Exalted is He!) that he would never marry; and he wandered the wilderness afterwards like a madman, weeping.

(As with Jewish and Christian, the notable lesser role of women can often be tracked in Islam as well. Here the theme seems to be celibacy as preferential to the disciple, and women are often portrayed as enticements that can lead a man astray from the true path to God. In most of the Jesus Hadith related to resurrection, Jesus provides little to no commentary but stands in the background to the central purpose of the tradition, which may have originally been used to deepen a community's commitment to celibacy or to the sect itself. Author paraphrase, based on Margoliouth)

It is related that the Messiah (God bless him and grant him peace!) passed in his wandering a man wrapped in his cloak; then he awakened him and said, "O sleeper, arise and glorify God (Exalted is He!)." Then the man said, "What do you want from me? Truly I have abandoned the world and its people." So he said to him, "Sleep then, my friend."

(—Margoliouth)

The Messiah used to say to his disciples, "I have only come from my Father and your Father to give you life from the death of ignorance, and to cure you from the disease of disobediences, and to heal you from the disease of perverse opinions and evil manners and wicked deeds, that your souls may be refined and made alive by the spirit of knowledge, and you may ascend to the kingdom of heaven beside my Father and your Father. There you will live the life of the happy ones and will be saved from the prison of the world, and the pains of the realm of existence, and the decay which is the dwelling of the miserable ones, and the neighborhood of devils, and the dominion of Iblis [Satan]."

(—Robson)

JESUS AS PROPHET OF LOVE

In traditional Muslim understanding, Jesus is often regarded as the most important prophet to precede Muhammad. And as the various Hadith about Jesus reveal, his place in Islam runs squarely through the place of honor and respect. In fact, to collect the entire Hadith related, to Jesus would be a monumental undertaking and would require a book of some considerable length—far more than I have devoted here.

Much like the Gospels (and the dozens of other alternative gospels spawned out of early church history), the Hadith attributed to Jesus was clearly a growth phenomenon, with traditions layered on top of other traditions and reflecting various times, places, and cultures. While it can be said that some of the Hadith about Jesus were meant to counter or correct the Christian insistence that Christ was God incarnate, there are a great many of the narratives that emerge from another center. Not all of the Hadith are counter-Christian or counter-Jewish, but, in fact, many possess remarkable similarity to earlier traditions and may have been adapted from them.

One interesting piece of Muslim history suggests that Muhammad, in an earlier period, lived among Jews and Christians while teaching and prophesying. He was quite at home among these respective traditions and scriptures. He would have known them.

There would not, then, have been any incongruity between the Jesus of Christian faith and the Muslim Jesus, the Prophet of Love. At least not in recognition. Not in honor.

Traditional Muslim understanding likely counters with the insistence that the Jesus of Christianity needed to be rescued from his own followers and—much like Ali being revered by the Shi'a sect—was simply given too much adoration. No doubt Jesus—like Ali to the Shi'a—was of such towering spiritual strength that some of the Hadith reflect this counterphenomenon. Some of the Hadith are pointed enough to make this leap.

But there are other possibilities, too.

As many scholars would point out, there seems to have been a widespread awareness of the Gospel of Matthew, especially in Islamic thought. As the comparison with the Sermon on the Mount demonstrates, this Gospel must have had some widespread use in the far reaches of the Arabian Peninsula in the age of Muhammad, and there were certainly points of interest in the teachings of Jesus as a resource for Muslim thought and practice. Even the Gospel of Matthew itself has been interpreted by some Muslim apologists as a tour de force for the Muslim faith—with Christ's references to "prophets being slaughtered, crucified, or scourged from town to town" (Matthew 23:34) as a prediction of the plight of Muhammad (his Hegira).

Although one cannot get to the heart of this matter here, suffice it to say that some of the Hadith of Jesus were certainly influenced by the gospel of Matthew, with the gospel of John not far behind. But whether adapted or redirected or retranslated for a Muslim faith, the Hadith do reflect a remarkable and wonderful symbiosis of Christian and Muslim thought. In the best of all possible worlds, one faith can receive the Jesus stories of the other without much reinterpretation or pretext. There is room for understanding.

Although, ultimately, Christianity and Islam would come to different conclusions about Jesus, these may reflect the ends rather than the origins. Christians would ultimately not agree upon the unity of God or the nature of the Trinity (think ecumenical councils and especially Nicaea) even as Muslims would not necessarily agree upon the nature of incarnation or the possibilities of a God who is both transcendent and immanent (think Shi'a and Sufi). Eventually religious history is told by the victors—and those who are marginalized to minority status are regarded as heretics or deficient of the truth.

Both Christians and Muslims have struggled, and do struggle, with their respective ideas about God—and how they relate to others *in the faith* as well as those *outside* the faith. Given these realities, it is all the more remarkable to note the profusion of Hadith about Jesus through the long history and interplay of both faiths. One might say that in the search for some center reference, Jesus could very well play the part.

Broken apart and analyzed, one might also arrive at the insight that at the center, all faiths share the importance of community. To the Jew, community is about *being Jewish*, practicing and observing both ritual and festival. To the Christian, the church is a fellowship of believers. To the Muslim, community is reflected in the *hajj* and the daily call to prayer.

It is fascinating, then, to note how often the Hadith make mention of the community that surrounded Jesus. Sometimes the "children of Israel" are mentioned or just "the disciples." There are also hints of larger community and pilgrimage being made. So—perhaps even more than Muhammad himself—Jesus is revered as a reformer of community, a charismatic though humble soul who brought others around him. Though in Islamic tradition Jesus points the way to Muhammad, there is also a sense in which Jesus had first formed the community. There were always prophets—dating as far back as Adam—and the prophets were often regarded as those who led the community from one place to another, from one dispensation to the next.

As we have seen, Jesus carries a great weight in the Hadith material—far more pronounced in later traditions of Islam than in the Qur'an—which may suggest that earlier Islamic and Christian communities lived both in proximity and in peace. When the story could be told, there was a uniqueness in the telling. We might even imagine Christian and Muslim pondering the same Hadith or Gospel pericope.

It is telling that Jesus was regarded as the Prophet of Love. There must have been a place for him amid the misunderstandings.

As one Hadith affirms, "Jesus asked the Israelites, 'Where does seed grow?' 'In the soil,' they answered. Jesus said, 'Truly I say to you, wisdom grows only in the soil-like heart'" (Robson).

Jesus—as reflected in the synoptic Gospels—was a teller of parables and observer of the natural order. He spoke of birds, of trees, of wind, of rain. There were storms, bushes, rocks. And there were seeds and soils as well. Inside these observations—whether Gospel or Hadith—there was the intent of the heart. As a seed grows in the soil, so wisdom grows in the heart. This is a Jesus teaching in both faiths—and predominant throughout.

Jesus as lover and beloved is affirmed in the Hadith. He points to the greater love of God. Much like the Gospel of John, there are metaphors and mysteries in the Jesus Hadith that one simply doesn't find in the traditions about Muhammad. There is a kind of high-mindedness in the Muhammad Hadith that one does not find in those attributed to Jesus. The Prophet speaks clearly. Jesus speaks in metaphor. This is often overlooked—but the arc back to shared community may again be reflected in this reality.

Consider, for example, this common attribute: "God revealed to Jesus, 'If you look into the secret thought of a servant and find in it no love of this world or the next, I fill it with love of me and take charge of guarding it'" (Robson).

Jesus as the Prophet of Love has an endearing charm, and although he can be harsh in other Hadith, he always seems content to reveal some deeper truth about God's mercy. The Jesus of Islam is not an icon or a stained-glass window but a receptacle of humility and simplicity. It is not just his life and manners that are simple—but his teachings as well. They seem easy enough—but yet contain a profound element to them that leaves one pondering how such a thing is possible or how it could be lived out. There is love . . . and then there is love of God. Jesus possesses both in ample portions, and he is often on the receiving end of God's adoration.

Whenever one undertakes a study of the Jesus Hadith, one comes away with a deeper appreciation of the faith that produced them. People were moved to remember, to retell, to record what Jesus did, what he said, how he lived. Jesus is not marginalized to small stature but is enlarged by measure of his greatness—regardless of how one, ultimately, refers to him.

The authority is there—even though theologies differ.

Like any great religious figure, we often measure the impact and influence by adherents. But we can also measure by sheer volume of the canon—the corpus of written and oral material that was memorized and immortalized and passed from one generation to the next. Taken as a whole, the Islamic Hadith of Jesus teachings may surpass the volume of the canonical Gospels—or at least rival it—and so there must be some weight given to the reasons behind this record. To overlook it would be paramount to glancing at a book and saying it has no pages.

The Hadith, much like the Gospels, possess some mixture of history and tradition, memory and mirth, teachings and ageless truths. We need not look at the Jesus of Islam through Christian lenses to see that he is larger than either. One of the reasons there are so many gospels, so many Hadith, is that Jesus cannot be contained in them. To keep him there would, indeed, be idolatry. The Jesus of Islam and the Jesus of the Christian faith must be freed from the confines in which he is often imprisoned. This is true of gospel. It is true of Hadith.

Somewhere in the long trajectory of both faiths, there was a time when Jesus was heard in terms and understandings far different from our own. He was not enslaved to culture, or class, or the vagaries of refined religions. He was Messiah, the Prophet of Love.

Whether Gospel or Hadith, it is far more difficult now to sift our own prejudices, like chaff, from the wheat at the core. We find it difficult—and perhaps impossible—to separate our respective treatments of Jesus, our certain theologies, from what the historical Jesus actually thought of himself, irrespective of religion. The layers run deep, and people have been searching for the historical Jesus for centuries. Not even Albert Schweitzer could locate him—and by now we have remaining some vestige of our own faces, with Jesus reflecting more of what we hope to believe, or can accept, about ourselves than what we hope to discover about the love of God.

As many have undertaken a study of Jesus, here is yet another—but one, it is hoped, that can help to bridge the gaps of misunderstandings and show not that Islam and Christianity are the same faith, but that even though profoundly different, they still have much the same regard for Jesus. The Gospel and the Hadith teach as much—and at the core of both faiths there is a regard for the mercy of God.

The name of Jesus is the same.

And as one Hadith notes, the heart of Jesus was ever on love, and on the love of God: "Jesus was asked to name the best of all works. He said, 'Contentment with God Almighty and love of Him'" (Robson).

5

"THE JESUS OF THE SOUL"

Understanding the Sufi Jesus

All in the created world will pass away, but the face of your Lord will remain. —Qur'an, Sura 55:26–27

The religion of Islam centers on a single mantra—the foremost revelation offered to the Prophet Muhammad on Mount Hira: "There is no God but Allah (God)." This is the first of the "five pillars" of Islam and is the principal foundation one must consider when undertaking a study of the faith. This creed, taken by itself, might well summarize the intent of Islam (to worship God alone) as well as the mission of Islam (to unite the world in devotion to the one God). From this first pillar of the faith, a Muslim is expected to gain an understanding of all that is required by God as well as to fulfill all that is required in life and relation to others.

From a purely Western viewpoint, however, one could make an argument that this pillar is the root source of much misunderstanding between Muslim and Jew and, subsequently, between Muslim and Christian. Judaism and Islam have had a long history of cultural and religious tension; and Christianity, from the Islamic viewpoint, seems to deviate from pure monotheism because of the doctrine of the Trinity. And yet, paradoxically, Islam has more connection with historic and theological Judaism and Christianity than many realize. This is true, in part, because of Islam's time frame: born in Arabia in the seventh century CE, long after both Judaism and Christianity were firmly established and were being practiced throughout the world. But it is also due, in part, to Islam's own traditions and, perhaps more importantly, to Islam's unique interpretations of these other monotheistic faiths.

Within the Qur'an—Islam's sacred book—one can find stories that are remarkably similar to those found in the Bible (the sacred text of Jews and Christians). Abraham and Moses are mentioned in the Qur'an along with many other figures found in the Hebrew Bible. Adam is here, and Noah, along with Ishmael. Prophets are mentioned by name as well as angels and the Virgin Mary. And remarkably, there is another prophet named Isa (Jesus), who occupies abundant space within the Qur'an—including many corresponding beliefs about Jesus which can be found in the New Testament Gospels and the letters of Paul the apostle.

To say, however, that Islam can be defined or understood solely from the writings of the Qur'an is, at least, limiting. As with most religions, Islam contains many traditions and variations—both in understanding and practice. Like Judaism and Christianity, there are fundamentalist and open expressions of the faith as well as various schools of thought and belief. Although Islam comprises two prominent sects— the Sunni and the Shi'a—there are many smaller sects that have arisen at various junctures in history (not all surviving). As with Christianity, many of these sects originally sprang from the teachings of a prominent leader or were based upon regional or cultural influences.

These various practices and understandings may well go back to the time of Muhammad himself who, although desiring to establish a just society, had some followers who were more inclined toward the mystical and interior way of life. Rather than focusing on outward practices and points of theology, these disciples desired an approach to Islam that was intended to offer God's presence through mystical union. Certainly by the eighth and ninth centuries it can be well documented that an ascetic form of Islam had developed alongside the traditional sects such as Sunni and Shi'ite. These ascetics, desiring to return to a simpler way of life and a deeper devotion to God, became known as Sufis (a name derived from the Arabic word for "wool" and the garment of choice worn by these disciples). These Sufis, particularly those associated with the Mawlawiyya order that originated in Turkey, often utilized a whirling dance as part of their trancelike ceremonies. Western observers thus coined the phrase "whirling dervishes" to describe this style of worship.

Sufism remains a vital force within Islam and a way of life for millions. Yet many of Sufism's great texts and traditions have remained hidden from practitioners of other faiths, particularly Christians, for centuries. One reason, of course, is that Islam's texts were, for many years, published almost exclusively in Arabic—the language of the Qur'an. Any study of the Qur'an or other Islamic literature was undertaken only in this tongue. And, on another front, the separation of Western and Near Eastern cultures and literatures has had a far-reaching effect even to this day, with much misunderstanding and a long history of struggle and suspicion. Throughout this history, it has been difficult for people to share ideas under such a cloud of anxiety.

Yet Islamic literature has not only existed but thrived. Sufi variations on ancient Islamic themes are a most important ingredient in the exploration of the Islamic faith and—to Western readers—may well serve as a more understandable and appreciated starting point for learning about Islam than the Qur'an itself.

It is necessary to note that among the traditions of Islam, the mystical Sufi way of life has produced an abundance of parables, teaching stories, and narratives that offer a wide array of vantage points and philosophies. Many Sufi stories resonate with symbolism, while others provide instruction or insights that might help the disciple in the quest for purity or wisdom or in relationships with others. It is worth noting that the sizable corpus of Sufi poems contains some of the finest devotional material in religious literature. Much like the biblical Psalms, these poems offer personal thoughts and feelings that would ring true in the experience of other believers. Some of these poems may speak of doubts, or fears, or even acts of contrition or unfaithfulness. Other Sufi poems provide glimpses into the interplay of religious ideas and expressions—sometimes between Christian and Muslim—especially as these traditions came into contact with each other in the centuries of Islam's infancy.

One example of this influence can be seen in the famous Sufi *tarji'-band* poetry written by Hatef of Esfahan, which offers a starting point for a discussion of the Jesus of Sufism. Here the poet has come into contact with the Christian doctrine of the Trinity—God expressed as Father, Son, and Holy Spirit—but instead of dismissing the doctrine outright, the poet ponders the meaning of this idea as he converses with a Christian woman.

"Lured by you, my heart is entangled
   in your snare," I pleaded in church
To a Christian maiden,
     "as though every stray strand of my hair
Were enmeshed in your cincture's skeins.
      How long will Unity's way remain unfound? Till
when will the One stand defamed by the trinity?
      How can it be laudable to call God The
Absolute, the Single, with Names like
    Father, Son and Holy Ghost?"
She parted her sugar-drenched lips,
   which disparaged sugar itself, and said:
"Were only you conscious of Unity's mystery,
   You'd never name me 'infidel'.
The radiant visage of Eternal Beauty
   illuminated three distinct mirrors;
Silk is not threefold in kind
   If named *parniyan, harir,* or *parand.*"[1]
Engaged in this parley, suddenly
   I heard the churchbells chime:
   There is only one;
   Nothing exists but He;
   He is One;
   No god but He exists.[2]

Any discussion of the Jesus of Sufism needs, from the outset, to distinguish between the Christian doctrine of the divinity of Jesus and the Sufi understanding of Jesus as a prophet committed to purity, submission, and holiness. While Islam affirms many of the basic tenets of Christian belief—including the virgin birth of Jesus, his prophetic role, and his ascension into heaven—the idea of Jesus as God, resurrected Lord, or Redeemer is not a part of the equation. Rather, Jesus is one of several major prophets, important in the way that Abraham is important, or Moses, or John the Baptizer. The Jesus of Sufism occupies a major place in the religion's literature and thought—even an exemplary one—and yet he is not central to the faith. This distinction cannot be overlooked.

However, one would be remiss to assert that Jesus has had no influence upon the Islamic (and especially Sufi) understanding of God. Sufism is replete with stories and tales of Jesus—his teachings, his life, his exploits. In many instances, Jesus is held to the light as an example of Sufi piety, as a great master of devotion to God, and as one who was, in his essence, humble and pure of heart. Just as the prophets of Israel often used the names of kings and sages to challenge the accepted beliefs of the time, so many of the Sufi storytellers enlisted the name of Jesus to challenge Islamic practice or complacency. Some Sufis even looked to Jesus as the prophet of the interior life and took it upon themselves to revise the first pillar of Islam to say: "There is no God but Allah (God), and Jesus is his prophet."

The Islamic sage Attar (who was born around 1136 in Persia) often used Jesus in his poetry and stories to direct the seeker toward a greater devotion to God. In many of Attar's stories and poetical discourses, Jesus occupies a prominent position. He is often mentioned among the great prophets of the faith and is offered as an example of pure love. One could make a strong argument that Attar himself saw in Jesus the symbolic representation of the life he longed to embrace.

According to tradition, Attar was floundering in his faith until one day a poor Sufi dervish entered his pharmacy and asked the wealthy merchant, "How are you going to die, knowing that you must leave all of this wealth behind?"

Attar replied, "I suppose I will die just as you will."

The dervish responded, "But I have no worries. All I possess is the clothing on my back and my beggar's bowl." Upon saying this, the dervish lay down on the floor, uttered the name of God, and died.

Attar was so moved by this expression of faith that he immediately forsook his business and took up the Sufi way of life. Over a course of years, Attar produced a monumental body of work—a rich collection of poems and tales that is nearly unrivaled in the vast canon of Sufi literature. Among Attar's arsenal of poetry and stories, one can find many centering on the person of Jesus. To the Sufi, Jesus possesses all of the qualities of humility and self-denial that would be required for one to enter into union with God.

In many of these stories attributed to Attar, Jesus comes into contact with the seeker who is struggling or, perhaps, offers his own affirmation to the seeker who is yearning for some word from the Lord. Two such examples follow:

Once, Jesus entered a cave and discovered a man sleeping on the floor. "Get up," Jesus said, "and get to work. Make a way for yourself. The world is passing you by."

"But I've done enough work to last two lifetimes," the man replied. "I've established a place for myself in the next life."

"What have you accomplished, then?" Jesus asked.

"The world to me is a piece of straw," the man answered. "It is like a crust of bread, or a bone that I might toss to the dogs. Oh, I've been free of the world a long time now, and I look for nothing from God. Why should I look for happiness in this life. I have no attachments, and I am free!"

When Jesus heard the man's reply, he said, "Sleep soundly, then. Go and do as you like. Since you are no longer bothered by the world, it cannot hinder you. You have accomplished everything at once."[3]

In a similar story, Jesus comes into contact with an ascetic whose devotion to God is all consuming:

Jesus once came across a man who had founded a retreat for himself in the desert. The little place was nestled next to a natural spring, and was walled off by hedges. Jesus asked the man, "Why have you secluded yourself from others?"

The seeker replied, "My devotion to God has been a life-long labor. Nevertheless, my deepest desire has not been granted."

"And what is that?" Jesus wanted to know.

"To drink one sip of the Divine Love," confessed the seeker.

So Jesus prayed with the man, that his request might be granted. Then Jesus went on his way.

Some years later, Jesus returned to that area and noticed that the little retreat was now in a state of disrepair. The desert had nearly covered it, the water supply had dried up, and the hedges had crumbled away. "Where is the man who once lived here?" Jesus prayed. God answered, "You will find him now on the mountaintop. But he is nothing but a knot of grief from head to toe."

Jesus sought the seeker out and found him just as God had directed. Sure enough, the man was a mere shadow of his former self. His face was pale and haggard, his body shrunken, his shoulders weighed with grief. Jesus greeted the man, but the seeker gave no reply. Jesus asked God to reveal what had happened to the seeker, and the Lord offered this answer:

"The man desired a drink of Divine Love and I gave it to him. However, once he possessed it, he ceased to care for himself. He gave up everything and became utterly helpless. Had I given him even an atom more of love, his human frame would have been shattered into a thousand pieces."[4]

These two stories reveal a common theme found among the Jesus tales of Sufism: those looking for a deeper relationship with God would do well to follow Isa's example.

For the Sufi, Jesus is not marginalized to the edges of the faith. Rather, Jesus—in true prophetic voice—reminds his disciples that God is not "out there" to be discovered or coerced into action but is present and near in the simple life of devotion, eager to assist the faithful as a lover cares for the beloved. There are numerous citations attributed to Jesus regarding these central concerns—teachings that call people to a life of dedication to God.

The devotion of the Sufis can be traced back to the eighth and ninth centuries, when this ascetical form of Islam developed alongside the other two prominent sects. These Muslims who attempted to return to a simpler form of life often wore wool garments, and this is where the term "Sufi" derived (meaning "wool"). Again, as in most religious traditions, the Sufi way of life may be understood within the historical framework of the origins of the movement—as Sufis were predominantly troubled by the tendencies that Islam had developed—essentially overlooking the spiritual nugget at the heart of the faith. Sufism was a movement to recover (some might say "reform") the heart and soul of Islam.

It is no small thing that Sufism developed during the centuries when Islam was beginning to emerge as a distinctive faith—set apart from Judaism, Christianity, or Zoroastrianism, for example. As Islam was moving away from an original idea of the unity of various faiths (or at least the idea that truths and true prophets were to be found in all), Sufism was a counterculture movement that sought to recover this unity of the interior life—and Jesus became the example. The love of God became the rule of Sufi life and its distinctive feature.

Sufism became a mystical way of life for those Muslims desiring to devote themselves completely to God. The Sufi hoped to achieve this through meditation and movement, through reflection and prayer—practices that they felt had become obscured by the concept of God who was completely transcendent (and therefore could not be experienced) or by devotion to shrines and human agents. This is not to say that all Sufis worshipped or conceived of God in the same manner, but as a minority movement, Sufism contained a core mysticism and direct experience with God.

It should also be noted that the terms "Sufi" or "Sufism" did not come into existence until some 150 years after the time of Muhammad. Up until that time, the Shari'a—or the rules of conduct as prescribed by Muhammad—were deemed to be the only method of achieving salvation and practicing Islam. There were mystics—to be sure—but these were forced to practice their faith (usually by prayer and fasting) apart from the predominant Muslim sects, and these mystics were generally regarded as suspect at best, or not true Muslims in many instances.

By 800–850 CE there were, however, certain practices that had made their way into the deeper layers of Islamic thought, and we can safely say that by then the Sufi way of life had been adopted by many. There were different prayers being said than those prescribed by Shari'a, and one of the new practices was *zikr*—which means "remembrance"—and was a practice of chanting God's name or God's attributes until one felt a oneness with God. *Zikr* was not an exclusive practice of the Sufis but was another layer of devotion over and above the prescribed religious laws. In time, Shari'a was regarded as the foundation by the Sufis, and once one learned these basics, a devotee could then seek to obtain deeper wisdom and attachment to God.

This secondary layer, called Tariqa (Path) was practiced in order that one might eventually accomplish the ultimate Haqiqa—which means Truth or Enlightenment. Schools and disciples sprang up around these methods.

This period of time, from 800 to around 1450 CE, is often regarded as the golden age of Sufism. A great many of the Sufi masters and traditions attributed to the Sufis emerged during this time period. The prophets, as well as many prominent Old Testament and New Testament figures, were regarded as having achieved the Haqiqa. It should be noted that much like Islam on the whole, Judaism and Christianity were regarded as former paths, or platforms from which God worked in the past. Islam is the corrective path, the ultimate, but the other platforms are not rejected outright, necessarily, in much of Sufi thought.

What matters ultimately is the love of God and achieving a unity in this love.

Dating back to the eleventh century there were well-known Sufi mystics, such as Ibn Sina and al-Ghazali, who helped to move Sufism into acceptance and, in some minds, into representation as the most authentic form of Islam. Both Ibn Sina and al-Ghazali had a deep appreciation of other faiths and traditions, and in time Sufism on the whole would adapt and adopt a much broader mind-set than traditional Islam with regard to other faiths. Again, at the center of much of the Sufi traditions one can find a rich assortment of Jesus stories. As the Prophet of Love, Jesus and the Jesus narrative would occupy a central place in the development of Sufism.

Other early Sufi masters, such as Hallaj (who is often regarded as the first Sufi martyr), often generated stories of their own—and their lives took on a place inside the tradition itself. Many of these stories related by and about the Sufi masters bear a remarkable resemblance to Jesus or Messiah stories found elsewhere in Islam. Abū Saʿīd, Attar, Nizami, and eventually Rumi were all Sufi masters who added other layers to the Hadith—many of them about Jesus or bearing striking similarities to the earlier traditions reviewed in an earlier chapter.

These masters—some of whom may be more accurately categorized as poets—each offered traditions and unique stories about Jesus or insights that would bear much resemblance, at times, to the teachings of Jesus. Many of these Sufi stories contain a humor that is not found in earlier traditions—and in point of fact, humor is often at the heart of much Sufi prayer. There is a joy in the Sufi way of life.

Likewise, in nearly all Sufi literature, Jesus can be found offering expression to the interior life—the mystical way of the Sufi. In many of these sayings, materialism in its various manifestations is renounced; simplicity is offered as a path to God; virtues are affirmed. The Jesus of the Sufis is a teacher who lives the true life to such a degree that others are drawn to his humility and devotion. Unlike Muhammad—the prophet of the revelation—Jesus is revered as the prophet of mystical union with God. This Jesus can converse with the living and the dead, make crooked paths straight, and even get an audience with God whenever the need arises.

The Jesus of the Sufis—much like the Jesus of the New Testament—offers teaching weighted with authority and bite. Taken alone, these statements may seem inapplicable to daily life. But to the Sufi, as to the Christian who might try to follow the teachings of Jesus as set forth in the Sermon on the Mount (Matthew 4–7), these statements hold the disciple to a high standard and call to attention the rivaling forces and interests which dominate human life.

> Jesus said, "Love of the world and love of the hereafter cannot be brought together in the heart of the believer, any more than fire and water can coexist in one place."

> Jesus said, "The world is a bridge, pass over it. Do not linger."

> Jesus told his disciples, "Many a lamp has been extinguished by the wind, and many a devotee, ruined by pride and conceit."

> The disciples asked Jesus what they must do to enter heaven. Jesus told them, "Keep forever silent." They replied that this was impossible. "Then," said Jesus, "say only what is good."[5]

Sufi teaching, like much of religious thought, contains metaphors and symbols that are not always perceived by the untrained or inattentive listener. As with many of the parables of Jesus found in the New Testament, one must be on the lookout for wordplay, listen for puns and other literary devices, and sometimes use the great storehouse of the imagination to gain access to a story's underlying meaning. Sufi stories are no different.

There is a well-known Sufi tale which can help to illustrate this point.

> Once, a shaykh was teaching among a group of dervishes. One of the dervishes asked him, "How do you understand Sufism?"
> The shaykh replied, "All I understand is where to sit to get the first cup of tea."
> Many of the dervishes laughed at this response, while others sat quietly, pondering the implications of his words.

This story, in the Sufi mind, works on two levels. The key to understanding its meaning lies in the fact that traditionally, a Sufi teacher is always served first. But how does one get to be a Sufi teacher? Only through years of study and dedication to the ways of God. In this instance, the shaykh's response invites both laughter and contemplation. The story itself can be retold as a joke and as a point in serious conversation.

When the Sufi masters used Jesus to convey their insights, they did so with an eye and ear toward this twofold interplay. The stories themselves entertain—as all great stories do. But they also work on the spiritual level, in the realm of philosophy, or as teaching methods designed to transport others into mystical association with God.

For the Sufis, Jesus is a popular figure to quote, to emulate, and to create. Although not venerated or adored, Jesus nevertheless holds a place of reverence and awe within the pantheon of prophets who have impacted the Sufi life. For the Sufi, Jesus is seen as a guardian of the sacred, a kind of icon—much like a lens through which one can observe and make sense of the world.

Consider again, for example, the well-known Sufi tale about Jesus and a dead dog. This story, recounted in various forms by Sufi masters through the ages, offers a glimpse of the world through the eyes of Jesus, who is able to appreciate beauty in the midst of ugliness.

> Jesus and his disciples were walking through an alley when they came upon a dead dog. The carcass was beginning to rot, and a foul stench filled the air. The disciples commented on the odor and made remarks about the ugliness of the decomposing creature. Jesus, however, leaned over, looked more closely at the animal, and pointed out to his followers the condition of the dog's teeth, as they were exceedingly white and clean.[6]

Much commentary has been offered on this story through the years, and the tale serves to remind the disciple to be attentive—even in difficult or trying circumstances. God's beauty and wonder is everywhere, and if one looks closely enough, one can discover the intricacies of this glory. Often, overwhelmed by the big picture, it is difficult for the disciple to appreciate details and to be renewed by the positive awareness of God's presence.

Sufi wisdom provides a vantage point from which to view the world. And Jesus is often used as the lens through which the disciple studies its meaning.

At its heart, the Sufi life was meant to be an ethical journey. Choices would have to be made, sacrifices undertaken. Respect and humility would be as lights along the path. For the Sufi, Jesus was also regarded as a *master* of the interior life—one who had subdued his passions and had learned how to make proper choices. As with other meditative traditions, the goal of prayer and service was meant to lift the pupil to the throne of God—to experience God in the moment. Wisdom was seen as the product of the ethical life; foolishness, as the antithesis.

Among the Sufi masters who looked to Jesus as the embodiment of perfected love was Jalaluddin Rumi—perhaps the most widely celebrated and translated Sufi master in history. Rumi, born in 1207, lived most of his life in Konya (located in present-day Turkey). His father was a respected speaker of the time and taught Islamic law in the mosques.

Early in his life, Rumi took a liking to the works of the famed Sufi master Attar, and his influences were many. After his education, Rumi became a most-sought-after professor, and people traveled for miles to hear him speak on a variety of Islamic issues and philosophies. His learning and intellect were great, but the turning point of his career came as the result of a chance meeting with a revered spiritual leader of the time: Shams-uddin Tabrizi.

Various versions of this meeting have been handed down through the centuries, but the most insightful, perhaps, involves an encounter which took place in Rumi's classroom. One day Rumi was lecturing a class at the university when Shams walked into the room and took a seat among the students, interrupting the talk. In the middle of the lecture, Shams pointed to a pile of books in the corner and asked, "What are these?"

Rumi paused, believing Shams to be a beggar, than answered softly, "You would not understand."

Moments later, flames shot from the pile of books, causing Rumi to cry out, "What is this?"

Shams replied, "You would not understand." Afterward, the tradition holds that Rumi fell at Shams's feet, vowed to be his disciple, and left his post at the university. For several months, Shams and Rumi were in retreat, and afterward Rumi was filled with a new love and devotion for God that changed his life. Shams had formed a special bond with Rumi (then thirty-eight years old), and the mystic soon began to possess great sway over the philosopher, even to the point where Rumi left behind the life of an intellectual and began to pursue the life of a mystic. His great masterpieces of poetry soon followed, the most important of which—the *Mathnawi-yi ma'nawi*—is commonly regarded as one of the world's finest pieces of spiritual writing.

Like Attar before him, Rumi felt a special kinship and devotion to Jesus. As Rumi's poetry reveals, he believed Jesus to be the embodiment of perfected love. Following the path of the Sufis before him, Rumi organized his thought around Jesus rather than the Prophet Muhammad when it came to practice and belief. He saw in Jesus the greatest example of detachment from the world—as a common Sufi tradition held that Jesus carried only a cup and a comb in his possession (and these he gave away).

Rumi's poetry offers a glimpse of the glory of God and speaks in intimate terms of a God who is both lover and beloved. Much of his poetry is woven with insightful narratives—both from his own life and in the form of parable—which speak to the journey of the Sufi heart and the beauty and love of God.

Jesus is given a place of honor in Rumi's poetry, and he is frequently held to the light as an example of supreme love. In the *Mathnawi*, especially, we see Jesus subduing wild beasts, teaching deep secrets, and even raising the dead. But all of these actions have little importance next to his love. Here is one of Rumi's classic stories retold:

One day Jesus was seen running among the hills as if a hungry lion were after him. A friend came upon Jesus in this state and asked him, "What are you running from? There is nothing in sight."

Jesus answered, "I am running away from a fool."

"But aren't you the Messiah?" the friend said. "Aren't you the Christ who has healed the sick, opened the eyes of the blind and the ears of the deaf?"

"I am," Jesus responded.

"And aren't you the same one who prayed over a dead man and brought him back to life?"

"Indeed."

"And aren't you the same one who fashioned birds out of clay, then clapped your hands and watched them fly away?"

"Yes. It is true."

"Then why, O pure spirit," said the friend, "are you afraid of a fool? Surely if such miracles reside in your power, you have no need to fear anyone."

But Jesus insisted: "I swear by the Exalted One who created all things before eternity, who made the body and fashioned the stars and the heavens, I have chanted God's name in many situations. I have raised the dead in God's name; I have brought forth existence itself by invoking the power of God; and I have even used the name of God to cleave a mountain in half. However, when I chanted God's name lovingly in the presence of a fool, it was no use. The heart of a fool, you see, is even harder than granite."

The friend continued: "But when you spoke the Divine Name in all other circumstances, you worked wonders. Why, in this case of the fool, has the name of God proven ineffective?"

Jesus said: "The pain of blindness is a tribulation, and only the wrath of God can cure stupidity. No hand can mend a fool's heart. The only cure is to flee from a fool!"[7]

The Sufi understanding of Jesus, as presented in the poetry of Rumi, is one of love and devotion. In fact, one of the most common terms used to describe the Sufi's mystical union with God is the "Jesus of the Soul." In philosophical and theological terms, the Sufi's goal was to find a union with God after the example of Jesus, who had forsaken the ways of the world to experience the glory of God.

Rumi often wrote of Jesus in this fashion.

> Grieve not that Mary's gone;
> The light that Jesus heavenward bore, has come.

> Only when the Jesus of the Soul
> Turns away from the world
> May one soar in spiritual flight
> Beyond the azure vault of the skies.[8]

The Sufi way, as testified in the images of the "whirling dervish" and the trancelike meditative practices of the various orders, often used repetition—especially repetition of the name of God—to instill a sense of peace and a union with the divine. Chanting and—as was common with Rumi—playing tunes on a reed pipe were often employed to bring the devotee into a state of ecstasy.

Since the goal of Sufism, unlike that of traditional Islamic practice and study, did not center on the intellect so much as the heart, it was imperative for the Sufi disciple to follow a master and learn of the supernatural mysteries through direct experience. The Sufis, however, did not agree as to the extent and intent of such experiences. Some, such as the mystics who followed Abu Yazid Bistami (d. 874), believed

that the goal of Sufism was to become lost in the love of God, completely devoid of self and removed from an awareness of the world. Such a
state was often referred to as "annihilation." Others, such as those led
by al-Junayd of Baghdad (d. 910), did not hold to this philosophy. They
regarded such a state as dangerous and taught that following each ec-
static encounter with God, a return to the self and an awareness of the
world was vital.

These differing philosophies, like those encountered in Jewish Kab-
balism or Christian Pentecostalism, have influenced Sufism to this day.
Yet there is a constant belief that repeating the name of God can and
does have a soothing effect upon the soul.

Attar thought as much. In one story about Jesus, the Sufi master
employed a snake charmer to make his point.

> Jesus saw a snake charmer crouching beside a hole, trying to coax the
> creature from its lair. The charmer was incanting and using magic
> potions and spells. As Jesus passed by, the snake poked its head out
> of the hole and said, "O Spirit of God, shining candle of all creatures.
> A thirty year old man is trying to lure me from my lair—though I am
> a full three hundred years of age."
>
> Some time later, Jesus revisited the area and saw the snake
> charmer sitting in the marketplace with his basket. "How is the spell-
> casting going?" Jesus asked.
>
> "I managed to charm the snake into my basket," he answered.
>
> Jesus lifted the wicker lid and peered in. Sure enough, there was
> the snake, coiled up.
>
> Jesus asked the snake, "How could you have allowed yourself to
> be captured? After all, you knew what the charmer was up to."
>
> "That's true," answered the snake. "Yet none of his charms
> worked on me. No, it was the repetition of God's name that mesmer-
> ized me. It was the Divine Name which charmed me. Oh, how I wish
> that a hundred souls like me could find joy in His Name."[9]

Sufi mystics often looked to Jesus as a guide through the labyrinth of
life. They believed that he possessed the qualities of the perfect Sufi—
one who had navigated the waters of temptation, isolation, greed, and
revenge—and had emerged on the other side unscathed. Through his
holiness, they envisioned the perfection of Allah. Through his humility,
they aspired to perfection. In his simplicity, they discovered joy in the
wandering life and the beggar's bowl. And in his love, they found peace.

To the Sufi, Jesus was the soul through which one could eventually see the glory of God. Although not worshipped as redeemer or messiah, this Jesus, this Isa, was a kind of living icon—a refined lens through which the Sufi learned obedience and mastered the art of being, of living in the majesty of the Beloved.

As both Attar and Rumi affirmed, Jesus had loosed a great compassion upon the world. Jesus loved his enemies, lived humbly, and submitted to God. And in this, the Sufi felt confident in his words and teachings. The best of Jesus awakened the Sufi soul to the mystical union with God . . . and this was enough. Jesus lived the five pillars and fulfilled them, earning him the reputation as one who had submitted fully and completely to God. His vision was not clouded, and his heart remained steadfast on the One Eternal God—the Merciful, the Beneficent.

Jesus has remained, to the Sufi, the soul's delight—pure, joyous, eternally blessed—and, as this final story demonstrates, the soul's refreshment.

Jesus once stopped to drink from a brook of running water and found its taste sweeter than honey. A man came along with an earthenware pot and dipped it into the water. When it was filled, he offered a drink to Jesus. But as soon as Jesus touched his lips to the earthenware pot, he recoiled, for the water had taken on a bitter, salty taste.

"Oh, Lord," Jesus prayed, "the water that is in the brook is the same water that is in the pot. Yet one is sweet and the other is salty. How can this be?"

The pot answered, "My essence is ancient, for I have been fashioned and refashioned a thousand times over the years—first as dirt, then into cask and mortar. Even if you refashioned me a thousand more times, I would still taste of death, for death is putrid.

"Likewise," the pot continued, "do not fashion yourself into a vessel of neglect. If you cannot know yourself when you are alive, how will you discover yourself when you are dead? Your quest consummated while in life—therefore your death is but a loss. Though born of human birth, you die a godlike death. A hundred thousand veils shroud the Sufi's vision. How can he ever find himself?"[10]

For the Sufi, Jesus was an ascetic Muslim who eschewed all pretenses of the world and loved only God. There are many variations of the cup and comb account in Islam (for example), but in Sufi expression Jesus often goes beyond these.

> Jesus (Peace be upon him!) used to take nothing with him but a comb and a jug. Then he saw a man combing his beard with his fingers, so he threw away the comb. Later, he saw a man drinking from the river by cupping his hands, so he threw away the jug. (Margoliouth)

While Sufism did not develop into a purely ascetic form of Islam, the origins of Sufism show tendencies in this direction. Simplicity, devotion, direct experience of God—these became the hallmarks. Many traditions referencing Jesus are no doubt of Sufi origin or intent, as these express the desire to fall away from the world's allures.

The following Hadith are from Margoliouth's collection and offer enough variety to demonstrate the allure of pure devotion to God.

> Jesus (Peace be upon him!) said, "Devotion has ten parts, nine of which are found in silence and one in flight from men."

> John (the Baptizer) said to Jesus (Peace be upon him!): "Do not be angry." He replied, "I am unable to keep from anger; I am only a man." John said, "Do not acquire wealth." He replied, "This is possible."

> And he said, "I have thrown down the world for you and you have sat on its back, so let not kings or women quarrel with you about it. As regards kings, do not quarrel with them about the world, for they will not oppose you so long as you leave them and their world alone; and as regards women, protect yourselves against them by fasting and prayer."

> And he said also, "The world is both seeing and sought. He who seeks the next world, this world seeks him until his provision in it is complete; and he who seeks the present world, the next world seeks him until death comes and seizes him by the neck."

> Jesus (Peace be upon him!) said, "The love of this world and of the next cannot stay in the heart of the believer, just as water and fire cannot stay in one vessel."

Someone said to Jesus (Peace be upon him!), "If you were to take a house to cover you (it would be good)." He replied, "The rags of those who lived before us are sufficient for us."

Jesus (Peace be upon him!) said, "O company of the disciples, be pleased with what is worthless in the world along with welfare in religion, just as the people in the world are pleased with what is worthless in religion along with welfare in the world."

The disciples asked Jesus (Peace be upon him!) to tell them how they might enter heaven. He told them, "Keep forever silent." They said, "This is impossible." He replied, "Then say only what is good."

Jesus (Peace be upon him!) said, "Seek after worldly goods in order to do good works, but be aware that to renounce the world is more virtuous."

Jesus (Peace be upon him!) said, "Smart dress shows a prideful heart."

Jesus (Peace be upon him!) said, "Many a lamp has been extinguished by the wind, and many a disciple ruined by pride and conceit."

Jesus (Peace be upon him!) said, "I tell you the truth, if you humble yourselves you will be lifted up and magnified, and as you show compassion you will be treated with mercy, and if you attend to the needs of people God will attend to your need."

It is related that Jesus (Peace be upon him!) said, "O company of the disciples, you fear to sin, while the prophets fear unbelief."

When Jesus (Peace be upon him!) was asked of his disciples, "With whom should we keep company?" he replied, "With those whose association causes you to remember God."

Jesus (Peace be upon him!) said, "Whoever turns a beggar away at his door will not be visited by angels for seven days."

Jesus (Peace be upon him!) said, "O company of disciples, keep your bellies empty that you may see the Lord full in your hearts."

Jesus (Peace be upon him!) said, "Blessed is the one who surrenders to God, for he will not die an oppressor."

There is a word at the end of the Gospel of John which reads: "Jesus did many other signs in the presence of his disciples, which are not written in this book" (John 20:30, NRSV). Much of the Sufi tradition, and Islam on the whole, offers a panoply of other signs concerning Jesus—and preserves both Gospel-related familiarities and extractions that are unique. Just as the Christian religion and the church's subsequent history eventually removed the Jewish Jesus from the Gospels, we discover in the Sufi Jesus, especially, that he is remembered and presented in a Muslim light.

The Sufi remembers Jesus as a prophet of God who was filled with love, sincerity, purity, and benevolence. Muhammad always referred to Jesus as a brother, and in traditional Islam some Hadith carry the weight and memory of both prophets. But to the Sufi, Jesus is something akin to a big brother—he is respected and looked upon as a guide and friend. Jesus, among the many Sufi traditions, is kept alive not only in the literature but in the heart.

Or, as Attar and Sana'i once noted, respectively:

> If for only a moment you free yourself
> From this prison around you,
> You will be like Jesus,
> Unique in detachment.

> One should be as Jesus, son of Mary,
> On the way of sincerity,
> To grasp the value and verity of the chapter
> And verse of the gospel. [11]

6

FROM THE FAR EAST

Jesus in Taoism and Buddhism

Hide your good deeds, and confess before the world the sins you have committed. —Buddha

Beware of practicing your piety before others to be seen by them. Forgive us our debts, as we forgive our debtors . . . . —Jesus, Matthew 6:1 and 6:12 NRSV

My words are very easy to understand and easy to practice. —Tao Te Ching (70)

Take my yoke upon you and learn from me; for I am gentle and humble of heart and you will find rest for your souls. For my yoke is easy and my burden is light. —(Jesus) Matthew 11:29–30 NRSV

Taoism, as a philosophy, originated in China some three hundred years before the common era (CE). The Tao, meaning "path" or "way," embraces not only teachings but also doctrine, method, principle, and order. As such, Tao has come to represent the source of all things, the matrix of existence, the way.

The Tao took written form over two thousand years ago in two collections: Tao Te Ching and Chuang-Tzu. These two works—which are now regarded as classics of world literature—contain the compilation of wisdom and mysticism that comprise the Tao. Chuang-Tzu contains many moralistic stories and lessons—though often mystical and meta-phorical in nature. And the Tao Te Ching has influenced many religious traditions and philosophies, including Taoist, Buddhist, Confucian, and various legalistic and martial schools of thought, including Zen.

But the original words—once written—do not make up the "way." Rather, to understand Taoism as a religion and as a faith capable of interacting with the Christian missionaries from the West who would introduce Jesus into Taoist thought, one must go back to the origins of Chinese dynasty and interact with a body of work—and a far more ancient philosophy—that emerged in prehistoric times.

These shamanistic practices and thoughts were eventually written down in a form by Lao Tzu—or at least attributed to him—and became known as the Tao Te Ching. This was in the sixth century BCE, and Lao Tzu—a distant historical figure shrouded in mystery—is commonly re-garded as the founder of philosophical Taoism. But Taoism developed, after this time, into two main schools of thought: Tao Chiao and Tao Chia. The latter refers to the philosophical aspects of the faith as exem-plified by Lao Tzu, Chuang Tzu, Lieh Tzu, and others. But the Tao Chiao refers to the religious aspects of Taoism. Both of these schools trace their foundations and practices back to the founder—Lao Tzu, as well as the Tao Te Ching—but the interpretations and traditions of each are considerably different.

Because the Tao Te Ching was read widely and utilized in different ways, it developed a wide appeal and multitude of uses, as evidenced by its place in Taoism, Buddhism, and Confucian thought and practice. The Tao Te Ching is believed to have been compiled in written form by 500 BCE.

Religious Taoism, however, did not emerge purely so until the dy-nasty of Chao Cheng (around 250 BCE). Cheng ascended the throne as a youth and quickly sought to unify all of the peoples of China through conquest, announcing that the established Ch'in Dynasty would last for ten thousand generations. This period was torn by upheaval, yes—but the Ch'in Dynasty is also where the word "China" comes from. Cheng's conquests also expanded China's reach to the south, and the emperor built larger portions of the Great Wall during this era and also built massive monuments for his own glory. In more recent times, the discov-ery of his terra-cotta soldiers in Xian, buried in lines as if pledging their undying service to the emperor, offers a glimpse into the splendor and the pervasive military and political reforms conducted under his watch.

However, Cheng's revolutions came at a price. In order to unify the peoples he also effectively instituted a central written language—nullifying the various dialects and pronunciations. In 213 BCE he ordered the burning of all ancient books—his intent, it seems, to ensure that there would be no variant political, philosophical, or social challengers. Some scholars, primarily Confucians, attempted to hide some of these ancient texts, but they paid for this with their lives, as one legend reports that some three hundred were buried alive. The cultural and social destruction of this time was immense.

Likewise, is it evident that Cheng also attempted to adopt many of the principles and ideas contained in the philosophies of Chuang Tzu. This glimpse into the history of the Tao offers the first hints of religious aspirations, as Cheng seemed obsessed with some Taoist ideas concerning immortality. When Cheng died in 210 BCE, his eleven-year reign was superseded, overthrown actually, by the Han dynasty.

But after this point, one can begin to speak of a Taoist religion—although Lao Tzu and Chaung Tzu would not have recognized what the Tao Te Ching had become . . . namely an ethical guidebook used for daily living. At the advent of a new millennium the Tao Te Ching had become a central text—not a scripture, exactly—but certainly used in varied philosophies and approaches to life.

What makes any discussion of Taoism so difficult, however—especially in the religious sense, and more specifically with any connection to Jesus—is that pure Taoists would never see themselves as adhering to a religion, a philosophy, or even certain practices. The Tao, after all, means "way" or "path" . . . and when one begins to discuss the Tao for the purposes of a book such as this, we must always be aware that we are approaching the Tao and Taoism through Western eyes and seeing it through lenses colored by other sensibilities, histories, and understandings.

In the broadest sense, it is simply inaccurate to speak of Taoism as a religion at all. And when one begins with this in mind or with this preconceived idea, it is easy to miss the true significance and meaning of the Tao.[1]

Having said this—and clearly stated—we can then proceed to undertake a study of some of the unique features of the Tao and how, later, they were translated—or, how Jesus was adopted and translated—into this structure. This is not easy to understand, nor is it a simple matter of comparative religion—as has been pointed out—but may prove to be more intriguing than looking at Jesus through the various Western traditions or through monotheistic lenses.

Again, using the Tao Te Ching as principal text, one would do well to understand Lao Tzu—who, regardless of one's religious or philosophical persuasions—must no doubt be considered one of the greatest teachers (and most influential) in history—even as a mythical figure. To many, Lao Tzu is known as the "Most Exalted One" and is often regarded as both sage himself and compiler of the ancient philosophies, including the I Ching.

Legend has it that, centuries before the Cheng dynasty, Lao Tzu sensed that a time of great upheaval was about to befall the empire, and so he rode westward on the back of a water buffalo. At the border, a government official requested the he write down the essence of his wisdom before leaving China forever, and this became what is known as the Tao Te Ching.

As many have pointed out—both East and West—the Tao Te Ching works on many levels. On the one hand, it is a gift of rational thought—practical advice that has been applied in myriad ways through centuries and in many cultures. And on the other hand, it is far more profound, a work of immense and immeasurable wisdom that confounds even the wisest sages and yet refreshes at one and the same time. One can read the Tao Te Ching through Western lenses and actually bring from it a sense of the familiar—a kind of common humanity that is accessible regardless of time or history. And one can also read the Tao Te Ching and drop away from it with a sense of frustration, as the poetic form and the language itself seems beyond comprehension.

One has, then, just encountered the yin and yang of Taoism. On the one hand, this—on the other hand, that. There is the one. There is the other.

When one reads the Tao Te Ching there are encounters that appear at first startling and then meld into the familiar.

Consider, for example, the familiar forty-second Tao:

> The universal essence gave birth to the One.
> One birthed Two.
> Two birthed Three.

And Three birthed the diversity of all things.
All lives bear yin and embrace yang.

This Tao, taken at face value, can be interpreted so many ways. Monotheists can see in it some essence of origins, or the unity of God. Trinitarians might give heed to the three in one. And the variety of religious insights that could be extracted from these five lines—perhaps endless. All could be correct. But all would also be incorrect. There is substance here, but more of the imaginative. There is poetry. And taken from the original Chinese tongue, a translator could make a solid play for many and varied word choices. There's no getting to the meaning of the Tao—which is part of its wonder and delight. But what one can find in the Tao is on the other hand practical and illuminating.

The ancient Taoist practitioners believed that the Tao (or way) was beyond human comprehension, and so they sought to find certain patters of the Tao in events, in nature, and in the social order. Various schools of thought developed, and in time Taoism became focused on three primary areas: the well-being of the individual, social harmony, and an increasing awareness of what was often described as "consciousness."

The Tao Te Ching was divided into eighty-one portions—a work comprising poetry, ancient wisdom, and proverbs. In it one can find political and social commentary, psychology and mysticism, and enough philosophy to provoke debate as well as introspection. The Chuang Tzu contains classical stories and narratives of the sage, and was likely written some two hundred years after the Tao Te Ching.

Although not easily accessible to Western minds, the Tao Te Ching and the Chuang Tzu contain concepts that would prove difficult for Western religions. And yet, as we shall see, eventually Jesus was interjected into the Tao following the advent of Christian missionaries to China.

But this was no easy matter.

Consider, for example, the extreme cultural, social, and even religious dissonance between East and West. From what commonalities would one begin to speak of Jesus—a first-century Jewish peasant-prophet then far removed from the Far Eastern philosophical traditions that were born out of caste and dynasty? What concepts (or even words) could form the basis of this conversation?

That a Jesus tradition developed in Taoism is surely one of the most ingenious and incomparable expressions of faith.

Consider the beginning of the Tao Te Ching:

> A way can be a guide, but not a fixed path;
> Names can be given, but not permanent labels. [2]

Surely the beginning of the Tao makes any connection to Jesus— especially regarding Jesus as the way, the truth, and the life (John 14:6)—quite difficult. The Tao even expresses that "the way that is deemed the way is not the way."

These dichotomies make the beginnings of the Jesus traditions in Taoism rather precarious. Yet still they exist.

In the year 635 CE, Aleben—an orthodox bishop from Persia— entered China with a small entourage. They had traveled along the "Silk Road"—a common passage east to west—and eventually made their way to Xian, where, as legend has it, Aleben met with the emperor Taizong at the Imperial Library, a vast trove of some two hundred thousand works that even then would have rivaled the famed library of Alexandria as one of the largest in the world.

Taizong, in a bold display as emperor, had been granting rights and privileges to foreigners, inviting them into his country, in no small part to prove the superiority of Chinese culture and ingenuity. To Taizong, his benevolence was meant to show the barbarian the strength of his empire, but at the same time he was offering a religious and philosophical freedom rarely seen before in China. Monks from across the land were also traveling to India and other realms, gathering Buddhist scriptures, or copying them before returning to China. The same can be said for Confucian and Taoist monks. It was a time when many other philosophies and thoughts were being brought to China.

When the emperor Taizong met with the bishop Aleben, he was fascinated by the bishop's scriptures. He ordered that a copy be made of these Christian texts—and monks set out to render the Bible into Chinese characters.

Aleben also established a monastery. But over time, both the monastery and the Chinese translations—or what became known as "the Jesus Sutras"—were lost in the sands of history. That is, until a Taoist monk cleared away a cave in 1900 CE and made a startling discovery.

In Dunhuang, a series of cave temples had been occupied by the monks for some centuries. One of these monks—Wang Yuanlu—had been cleaning out some of these chambers, long since abandoned. After clearing away a small wall composed of brick and mortar, the monk entered a clandestine chamber that was piled high with some fifty thousand scrolls—a cave that had been sealed for nearly nine hundred years. Most of these scrolls were Buddhist in origin, and some contained poetry and song. But five of these scrolls, surprisingly, contained marvelous stories and copious references to Jesus—teachings couched in Taoist language to be sure—that eventually became known as the Jesus Sutras.

How these scrolls survived for nearly nine hundred years in an arid cave is something of a mystery. But history does reveal that soon after Aleben's journey to China, the Christian faith did spread throughout Asia. These early Christian missionaries borrowed heavily from Taoism and Buddhism and, being of Eastern Orthodox persuasion, had a more open acceptance and willingness to adapt these ancient teachings to the Christian faith. Unlike the Roman Catholic and Protestant missionaries who would enter China later, the earliest Christian communities in China bridged these religious and cultural gaps by placing Jesus in the Tao. These communities possessed, obviously, a more Eastern outlook on the faith and were able to adopt alternative expressions and language—even in regard to Christ's divinity and an understanding of the Trinity. Some centuries before, the church had split over the language of the Trinity, a reality that dated back to the time of the great ecumenical councils that culminated in Nicaea. But the missionaries who first came to China—such as Aleben—would not necessarily have been deemed staunchly orthodox even by these early standards. Orthodoxy was defined by creed. And the church had taken centuries to find agreement—only to end in schism.

Certainly, under Aleben's leadership, the first Christian churches were founded in China, but soon afterward there was persecution. Less than a century later, many religious groups were subjected to threat of death. Only the Taoist and Confucian ways were tolerated, and Christians, as well as Buddhists and other minority sects, were ferreted out for extinction. And as Muslims seized control of long stretches of the Silk Road leading into China, new missionaries and converts were fewer in number. Travel to China waned. And eventually the memory of and community cherishing the Jesus Sutras were lost.

Likely, during this time of intense persecution, the Buddhist and Christian disciples inside China spirited the scrolls into the Dunhuang cave complex, where they remained, undisturbed, for nearly a millennium.[3]

The Jesus Sutras, however, provide some of the most intriguing background to early Christianity in Asia—but more importantly, they broaden our understanding of how Jesus was understood, discussed, and remembered in cultures that were wildly divergent from first-century Judea, the Roman era of Christianity under Constantine, and the developing orthodoxy of the West. The Jesus Sutras demonstrate how the teachings of Jesus were applied or even modified to fit predominant philosophies of the age and how these teachings were incorporated into schools of thought that are a far cry from the much earlier rabbinical Judaism of the New Testament. The Sutras also demonstrate how Taoist, Confucian, and Buddhist thought (among others) have impacted Christian teaching—and how there was, or perhaps always has been, a living conversation between faiths. The Sutras show how Buddhism and Taoism have impacted Christian understanding and also demonstrate what different faiths can offer to each other.

In many respects, we can regard Taoism and Confucianism as indigenous philosophies—as these are the only two belief systems that have emerged and, in many respects, remain predominantly Chinese. As we shall see, however, even these philosophies were not without adaptation. And the fact that these philosophies merged with Christian thought—and were used as scripture in early Christian communities in China—is a most remarkable way (Tao) unto itself.

As indicated earlier, the origins of the Tao are shrouded in mystery. Although much of the writing attributed to Chuang Tzu may have come from various sources and times, there is nevertheless a playfulness of wordplay and story that surrounds the mystic. One might even say that Chuang Tzu told *parables*—though this is a word associated with rabbinical Jewish storytelling, of which Jesus was a master.

Given these similarities then, it may not be surprising that these early Christian communities in China were able to adapt the Tao and strands of Buddhist thought heavily tied to story and social ethic into a new expression of Christian gospel. And while the Tao would remain deeply Chinese (and Buddhism would come to be regarded in China as a "foreign" philosophy and belief system), both can be said to have had an impact on the Jesus Sutras as they were developed and written.

What the Jesus Sutras reveal is not only historical but also cultural. There have always been ways to bridge beliefs and to express one faith in the language of another. In modern times we seem to have lost this ability—or perhaps the willingness—but it was not so in certain eras of the past. One way of speaking of Jesus does not negate the language or faith of another.

In the Jesus Sutras—all of which were most likely discovered in the cave at Dunhuang—we find a remarkable meld of Christian, Taoist, and Buddhist beliefs. The Jesus Sutras might be understood as a fifth gospel, one couched in the language of these older beliefs, including reincarnation and karma. Buddha is regarded as a brother to Jesus, and the Messianic portrayal of Jesus is steeped in Buddhist imageries of enlightenment, of salvation from worldly attractions, and contains Buddhist imageries of heaven and hell. One might regard the Jesus Sutras and the many variant sutras detailing Old Testament and New Testament concepts such as creation, sin, and law as a Christian adaptation of Buddhism and the Tao Te Ching. In these sutras we discover how these early Christian communities in China adapted Eastern Christianity concepts to form a most unique presentation of the life and teachings of Jesus—a gospel, indeed, that could be heard and accepted inside the traditional concepts of Buddhism and the Tao.

In the Jesus Sutras themselves we continue to discover this remarkable blend of East and West, past and present—and find here a Jesus adorned with the humility of the Buddha and Tao that leads to life.

As with many of the Islamic stories attributed to Jesus, the sutras contain words and wordplay familiar to that portion of the Gospel of Matthew, chapters 5–7, which is commonly called the Sermon on the Mount. Noting the emphasis on this portion of the Gospel and how it was carried into the East by missionaries, one also discovers that this portion of Gospel must have been considered the core of the teachings of Jesus—or was at least regarded as teachings that could be adopted into those cultures and languages where there was interaction.

The fact that this portion of the Gospel of Matthew was so heavily imbued in the Islamic Hadith and the Chinese sutras does tell us much about the kerygma as it existed among missionaries and within the cultural interactions of the Eastern world—especially in the centuries immediately following the councils and the formation of the creeds. These particular teachings of Jesus seemed to occupy a central place in the meaning of discipleship—or what it meant to be a follower of Jesus.

This may seem like a historic oddity—especially given certain contemporary mores and evangelical emphasis on lifting up those portions of the Gospels that demonstrate the importance of worshipping Jesus or declaring him as the true way. There is little in the Sermon on the Mount (Matthew 5–7) that would point to Jesus as an exclusive teacher, though certainly a challenging one. But the ethic here attributed to Jesus and his teachings has a more universal appeal, and we can come away from this portion of the Gospel with the sense that Jesus offers certain ends and attitudes which can be practiced by all who accept his authority to teach. One would not necessarily have to affirm Jesus as Messiah in order to follow these teachings. Though, of course, the teachings are so fundamentally difficult (i.e., forgiving one's enemies, giving and praying in private, generosity toward strangers) that if one did not have a religion or philosophy to rely upon in practice, they could scarcely be achievable.

This portion of the Matthew Gospel contains no lofty attributions of Jesus but centers on ethical behaviors and attitudes that could play well in any culture—provided one could see the value in forgiveness, generosity, and the like. The teachings we find here in the Gospel are, to say the least, demanding . . . but they are not of the variety that would lead those of another faith to scratch their heads in confusion or balk at Jesus as he is presented as an ethical or moralistic teacher.

One doesn't have to read far into the sutras to see how this Gospel was adapted into the Tao. The sutra will be startlingly familiar to the Christian. We can begin with the beginning of the sutra.

The Lord of the Universe thus spoke:
If anyone gives alms he should not give it to man, but first of all must give it to the Almighty Lord, and only then shall he give his alms.
Let not your right hand know what your left hand giveth.
When you worship you should not allow it to be seen or heard by others.
When you pray you should not be selfish or wordy in your prayer.
When you pray you must first of all forgive other men's transgressions against you.
And then, if you turn toward God and pray for the forgiveness of sins which you yourself have committed, you will be forgiven.

If you forgive those who trespass against you, only then will the One also forgive you.

By your forgiveness of others will you know that your sins are forgiven.

For this One is no other than the *K'o-nu I-Shu* (Holy Jesus).[4]

Though not far removed from the language and wording of Matthew's Gospel in many places, the sutras do diverge into Taoistic language and thought at other junctures. For example, as the sutras diverge into Christ's teachings about food and raiment (clothing) and the injunction against worry, the Taoist (and Buddhist) philosophy of the five elements appears.

Whatever food or raiment you are in need of, all belong to the one God's own will.

At one time, the One gives food and drink, while at another, raiment.

Other gods can give us nothing at all.

Man at his birth is invested with both "an upper clothing of soul" and another "upper clothing of the five elements."

Here is a reference to the five elements of Taoist thought: earth, fire, metal, water, and wood. These five elements, or attributes—or as they are sometimes called today, aggregates—are not only regarded as the building blocks of all of the physical universe but comprise the mental and emotional attachments and processes as well. This is as much philosophical—perhaps even more so—as elemental.

The five elements are not only central to Taoist and Buddhist thought but also to Confucian, and, to certain degrees, they entered the philosophies of the ancient Babylonians and, later, the Greeks.

Attributed to Jesus, here the five elements take on a spiritual quality, a type of clothing. The elements, then, are more than the makeup of the body (as we might read in Matthew's Gospel), but presented through the Tao they are also the mystical and spiritual manner in which God (the One) relates to us, nurtures us, and redeems us. In Matthew's Gospel the emphasis of Jesus is centered on putting aside "worry" over one's physical needs—namely food and clothing—as God knows these are what we need and will provide such. But in the sutras this teaching is deepened considerably to include a universal teaching about the nature of "soul" and at the same time hold up a monotheistic vision of the One who clothes the cosmos in the spiritual, physical, and mystical elements of creation.

Elsewhere, we see how the sutras use Matthew's Gospel to portray the spiritual quest—especially seeking through prayer.

Try only to find the uprightness of another's conduct and try to find why you can not yourself be so upright.

For if you try to make another upright, it is something like asking the other person to allow you to take a mote from the other's eye, while you have a beam in your own eye.

Therefore . . . first, cast out the beam out of your own eye.

Do not put what is holy and pure before "quasi-persons" lest they despise it.

Ask The One and you shall be given.

Knock at the door, and He will open it for you.

For everyone that asks the one God will surely be given what he asks,

If you knock at the door, He will open it for you.

But if you do not obtain what you ask, that is because you are not permitted to ask erroneously.

Indeed, even if you should ask, you would not obtain that which is harmful to yourself.

If you go to your father and ask him for bread, you will immediately get it.

But, if you should ask for a stone, you would not get it for fear it may hurt you.

Then how much more will Our Father, who is compassionate and merciful and gracious, be willing to give all of these!

Whatsoever you would have others do for you, others would also have the same be done by you.

Whatever others would do to you, you should again do to them so as to reward and compensate them.

Depart from the wicked way, but enter the narrow path, and it will lead you to Heaven.

The sutras, though not necessarily written as an evangelistic tool, do capture an essence of Jesus that is markedly different from the Western creedal expressions of faith. The sutras, for example, also relate the Passion narrative—those final days leading up to the arrest, trial, and crucifixion of Jesus. This Passion narrative deviates little, if any, from the Gospel accounts—though it is a summary as opposed to the biblical presentations of the synoptics.

After the Passion narrative, the sutras also incorporate borrowings from the apostle Paul—especially the book of Romans—and form a kind of apologetic and theological centerpiece from which one might understand the Messiah (Jesus).

Now, who in the world would say, "I am the Lord of the Universe?"

But let us cease from arguing! When the time to tell the truth comes, you will find that the temptation to deceive is not confined to yourself alone. Such is the nature of Adam.

That man (Adam) was the very first, and from the very fact that all human beings have descended from him, we know that such a man existed.

Now, who could boldly come forward and dare pretend, "I am the Lord of the Universe?" Would not such an imposter be discovered immediately?

That man (Adam) not obeying the commandment of the Lord ate the fruit of that tree.

This act of eating the fruit of the tree was no other than eating of the fruit "in one's mind."

From the moment when he ate the fruit he made himself equal to the Lord of the Universe. Apparently, in his mind, it seems that he made himself equal to the Lord Himself.

This man, Adam, therefore lost peace with God.

Likewise, if any man should pretend himself to be God, then that very man ought to be put to death.

The Messiah, therefore, is not the Lord of the Universe, but he made the Lord of the Universe known to all mankind.

The Messiah Himself did the work of Sanctifying Transformation in a limitless measure. What he did shows that he is not the seed of man. But what he did shows that he is the seed of the Lord of the Universe.

[and sixty verses later in the sutra] But, all human beings who have faith will come to the Lord of the Universe.

The Jesus Sutras, perhaps more than the ecumenical councils which led to the split between Catholicism and Orthodoxy, demonstrate the remarkable pliability of the Gospel before the creeds boxed Christian expression—both in form and function. In no small way, the language of the creeds themselves disallowed any other words, phrases, or alternative expressions to speak for the Christian faith. But the Jesus Sutras offer a variant Messiah—though in most ways "orthodox"—who offered his teachings and, indeed, his own life as a means of redeeming the universe (the five elements) and humanity. The sutras are not universalistic in their outlook. Far from it. But the sutras do offer a somewhat apocalyptic vision of a salvation that contains strong elements of the Tao.

Behold! Who is this man that has come to this world from your Father and perfected the work of Sanctifying Transformation?

For our own transgressions and sins, from His own choices He made His own
Person responsible and suffered the death of His five attributes of body.
He will make all people without exception rise again.
All the human beings that are dead will rise into this world, while those that
died without hearing the Gospel will also be made to submit to the judgment
of the Messiah at the end of this world.
Those that worship the Lord of the Universe will enter the place of the
Messiah's Father, or heavenly abode, and dwell there everlastingly.
They shall be given the joy of eternal life there.

Among the sutras one can also find several hymns. These poetic and
musical expressions—some adoring the Trinity, others more theological
in nature—may provide the most profound expressions about Jesus
using the language of the Tao. One sutra—"On Mysterious Rest and
Joy"—paints a majestic portrait of Jesus, captured through a dialogue
between Jesus and Simon (Peter). Here, Jesus reveals the truth because
he is "all illuminating" and "all pervading."

Jesus points out that he has been transfigured (as was Lao Tzu,
according to tradition) with the "ten streaks" to signify his attainment of
wisdom penetrating the four quarters (vs. ten). Elsewhere in the sutra,
Jesus continues with these insights that lead to the "Way of Rest and
Joy."

Therefore I say unto you that "non-desire," "non-action," "non-virtue" and
"non-demonstration" will be known by the term of "the four laws."
Those laws will not make people praise themselves, but will make them free
from all other doctrines. Being tender and merciful to all, and doing "the great
act of compassion" quietly and silently, people will become free from
boundless desire, and will make all people to obtain "the most Victorious (law)"
of all the teachings.
And as this teaching makes all people to obtain "the most Victorious law" it is
called "the Way of Rest and Joy."

In the "Luminous Religion Sutra on the Origin of Origins," we see a
still deeper expression of Taoist thought—a merging of Taoism with
Christianity. This yin and yang sutra is remarkable for its complexity
and poetry. There are also hints of the Gnostic. But there is a delightful
play of words and theology which makes this brief piece of writing
reminiscent of portions of the Gospel of John, where Jesus as the divine
Son of God speaks of himself as the Way, as Truth, as Life. The sutra,
which is incomplete as it stands, ends with these words:

Let each of you, therefore, understand the true meaning of our teaching, according to the position and knowledge of each.

If you understand the meaning of non-origin and non-creation, your stumbling block of doubt will melt away at once.

And at that moment when you understand the Truthfulness of Mysterious Creator you will attain the state of non-creation, non-expression, non-religion, and non-connection as well as mysterious existence and mysterious non-existence both profound and serene.

Indeed, the beauty of the Jesus Sutras is that they invite the reader to focus on an interior life while also practicing the precepts of faith toward others. This is yin and yang, while in classical Christian thought it might be regarded as the tension between personal piety (holiness) and concern for the other. The sutras are not divisive but unifying, and their spirit is both immanent and transcendent.

THE TAOIST PARALLELS

Without implying that Jesus was directly incorporated into the Tao or that these two philosophies/religions are the same, there are certainly parallels between the teachings of Jesus and the earlier philosophies of Lao Tzu and the Tao Te Ching. One can see how the Jesus Sutras were, in part, a gathering place for similar teachings as East (Tao) met West (Christianity).

Amazingly, we shall see how certain elements of the Tao (and Buddhist thought later) offered a lively interplay with Jesus. Or, to put it in historic terms, ancient Hinduism certainly formed the foundation of Buddhism—which, at its origin, was at first considered a Hindu sect. Both Hinduism and Buddhism had some impact upon Greek philosophy and later, as Judaism and Christianity interacted inside the crucible of the Greco-Roman world, we can see how Greek thought impacted Christianity (certainly through Paul and the church after Constantine) and, to a much larger extent, the Gnostic expressions of the Christian faith.

As developed, the parallels between certain teachings of Jesus and those of Lao Tzu and the Tao Te Ching have a remarkable similarity.

Consider, for example:

Jesus: "Behold the Kingdom of God is within you." (Luke 17:21, KJV)
Lao Tzu: "The Way is empty, the Way is full. There is no way to describe what it is. Find it within yourselves."

Jesus: "Enter through the narrow gate." (Matthew 7:13, KJV)
Tao Te Ching: "I seek to comprehend and walk in the Way so I do not lose sight of it. The Way is not complex, nor is it shrouded in mystery. People just ignore it." (my paraphrase)

"The Word became flesh and lived among us." (John 1:14, NRSV)
Tao Te Ching: "Since the beginning It has assumed many names. I know neither its beginning or its nature, but I understand It through the Way."

Jesus: "What is born of the flesh is flesh and what is born of the Spirit is spirit." (John 3:6, KJV)
Psalm 46:10: "Be still and know that I am God." (KJV)
Chuang Tzu: "Tao is beyond all words. It can only be comprehended in silence."

While the parallels between the Tao and some of the teachings of Jesus have a similar voice to them with regard to the Way, we discover a deeper familiarity in the ethical and social teachings of the two. Wealth, status, pride, envy: all of these vices and earthly pursuits are noted in the teachings of either and likewise challenged. The spiritual path that moves through all things in the Tao is not far from the spiritual insights that Jesus offers.

Again, there is an almost universal quality to both.

Loss, love, and personal pride are just a few of these noteworthy teachings. And by definition and effect we are asked to follow the Way that leads to life.

Jesus: "For those who want to save their life will lose it. What does it profit them if they gain the whole world, but lose themselves?" (Luke 9:24–25, NRSV)
Tao Te Ching:
"Or fame or life,
Which do you hold more dear?
Or life or wealth,

To which would you adhere?
Keep life and lose those other things;
Keep them and lose your life."[5]

Jesus: "You cannot serve God and mammon." (Luke 16:13, KJV)
Tao Te Ching: "True riches come from giving out of abundance to those in need."
Tao Te Ching: "Who can take his abundance and serve all under heaven? Only the one who is in possession of the Way."[6]

Jesus: "You must be born anew." (John 3:7, KJV)
Tao Te Ching: "Achieve the state of a newborn child."

Jesus: "When you pray, pray to your Father who is secret." (Matthew 6:6, KJV)
Tao Te Ching: "Close the door and shut out the senses."

Jesus: "Love thy neighbor as thyself." (Mark 12:31, KJV)
Tao Te Ching: "Nothing but good comes to him who loves others as he loves himself."
"The wise man feels compassion equally for those who are concerned about others, and those who are not."
"The world is transformed by those who love all people, just as you love yourself."

Jesus: "Be merciful, as your Father in heaven also is merciful." (Luke 6:36, KJV)
Tao Te Ching: "Do not turn away those you consider sinful and unworthy. If you have wisdom, you will try to save everyone."

Jesus: "Beware of practicing your piety before others." (Matthew 6:1, KJV)
Tao Te Ching: "Be careful not to display yourself in public."
"Follow the Way. But boasting and seeking recognition is not the Way."

Regardless of how one reads the Jesus Sutras or the Tao Te Ching, one can find some aspect of another Jesus—a fresh face, a Jesus newly discovered—inside the ancient texts. As the prologue of the Gospel of John declares: "In the beginning was the Word."

The word, or the words, have indeed endured—and in spite of the cultural, social, and historical divides, there is something of the prophet Jesus, the rabbi Jesus, the mystical Jesus in the words that have been preserved in the Tao. Whether the Way or the Way . . . one does not arrive at that end without first having journeyed forth in faith and humility—the latter being of prime importance to the discovery of the unknown.

And then, as soon as one believes he or she has arrived, even the Way vanishes.

This is both Gospel and Tao. And the path is narrow.

THE BUDDHA AND JESUS AS BROTHERS

For centuries, Buddhists and Christians alike have noted the similarities between the Buddha and Jesus. These similarities are not born of time or place, nor of background or family origins, and certainly not of any shared religious practices or understandings. But in terms of wisdom and teaching—one might even say "spirit"—the Buddha and Jesus are brothers. There is recognition.

In terms of history, Siddhartha Gautama, who became known as the Buddha, was born more than five hundred years before Jesus. This alone makes any contrived attempts toward similarity difficult—and when one considers the vast differences of culture (Nepal vs. Galilee), privilege (wealth vs. poverty), and background (Taoism vs. Judaism) between the early lives of the two, one quickly bumps against formidable opposition. And yet . . . these differences seem somewhat negated when one begins to delve deeply into the life and teachings of either, and what emerges on the other side of this comparison is nothing short of remarkable.

Again, these comparisons cannot be maintained if one concentrates on the peripheries of culture, time, place, religion, or the various communities and understandings that blossomed from their lives and teachings—but if one is open, especially, to the study of the other's words, there is a kind of symbiosis that does not exist anywhere else between such prominent spirits.

It could also be said that to understand one is not to detract from the impact of the other—which is also remarkable. Indeed, one could be fundamentally Christian and yet find in the Buddha's words and actions a recognizable witness. And one could be Buddhist to the core and yet find in the words and actions of Jesus a kindred spirit of self-emptiness. Both Buddha and Jesus possess a kind of humanity and universal wisdom that transcend the constraints and prejudices of religion or practice. Neither Jesus nor the Buddha are exclusively known by their disciples, for they possess both a fame and a transcendence that have carried forward through the ages, touching one generation as the next, regardless of race, class, or culture.

Anyone looking at the life and teaching of the Buddha through objective eyes will see more than a common teacher or spiritual leader. And the same could be said for Jesus. As we have already noted, Jesus transcends Christianity or Orthodoxy or any of a thousand ideologies or theologies that would desire to possess him exclusively. Jesus—even as proclaimed in traditional Christian language—has given himself for "the world." He cannot be possessed by a few or confined to a theological box—he will always break free.

And the same could be said of the Buddha. His life, his thought, his teachings . . . all transcend the outward forms of Buddhism or the inner work of Zen. Buddha is more than religion. And as one might point out from the outset, Buddhism indeed is not a religion at all but a spiritual quest and life without religious forms. Buddhism *is a goal*—to become one with the Buddha. To become *a buddha*. Which is Nirvana.

Comparing the life and teaching of Buddha and Jesus is not an exercise in comparative religion. Such a thing, indeed, is not possible. Buddhism is not Christianity. Christianity is not Buddhism. And Jesus and Buddha are not interchangeable—rather, each stands aloft on his own pedestal of life, death, and teachings.

However, once one gets acquainted with the intricacies and intimacies of both Jesus and Buddha, there is a kinship. There is recognition. One has the feeling that Jesus and Buddha are brothers—that some of what each taught and lived could easily have been lived and taught by the other. This recognition does not diminish either—but affirms both the stark differences and the similarities.

Living inside both one can find a spirit that is compelling and unlimited. Both Jesus and Buddha are timeless. One has a faith—as both Buddhism and Christianity profess—that Jesus and the Buddha live on, that others can reach them, or that they have been both example and guide to realities beyond this life.

Again, this is not to say that Buddha and Jesus are one and the same or that their teachings are not, at certain junctures, exclusive or limiting. But there are certainly similarities in their scope, their impact, their direction. Taken from the standpoint of wisdom alone, one discovers an even more compelling brotherhood between the two, and many contemporary authors such as Thomas Merton (Christian) and Thich Nhat Hanh (Buddhist) have written extensively on these commonalities. Even the Dalai Lama himself has noted the importance of both Buddha and Jesus in his life and teachings. One does not negate the other. They are like brothers.

There are, of course, other parallels that could be drawn—and shall be later in this chapter—but it is perhaps best to start at the beginning and flesh out the life of the Buddha so that we can more readily understand how Jesus enters into the frame of reference.

From the outset, however, any attempt to create a historically accurate account of the life of Siddhartha Gautama is fraught with difficulties (much like the quest for the historical Jesus has challenged and frustrated Christian scholars). But the sketch of Gautama's life is traditionally recounted as follows.

Gautama was born around 563 BCE in Nepal into royalty, though by tradition his mother, the queen, died at his birth. Gautama (the family name) was given the birth name *Siddhartha*, which means "one who achieves his aim." Evidently, Siddhartha's father shielded him from human suffering, had palaces built for him, and essentially had prepared a life of leisure for his son. But at the age of sixteen, Siddhartha traveled beyond the palace walls for the first time following his marriage, and there he encountered many forms of human suffering— realities he had been shielded from up to this point. Eventually, when Siddharta was around thirty years of age, he essentially renounced the life of a prince and began living life as an ascetic—begging for coins on the street and seeking true enlightenment.

Siddhartha tried many paths on his quest for enlightenment but eventually reached a state of mind/being that he called *jhana*, "bliss" or "refreshing." This path—which traditional Buddhists call "the Middle Way"—did not require mortification of the flesh or extreme forms of ascetic life, all of which Siddhartha had attempted, but rather a moderate path that led away from the excesses of materialism and self-mortification. It is said that after forty-nine days of meditation and confrontation with evil, Siddhartha achieved "enlightenment" at the age of thirty-five. This enlightenment led Siddhartha to new understandings about the source of human suffering and how to eliminate it. His discoveries became known as the "Four Noble Truths," and those who, like Siddhartha, are/were able to achieve enlightenment are said to possess the Ten Characteristics—which makes one a Buddha.

Siddhartha, like Jesus, had disciples. But unlike the relatively brief span of Christ's public teaching, the Buddha taught for forty-five years and gathered around him a tribe of seekers. Like Jesus, Buddha had his detractors and also countered many death threats. The teachings of the Buddha, though similar to Taoist and Confucian thought in some respects, were nevertheless unique—and there were many instances in which he and his followers were not accepted, understood, or welcomed. The Buddha, like Jesus, did not seek adulation or followers for himself but insisted that he was only providing a way that others could follow. It is believed that the Buddha died at the age of eighty—and that his last request was that his disciples follow no leader.

Historically, all of these details are sketchy, and what we have now are the various traditions about the Buddha, his teachings, and many narratives attributed to him. All of these, in their origins, were no doubt of oral memory and were only later written down. Nevertheless, the Buddha's teachings are rich in wisdom and insight and, as we shall see, often have a similar spirit to the teachings of Jesus.

To say that there is a Buddhist Jesus is a misnomer. Jesus, unlike with Islam, for example, is essentially unrecognized. He is neither prophet nor sage, teacher nor example. Jesus offers no Buddhist wisdom—and the Buddha offers no wisdom that would be regarded as Christian at its source—yet . . .

What we do have is the Buddha's teaching that—at many points—bears remarkable similarity to the teachings of Jesus.

Even in *the method* of teaching there is similarity.

For example, unlike Islam, where parables cannot be found in the sacred texts (the Qur'an), there is an ample supply of Buddhist parables. Many of these are attributed to the Buddha himself—or emerged as commentary, perhaps, on the Buddha's life. But the parables teach certain themes or lessons that often have a similar theme to those taught by Jesus.

Take this traditional and famous parable attributed to the Buddha. After reading it, one may indeed catch the similarities between its lessons and the life (and death) of Jesus himself. That is not to say that the latter borrowed from the former. Far from it. But again—note the spirit. Often, parables are the only form of teaching that can transcend cultures. Everyone, after all, can understand a story.

The Parable of the Beautiful White Elephant

Queen Videha of India once dreamed of a beautiful white elephant with six ivory tusks. When she awoke, she desired these tusks more than anything else in the world. She asked the king to get them for her. Although this was a difficult task, the king wanted to please the queen. He sent word to all of the finest hunters in his kingdom. "I will pay a great reward for these six ivory tusks," he told them. "The hunter who can find the white elephant, kill it, and bring me the animal's ivory will be given great riches."

Now it happened that there was a beautiful white elephant with six ivory tusks that lived high in the Himalayan mountains in a secret place. Few people had ever seen this elephant. It was not only beautiful, however, but also very intelligent and kind, for it had saved the life of a hunter many years before. This hunter's name was Iskander.

When Iskander heard about the king's reward, however, he was filled with greed. He forgot about the elephant's kindness to him those many years before. "I know where the elephant lives," he thought. "Soon the elephant's ivory tusks will be mine!"

So Iskander packed his bags and set out on a journey into the mountains to look for the giant elephant. The mountains were cold and snowy, but the hunter didn't give up. He wanted the king's reward more than anything else.

As the hunter trudged through the snow he thought, "Perhaps the elephant will remember me. They say an elephant never forgets. So I will act like I am a friend. And when the elephant comes close, I will kill it."

So the hunter journeyed on—through the snow, the ice, and the wind. He climbed high into the mountains, into the secret place where the elephants lived.

After many days, Iskander finally came to the elephant's lair. "Hello," he called out. "I am the hunter, Iskander, and I have come as a friend."

Sure enough, the beautiful white elephant suddenly appeared out of the snow. It shook itself, and blew snow from its trunk, and then smiled. The beautiful white elephant remembered the hunter from many years before. It could never forget a friend.

Soon, other elephants appeared in the clearing. The beautiful white elephant spoke and said, "It's all right! I know this man. He is an old friend."

Approaching the hunter, the beautiful white elephant reached out its trunk in friendship. It had been a long time since the elephant had seen Iskander, but he wanted to say hello.

Suddenly, the elephant's eyes grew large as plates when the hunter pulled a bow and arrow from his quiver. The hunter pulled back his bow and shot the elephant in the heart with a poisoned arrow.

The beautiful white elephant shook the ground when it fell, and the mountain trembled. But when the other elephants saw this, they were very angry, and they rose up to attack the hunter. Iskander ran for his life.

The elephants chased the hunter around the clearing, blowing their trunks and whipping the ground into giant plumes of snow. Ice broke away from the mountains, and many in the village below said that it thundered. As the hunter ran, he grew tired. He fainted into the snow. Soon, all of the elephants had surrounded the hunter. They moved closer, ready to kill him.

Not far away, the beautiful white elephant watched as it lay dying in the snow. Although the elephant could feel the hunter's arrow in its heart, it was filled with compassion. "The hunter is only a man," the elephant thought to itself. "And sometimes men are greedy. They want things that they cannot have, and they kill to get what they do not possess. But I must forgive the hunter for his weakness before I die and teach him how to rid himself of greed."

Suddenly, just as the other elephants were ready to charge and kill Iskander, the beautiful white elephant struggled to its feet, broke through the circle of elephants, and hurled itself next to the hunter in a great act of kindness. The hunter, fearful that the beautiful white elephant would spear him with one of its six ivory tusks, trembled in his shoes. He closed his eyes, afraid of what the white elephant would do to him.

But when the other elephants charged toward Iskander, the beautiful white elephant stood over the hunter and protected him. The beautiful white elephant was so big and strong that all of the other elephants were tossed into the snow. At last, sheltered in the protection of the beautiful white elephant, the hunter began to cry. "I'm sorry," he said, "I pretended to be a friend, but I was greedy. I came to kill you and take your six ivory tusks."

When the beautiful white elephant heard this, it walked its last steps to a nearby tree and broke off its own tusks by smashing them against the tree trunk. The elephant gave its tusks to the hunter and said, "I will soon be reborn in the Pure Land. But after I am gone, I will return to you, and will help you to rid yourself of the poison arrow of greed that is lodged in your heart."

And with those words, the elephant died.

When Iskander saw that the beautiful white elephant had saved his life again and had also given him its tusks, he was very sad. He thanked the other elephants, put the tusks in his pack, and journeyed back down the mountain toward the village. When Iskander returned with the elephant's tusks, he was welcomed as a hero. The other hunters cheered him. The king and queen embraced him and began to shower him with great riches.

But Iskander said, "I cannot receive these gifts, for I have taken these tusks from a true friend. I give these tusks to the king in hope that all will remember the true nature of love and will never forget the sacrifice of the beautiful white elephant."

When the queen heard of Iskander's change of heart and realized her own greed, she returned the tusks to Iskander and said, "Let us not forget this gift of peace. Let this story of sacrifice be told throughout the kingdom."

And so the story of the beautiful white elephant was born.

And Iskander, no longer a hunter, and no longer filled with greed, returned to the secret place on the mountain of the beautiful white elephant. It is there that he buried the six ivory tusks. And it is there that Iskander remains to this day, waiting for his friend, the beautiful white elephant, to return.[7]

In traditional Buddhist understanding, this collection of Buddha teachings is called the Dhammapada—which means, actually, "collection." On the whole, the trove of Buddhist literature (much more comprehensive than the formal Dhammapada itself) is much larger than the Bible. And is it quite different.

But as some people have suggested, if the New Testament were lost and only Jesus's teachings as found in the Sermon on the Mount (Matthew 5–7) survived, we would still have all that we needed to follow the teachings of Jesus. Likewise, a similar claim has been made regarding the Dhammapada. It contains the essential teachings needed to follow the Buddha.

Because of these similar teachings, there have been attempts to bring Buddha to Jesus—or to suggest that certain first-century Jewish sects, such as the Essenes, adopted the much earlier Buddhist teachings into their Messianic expectations. Others suggested that the Gospel writers adapted, in particular, these earlier traditions of the Buddha's birth to convey the birth of Christ. And some have suggested that Jesus was familiar with the Buddha's teachings and incorporated these philosophies into his own. (See Earnest de Bunsen's 1880 title, *The Angel-Messiah of Buddhists, Essenes, and Christians*; *Buddhism in Christianity* and *India in Primitive Christianity*, by Arthur Lillie; and *Was Jesus Influenced by Buddha?* by Dwight Goddard, for these respective ideas.)

Certainly, there could have been some overlap and interplay of culture and oral tradition between fifth-century BCE Tibet and first-century Judea, but the evidence for such is sparse at best, and if there was an interchange of ideas and literature, for example, it is more likely to have existed among those who traveled the trade routes or who had access to stations of wealth or power. It seems unlikely that a first-century peasant rabbi would have been aware of another teacher distanced by geography and time.

In spite of this lack of direct awareness, however, one cannot overlook the spiritual essence, the similarities evidenced by all great religious teachers. While Christianity certainly makes some exclusive claims about Jesus, the teachings of Jesus himself as found in the New Testament are not predominantly such but contain a rich universality that Jesus himself defined as "loving God" and "loving neighbor as self." If the exclusive claims are put aside for a moment and one is given to digesting the full scope of his teachings, most people will discover a rabbi who was more often concerned about right living, right loving, and whole human relationships. One would discover, in essence, a richness of parable, metaphor, and practical—though authoritative—teachings about forgiveness, reconciliation, generosity, and love.

The same may be said of the Buddha and, as the centuries have attested, those exclusive claims aligned with him. Dig deeper and one discovers teachings that contain universal truths and even practical instruction for living in a world of suffering, despair, greed, and death.

One would not have to claim allegiance to either Buddha or Jesus to gain something, to learn something from either. But to live by their teachings, of course, is where the structures of religion, tradition, and faith come into play. It is one thing to note a teaching, to understand it on an intellectual level, and quite another to incorporate that same ideology into a practice—especially as one encounters pushback through the predominant culture, or attitudes, or prevailing winds of the political or the social. Not everyone is a Buddhist who affirms a belief in the Buddha. Nor is everyone a Christian who affirms belief in Jesus. (Both teachers also warned of these superficial affinities, as when Jesus said, "Not everyone who says to me Lord, Lord will enter the kingdom of God," or the Buddha, "The way is the heart, and not all find the way.")

Likewise, when one reads the synoptic Gospels (Matthew, Mark, Luke) in particular, one comes away with an image of Jesus as a storyteller. Or at least Jesus uses the parable as the primary method of teaching, of revealing the nature of the kingdom of God.

The Buddha's teachings are also captured in these traditional stories—of which there are hundreds. These "Jatakas"—a Pali word which means literally "a born thing" or "a happening thing"—have been passed along for centuries and adapted, expanded, and codified. As with the teachings of Jesus, many of these Jatakas serve to illustrate some finer point of the Buddha's philosophy or were originally meant to address issues within the early Buddhist communities.

Among the Jatakas there are parables and fables that were meant to deepen a disciple's understanding of enlightenment, or faith, or compassion, or any number of pressing concerns. With some parables—much like those told by Jesus—the original meaning has been swallowed up by historical and cultural overlay, and we are forced to look back at these teachings and attempt to decipher what they mean. Some translate well to modern-day concerns, while the meaning of others has been lost altogether.

But one can also see through many of these respective parables how similar they are—and the common issues they address. There are also certain Gospel accounts which parallel certain episodes attributed to the Buddha, including this Jataka that holds similarities to Matthew 14:24–32 (my paraphrase):

> The ship was now in a terrible storm, tossed by waves and wind. In the middle of the night the disciples awoke and saw Jesus walking toward them over the water. They were terrified, thinking they were seeing a ghost. But Jesus called out to them, "Cheer up! It's me!" Right away Peter spoke up and said, "Lord, if it is really you, then let me walk out to you on the water." Jesus invited him out of the boat, and Peter began to walk on the water. But no sooner had he stepped out of the boat but he became afraid, seeing the waves and feeling the wind, and he began to sink. He cried out, "Lord, save me!" Immediately, Jesus caught hold of his hand, lifted him up, and brought him back into the boat and then said, "You have such little faith. Why did you doubt?"

The Jataka (190) is told as follows:

> A convinced believer was going, one day, to the river, coming at evening to the shore. But seeing no ferry to take him to the other side, he began to think of the Buddha and stepped out onto the water. His feet did not sink as he strode across. But as he stepped into the middle of the river he noticed the waves, and he lost his concentration upon the Buddha, and he began to sink. Regaining his composure, he focused again upon the ecstasy of the Buddha, was lifted up, and continued safely to the other side.[8]

One of the most similar parables told by the Buddha can be found in Mark 4:2–8:

Jesus told them a parable: A sower went out to sow seed. Some of the seed fell along the way and the birds ate it. Other seed fell upon the stones, so because it could not take root, it grew quickly but then withered. Some of the seeds fell among thorns, which choked off the nutrients and killed the plant. And then there were seeds that fell on good ground and produced a harvest of varying abundance. This is how it is with the kingdom of God.

Before a farmer gathers a harvest in the fall he must first plow the ground, sow the seed, irrigate the soil, and pull the weeds when they spring up. This is how it is with enlightenment. A farmer cannot expect to sow seeds one day, see plants grow the following day, and then reap a harvest the day after that. That's the way it is with enlightenment. First worldly desires must be removed, and then attachments, then evil desires the next day. Those who seek to understand Enlightenment will understand.[9]

Throughout the synoptic Gospels, Jesus often remarks, "Let him who has ears hear the meaning of the parable." Likewise, in typical rabbinic fashion, Jesus appeals to his authority as a teacher and offers the assurance of truth to those who would follow. Mark 7:24–25 would be typical of these pericopes. And the corresponding selections of the Buddha's teachings relate a similar vein of thought.

Whoever hears my words and does them is like a wise man who built his house upon a rock. Even though the rains descended, the flood came, and the winds blew, it withstood for it was built upon rock.

The disciples of Buddha have faith in Buddha's perfect wisdom. Those who regard Buddha will be supported by his wisdom and perfumed by his grace. It is hard to meet a teacher who can explain the Dharma; it will be harder to meet a Buddha; but it is hardest of all to believe in his teaching. A great rock is not disturbed by the wind; neither is a wise man disturbed by honor or abuse. Endurance is one of the most difficult disciplines, but it is to him who endures that the final victory comes.[10]

While parables of Jesus and Buddha may have similarities of theme, we find a much greater familiarity among their respective insights.

Digging deep through these layers of teaching, we soon discover that certain teachings of the Buddha could well have been said by Jesus and that certain parables and metaphors used by Jesus existed in similar strains and themes in the philosophy of the Buddha. Or, to use a modern idiom, if the two were to sit across from each other at one table, they would nod in agreement on many points.

There is a wonderful beauty to this realization—as this does not denigrate the teachings of either but enriches them beyond the time and culture in which each came into existence and blossomed into full-blown faiths. If there is any difficulty or exclusivity in the teachings of either Jesus or the Buddha, one is far more likely to encounter it in their "followers" than in the teachers themselves. Rather, both exhibit a wide embrace. This great spirit of acceptance and joy and love, in fact, was the very type of openness and eagerness of warmth that landed both of these teachers in trouble—particularly with the ultrareligious of their day.

One also has the sense that if the layers of tradition and interpretation could be cast off or pried away from the original intent of their teachings, both Buddha and Jesus would enjoy a much wider receptivity, and others would be able to hear them speaking instead of the din of conflicting voices and self-imposed guardians of their truths who claim to speak *for them*. At the core, Jesus and Buddha are timeless—as their teachings transcend culture, faith, and history.

As with Jesus, the Buddha of history is not easy to discover. The Buddha's teachings, in similarity to those of Jesus, have taken on various forms and strands. Just as there are four Gospels that comprise the collection of Jesus's teaching, so there are various forms attributed to the Buddha.

The Dhammapada, for example, which means "the path of dharma," is a classic Buddhist text that is based on the oldest and best-known version of Pali teaching. The Dhammapada, or path of harmony and righteousness, is a spiritual text of the Buddhist canon of scripture that seeks to introduce the path of the Buddha to the world. In the Dhammapada we find both ethical instruction and story. It is a text that, most like the New Testament gospels, is more available and readable as a narrative or a collection of sayings. One doesn't have to read deep or long into the Dhammapada to discover the Buddha's heart and, subsequently, similarities to the later teachings of Jesus.

As far as Eastern spirituality is concerned, the Dhammapada, the Bhagavad Gita, and the Upanishads serve as a triune expression of the various philosophies and religions that have since emerged from their expressions. But the Dhammapada is certainly most closely aligned to the Buddha himself and, by tradition, contains the essence of his heart. Just as the scribes of Judaism and Christianity preserved their sacred literature by copying, so the monks preserved these sacred texts and traditions by copying them in Pali and Sanskrit.

As we find the teachings of the Buddha today, we can note how many bear remarkable resemblance to those of Jesus, the Galilean rabbi, who taught some six hundred years later. Comparisons and cultural leaps are not always easy to make, but in the case of the Buddha and Jesus, we find an affinity of expression and heart.

COMPARATIVE SAYINGS

As with the Tao and the Jesus Sutras, the ethical dimensions and attachments of both Buddha and Jesus are noteworthy. The great themes of love, forgiveness, generosity, humility and peace can be found throughout. And without a deeper knowledge of either set of scriptures, the casual seeker might be hard pressed to tell the difference between the two.

Over the years there have been parallel lists developed, similarities of various import and weight—one of the earliest being Albert Joseph Edmunds, *Buddhist and Christian Gospels*. This vast work, still highly accessible, is likely the most comprehensive attempt to compare the words of Jesus and the words of Buddha side by side.

Edmunds begins with Christ's admonition, "All things are possible to the one who believes" (Mark 9:23) . . . and demonstrates a corresponding teaching of the Buddha, which reads, "Those possessing right belief, O Monks, at the time of death will rise again in the world of paradise."[11]

But there are, of course, dozens of others—and the deeper one is immersed in either the teachings of Jesus or Buddha, the more resonant the other becomes when the words are encountered. The ring of the familiar is not far off.

Although what follows is in no way a comprehensive parallel of these sayings, it is a beginning, and one can follow the trail more deeply into the forest by reading any number of books listed in the bibliography at the end of this book. But every journey begins with a first step, and so we must start somewhere.

Here is a breviary, a selection of parallel sayings that will set you on the way.

> Therefore I say unto you: Take no thought for your life, what you shall eat or what you shall drink, nor for your body, what you shall put on. Therefore, take no thought saying, "What shall we eat? or what shall we drink? Or with what shall we be clothed?" Take no thought for the morrow, but the morrow shall take thought of the things of itself. (Matthew 7:25, 31, 34, KJV)
> To worry in anticipation or to cherish regret for the past is like the reeds that are cut and wither away. The secret of health for both mind and body is not to mourn the past, not to worry about the future, or not to anticipate troubles, but to live wisely and earnestly in the present. Do not dwell in the past, do not dream of the future, concentrate the mind on the present moment. By acting now you can live a good day. [12]

> If anyone will come after me, let him deny himself. (Matthew 16:24)
> He that loveth father or mother more than me is not worthy of me. (Matthew 10:37)
> Anyone who wishes to become my disciple must be willing to give up all direct relations with his family. [13]

> Take my yoke upon you, and learn of me . . . for my yoke is easy, and my burden is light. (Matthew 11:29–30)
> The mission of a homeless brother is not an easy one, so he who aspires to it should wear Buddha's clothes, sit on Buddha's seat and enter into Buddha's room. [14]

> You must be born again. (John 3:7)
> It is, indeed, hard to be born in this world; it is harder to awaken in faith. [15]

> It is more blessed to give than to receive. (Matthew 6:11)
> In as much as you have done it unto one of the least of these my brethren, you have done it unto me. (Matthew 25:41)

It is a very good deed to cast away greed and to cherish a mind of charity. One should get rid of a selfish mind and replace it with a mind that is earnest to help others. An act to make another happy inspires the other to make still another happy, and so happiness is born from such an act. [16]

Blessed are the pure in heart: for they shall see God. (Matthew 5:8) If a man's mind becomes pure, his surroundings will also become pure. [17]

The light of the body is the eye: if therefore thine eye be single, thy whole body shall be full of light. But if thine eye be evil, thy whole body shall be full of darkness. (Matthew 6:22–23) If a man's body and mind are under control he should give evidence of it in virtuous deeds. One must try to escape from the darkness of ignorance and suffering, and seek the light of Enlightenment. [18]

Blessed are those who mourn: for they shall be comforted. (Matthew 5:4) Happiness follows sorrow, sorrow follows happiness. [19]

Love your enemies, bless them that curse you, do good to them that hate you. (Matthew 5:44) Anger will never disappear so long as there are thoughts of resentment in the mind. Anger will disappear just as soon as thoughts of resentment are forgotten. [20]

Lay not up for yourselves treasures upon earth, where moth and rust doth corrupt, and where thieves break through and steal. But lay up for yourselves treasures in heaven. (Matthew 6:19–20) Let the wise man store up a treasure which others cannot share, which no thief can steal: a treasure which does not pass away. [21]

You will know the truth and the truth shall set you free. (John 8:32) One who acts on truth is happy in this world and the world to come. [22]

You have heard it said by those of old: you shall not commit adultery. (Matthew 5:27) Let him not transgress with another man's wife. [23]

Do unto others as you would have them do unto you. (Luke 6:31)
Consider others as yourself.[24]

If anyone strikes you on the right cheek, offer the left cheek as well.
(Luke 6:29)
If anyone should give you a blow with his hand, with a stick or a
knife, you should abandon all desires and utter no evil words.[25]

Go and make disciples of all nations. (Matthew 28:19)
Teach the Dharma which is lovely at the beginning, middle and
end.[26]

Although the teachings of Buddha and Jesus have great similarity,
that is not to say that they are one and the same—or that Buddhism and
Christianity are identical faiths. Hardly so. Rather, it is the uniqueness
of both the Buddha and Jesus and their respective teaching that makes
the whole of both all the more compelling. In many respects both
Buddha and Jesus espoused a path that would lead to life—different
concepts of what this life entailed—but life, nonetheless. Each espoused a path of humility and service to others. Both Buddha and Jesus
taught the way in story, precept, and example, by personal acts of kindness and self-sacrifice. Both espoused a path of discipleship and sought
to bring followers along on the journey. Theirs was both a solitary way
and also a way filled with laughter, inclusion, and community. Both
practiced hospitality and acceptance and insisted that their own disciples show restraint, tenderness, peacefulness, and self-denial. Both also
insisted that the path was difficult and that certain sacrifices would have
to be made in order to attain the final goal—which is a life beyond this
one.

The symbols that Buddha and Jesus used to describe this path were,
however, quite different. We can see how the teachings of the Buddha
reflect his time and place, his culture and geography. And we can see
how the parables of Jesus, especially, reflect the intimate and well-worn
paths of Galilee and the living waters of lake and river.

Nevertheless, there is a strong connection at the heart.

As Buddhism morphed from a simple path of discipleship into a
system of belief and practice—one fraught with the new difficulties of
community and an expanding culture and impact—Buddhism became a

faith, or, perhaps more accurately, a philosophical system and set of practices that would bring one to enlightenment.

As Christianity morphed from Jewish roots (and in its origins from Judaism to Jewish sect to a new faith), Christian thought also adapted to its surroundings and culture. And in time there were so many various faces of Christianity that the Jesus of history became an academic pursuit and a set of creedal affirmations. The new life that Jesus spoke of along the shores of Galilee, the present kingdom of God that had already come and was proclaimed in word and deed, was no longer viewed as a present reality but a promise of heaven.

But the same might also be said of Buddhism.

In time the teachings of the Buddha, much like Christ's, were translated from this world to the next. And so, with either Buddha or Jesus, the challenge is to find the path of compassion and self-sacrifice that informs the present and changes reality.

Regardless of the source, there seems to be a vision shared by Buddha and Jesus that in its ethereal "otherness" may also impact how one lives into the compassion they taught. Or in the words of the Buddha we may also hear echoes of the words of Jesus.

> This Pure Land, wherein there is no suffering, is, indeed, most peaceful and happy. Clothing, food and all beautiful things appear when those who live there wish for them. When a gentle breeze passes through its jewel-laden trees, the music of its holy teachings fills the air and cleanses the minds of all who listen to it.
>
> In this Pure Land there are many fragrant lotus blossoms, and each blossom has many precious petals, and each petal shines with ineffable beauty. The radiance of these lotus blossoms brightens the path of Wisdom, and those who listen to the music of the holy teaching are led into perfect peace. [27]

7

JESUS AS THEY SAW HIM

Images and Ideas about Christ throughout History

Jesus was asked by some men to guide them to some course by which they might enter Paradise. He said to them, "Do not speak at all." They said, "We cannot do this." He said, "Then only say what is good." —Al-Ghazali, *Revival of the Religious Sciences*

For Christ plays in ten thousand places . . . —Gerard Manley Hopkins, "As Kingfishers Catch Fire, Dragonflies Draw Flame"

At the beginning of his opus *The Quest of the Historical Jesus*, Albert Schweitzer explores the difficulty of finding Jesus amid the myriad of images and ideas that history offers about him. Though Schweitzer wrote long before the contemporary scholarship that has explored so much of the historical Jesus, his insights still hold up in the fray. Jesus, as he points out, is difficult to get at. He is as much elusive as pervasive.

He writes: "We can, at the present day, scarcely imagine the long agony in which the historical view of the life of Jesus came to birth. And even when He was once more recalled to life, He was still, like Lazarus of old, bound hand and foot with grave-clothes—the grave-clothes of dogma."[1]

Indeed, as the life and teachings of Jesus were circulated among those early generations of Christians, some extrapolated from Judaism and others not, the images of Jesus multiplied with the times. Jesus was, at various junctures, viewed as a peasant rabbi and exorcist, a healer, a prophet, and a martyr. He was also regarded as Messiah and Savior, Son of God, and eventually as God in the flesh. He was at once a humble servant and the all-powerful Creator.

These ideas, coupled with concepts from other cultures and times, create a rich tapestry of iconography. Jesus—unlike any personality in history—can be many things to many people. Even with Christianity itself, there was a Jesus interpreted in the light of early challenges as represented by Gnosticism or Docetism and then reinterpreted at the intersection of latter times and cultures through the Tao and the lenses of history.

Add to this mix the incredibly deep and diverse Jesus of Islam and the images of some early Eastern Christian communities and Jesus becomes prophet, sage, and friend. There is a sense in which Jesus cannot be contained in any of these singular concepts—but rises above them and through them. Or, perhaps as Schweitzer indicated, inasmuch as we carry the spirit of Jesus forward, we find Him there.[2]

There have always been other Jesuses. From the beginning, the ideas about Jesus varied as much between Mark and John (Gospels) as they did between Peter and Paul and those early debates about the usefulness of circumcision and the Jewish law. To say that these debates did not involve ideas about Jesus is to shortchange the very nature of his impact. From the beginning of the Jesus movement, some regarded Jesus as the Messiah of the Jews while others regarded him as the Savior of the world (including Gentiles). These ideas were diverse. A common image of Jesus did not arrive easily—if it ever arrived at all.

Even if we focused on Christianity alone—without the myriad other voices and visions—we would arrive at the conclusion that Jesus has continually been reimaged and imagined in the church for centuries. This would be true not only for his teachings—which have been both conservatively and wildly interpreted—but also of his life and purpose. In short, we would be hard pressed to find any two Christians from any juncture of history—including our own times—who would express their faith in him or admiration of him in the same words. The same may be said of the Isa of Islam or the Jesus imagined by the many cultures and peoples of history.

This insight, of course, is not to denigrate Jesus or his impact—quite the opposite.

In fact, no single idea about Jesus can contain him. That is why songs are written, or poetry. That is why the painted images of Jesus vary and why literature continues to be produced. Jesus is more than meets the eye or the mind. The whole of his life and teachings cannot be reduced to a single concept or expression. It takes the many to create the one.

What follows in this final chapter is a kind of extrapolated history of Jesus imagery. There was certainly a Jesus of Galilee. But the Jesus who followed after could be described more accurately by song or poetry, perhaps. To read the New Testament, in particular, as merely a set of statements or hard facts about Jesus is to undermine those early voices who attempted to capture his spirit and his purpose in story and narration. Mark wrote a short story. John wrote poetry. Paul was a practical theologian interpreting Jesus for a mostly Gentile audience through handcrafted letters fraught with personal tragedy and emotion.

Where is the *real* Jesus?

This isn't a question that his friends were asking. They wanted to tell others about the Jesus *they knew*. They wanted to relate their ideas about Jesus in their own words, hoping that they could pass along some aspect of his life and teachings to those who did not walk the dusty streets of Galilee and Judea with him. And not just his teachings—but the meaning of his death and his life.

Christ does play in ten thousand places—as Gerard Manley Hopkins wrote. But perhaps it's more like ten million places, or ten billion by now.

One aspect of Jesus we don't seem to appreciate or enjoy is his diversity. But perhaps, as we read more about him or consider the ideas and images that others have expressed, we do find another Jesus we never knew. Christ plays in ten thousand places. We would be all the richer, I think, to have ten thousand concepts of him, too.

IMAGES OF JESUS: THE HISTORY AND THE POETRY

Love your neighbor like your soul; guard your neighbor like the pupil of your eye. —*The Gospel of Thomas*[3]

It is impossible to mount two horses or to stretch two bows. —*The Gospel of Thomas*

Split a piece of wood, and I am there. Lift up the stone, and you will find me there. —*The Gospel of Thomas*

Now, there was about this time, Jesus, a wise man, if it be lawful to call him a man, for he was a doer of wonderful works—a teacher of such men as receive the truth with pleasure. He drew over to him both many of the Jews, and many of the Gentiles. He was Christ; and when Pilate, at the suggestion of the principal men against us, had condemned him to the cross, those that loved him at the first did not forsake him, for he appeared to them alive again the third day, as the divine prophets had foretold these and ten thousand other wonderful things concerning him; and the tribe of Christians, so named for him, are not extinct at this day. —Flavius Josephus, 37–100 CE, *Antiquities of the Jews*[4]

Wherein I find you, there will I judge you. —Jesus, as quoted by Justin Martyr in *Dialogue with Trypho*, 47, and by Clement of Alexandria

And when Paul entered into the house of Onesiphorus, there was great joy, and bowing of knees and breaking of bread, and the word of God concerning abstinence and resurrection. For Paul said:

Blessed are the pure in heart, for they shall see God.

Blessed are they that keep the flesh chaste, for they shall become the temple of God.

Blessed are they that abstain, for unto them shall God speak.

Blessed are they that have renounced the world, for they shall be well-pleasing unto God.

Blessed are they that possess their wives as though they had them not, for they shall inherit God.

Blessed are they that have the fear of God, for they shall become angels of God.

Blessed are they that tremble at the oracles of God, for they shall be comforted.

Blessed are they that receive the wisdom of Jesus Christ, for they shall be called the sons of the Most High.

Blessed are they that have kept their baptism pure, for they shall rest with the Father and the Son.

Blessed are they that have compassed the understanding of Jesus Christ, for they shall be light.

Blessed are they that for love of God have departed from the fashions of this world, for they shall judge the angels, and shall be blessed at the right hand of the Father.

Blessed are the merciful, for they shall obtain mercy and shall not see the bitter day of judgment.

Blessed are the bodies of the virgins, for they shall be well-pleasing unto God and shall not lose the reward of their chastity, for the word of the Father shall be unto them a work of salvation in the day of the Son, and they shall have rest without end. —*Acts of Paul*[5]

This did our Lord Jesus Christ, who was sent by Joseph and Mary his mother to be taught.

Thereafter there was a marriage in Cana of Galilee; and they bade him with his mother and his brethren, and he changed water into wine. He raised the dead, he caused the lame to walk; him whose hand was withered he caused to stretch it out, and the woman which had suffered an issue of blood twelve years touched the hem of his garment and was healed in the same hour. And when we marveled at the miracle which was done, he said: Who touched me? I perceive a virtue has gone out of me. Thereafter he made the deaf to hear and the blind to see; out of them that were possessed he cast out unclean spirits and cleansed lepers.

Thereafter he did walk upon the sea, and the winds blew, and he cried out against them (rebuked them), and the waves of the sea were made calm. And when we his disciples had no money, we asked him: What shall we do because of the tax-gatherer? And he answered and told us: Let one of you cast a hook into the deep, and take out a fish, and he shall find therein a penny: that give unto the tax-gatherer for me and you. And thereafter when we had no bread, but only five loaves and two fishes, he commanded the people to sit them down, and the number of them was five thousand, besides women and children. We did set pieces of bread before them, and they ate and were filled, and there remained over, and we filled twelve baskets full of the fragments, asking one another and saying: What mean these five loaves? They are the symbol of our faith in the Lord of the Christians (in the great Christendom), even in the Father, the Lord Almighty, and in Jesus Christ our redeemer, in the Holy Ghost the comforter, in the holy church, and in the remission of sins.

These things did our Lord and Savior reveal to us and teach us. —*The Epistle of the Apostles*[6]

And Bartholomew answered and said unto Jesus: Lord, what is the sacrifice which is offered in paradise? And Jesus said: There be souls of the righteous which today have departed out of the body and go unto paradise, and unless I be present they cannot enter into paradise.

And Bartholomew said: Lord, how many souls depart out of the world daily? Jesus said to him: Thirty thousand. —*Gospel of Bartholomew*[7]

Ask for the greater things, and the small things shall be added to you. Ask for the heavenly things, and the earthly things shall be added to you. —Jesus, as quoted by Origen in *On Prayer*, and by Clement of Alexandria

I have read somewhere that the Savior said—and I question whether someone has assumed the person of the Savior, or recalled the words to memory, or whether it be true that he said it—but at any rate the Savior himself says: "He that is near me is near the fire. He that is far from me is far from the kingdom." —Origen, writing in *Commentary on Jeremiah*, 3:3, from a Latin text

For we remember our Lord and Teacher, how he charged us saying, "You shall keep my secrets (mysteries) for me and for the children of my house." —Clement of Alexandria, from *Clementine Homilies* 19:20

For the Lord said to me: "If you don't make the things from below like the things above, and neither the left hand to be like the right, you shall not enter into my kingdom." —this quote, from *The Acts of Philip*, contains similar language to that found in *The Gospel of Thomas* and *The Martyrdom of Peter*, as quoted by Linus

These are the words which Jesus spoke to Thomas. He said, "Whoever hears these words shall not taste death. Let him who is seeking cease his seeking until he finds—and thus having marveled he shall reign, and when he reigns he will find rest."

Jesus said, "Wherever there are two, they are not without God; and wherever there is one I say I am with him. Lift up the stone and you shall find me there. Cleave the wood, and I am there."

Jesus said, "A prophet is not acceptable in his own country, nor does a physician cure those who know him."

Jesus said, "A city built upon a high mountain once established cannot either fall nor be hidden."

Jesus said, "You hear with one ear but close the other."

Judas asked, "Who then are they that draw us, and when will the kingdom come?"

Jesus answered, "The birds of heaven and the beasts of the earth and the fish of the sea are the ones that draw you; for the kingdom of heaven is within you. Whoever knows himself shall find it, and having found it, you will know yourselves, that you are children and heirs of God Almighty and you will know that you are in God and God in you, for you are the very habitation of God." —various quotes from the *Oxyrhynchus Papyrus*, dated third century[8]

The other rich man said to him, "Master, what good thing should I do, that I might live?"

He said to him, "Man, do what is in the law and the prophets."

He answered, "I have done all that."

Jesus said, "Go and sell all that you own, distribute that among the poor, then come and follow me."

But the rich man began to scratch his head and was not pleased. Jesus said to him, "How can you say that you have fulfilled the law and the prophets, for in the law it is written, 'Love your neighbor as yourself,' and look, many of your brothers, who are sons of Adam, are clothed with filth and dying of hunger, and your house is full of many good things, and nothing is brought out from it to them."

Jesus turned and said to his disciple, Simon, who was sitting nearby, "Simon, son of Jonah, it is easier for a camel to pass through the eye of a needle than it is for a rich man to enter the kingdom of heaven." —Origen, quoting from *Gospel of the Nazareans* in his "Commentary on Matthew" 15:4[9]

Jesus said, "If your brother has sinned with a word and has apologized to you, receive him seven times in a day." His disciple, Simon, said to him, "Seven times in a day?" Jesus answered, "Yes, I tell you, and as many as seventy times seven. For in the prophets too, the word of sin was found, even after they were anointed with the Holy Spirit." —Jerome, quoting from *The Gospel of the Nazareans* in *Dialogue Against Pelagius* 3:2[10]

And when the Lord had handed the linen cloth to the priest's servant, he went to James and appeared to him. For James had vowed that he would not eat bread from the time he drank the cup of the Lord until he would see him arisen from among those who sleep. And shortly after, the Lord said, "Bring a table and bread."

He took the bread, blessed and broke it, gave it to James the Just and said to him, "Brother, eat your bread, for the Son of Man is arisen from among those who sleep." —Jerome, quoting from *Gospel of the Hebrews* in *On Illustrious Men* 2 [11]

Whoever owns anything is not worthy of me. —*Liber Graduum* 3:6 [12]

The doctor runs to where the sickness is. I go to the stone-throwers because they will become interpreters instead of stone-throwers. — Ephram quoting Jesus, *Commentary on the Diatessaron* 17:1 [13]

Jesus struck the ground with his hand and took up some of it and spread it out, and behold, he had gold in one hand and clay in the other. Then he said to his companions, "Which of them is sweeter to your hearts?" They said, "The gold." He said, "They are both alike to me." —an Islamic Hadith [14]

God revealed to Jesus (Peace be upon Him!), "When I consider the secret thoughts of a worshipper and do not find in him love of this world or of the next, I fill him with love of Me and take him under my care." —an Islamic Hadith [15]

The Messiah (Peace be upon Him!) said, "O, you who seek the world to be charitable with it, your leaving of it alone is more charitable." And he said, "The least thing is such that looking after it occupies one to the exclusion of glorifying God, and glorifying God is greater and more important." —an Islamic Hadith [16]

On me God's Son suffered a while; therefore I tower now glorious under the heavens, and I may heal every one of those who hold me in awe. Behold the Lord of Glory honored me over all the trees of the wood, the Ruler of Heaven. —from *The Dream of the Rood* [17]

Your majesty, when we compare the present life of man on earth with that time of which we have no knowledge, it seems to me like the swift flight of a sparrow through the banqueting-hall where you are sitting at dinner on a winter's day with your thanes and counselors. In the midst there is the comforting fire to warm the hall; outside, the storms of winter rain or snow are raging. This sparrow flies swiftly in through one door of the hall, and out through the other. While he is inside, he is safe from the winter storms; but after a few moments of comfort, he vanishes from sight into the wintry world from which he came. Even so, man appears on earth for a little while; but what went before and what follows, we know nothing. — The Venerable Bede (672–735 CE)

I pray thee, loving Jesus, that as thou hast graciously given me to drink in with delight the words of Thy knowledge, so thou wouldst mercifully grant me to attain one day to Thee, the fountain of all wisdom and to appear forever before Thy face. —The Venerable Bede

Redemption

Having been tenant long to a rich Lord,
Not thriving, I resolved to be bold,
And make a suit unto Him, to afford
A new small-rented lease, and cancel th' old.

In heaven at His manor I Him sought:
They told me there that He was lately gone
About some land which He had dearly bought
Long since on earth, to take possession.

I straight returned, and knowing His great truth,
Sought Him accordingly in great resorts—
In cities, theatres, gardens, parks, and courts;
At length I heard a ragged noise and mirth

Of thieves and murderers; there I Him espied
Who straight, "Your suit is granted," said, and died. —George Herbert[18]

As Kingfishers Catch Fire, Dragonflies Draw Flame

As kingfishers catch fire, dragonflies draw flame;
As tumbled over rim in roundy wells
Stones ring; like each tucked string tells, each hung bell's
Bow swung finds tongue to fling out broad its name;
Each mortal thing does one thing and the same:
Deals out that being indoors each one dwells;
Selves—goes itself; *myself* it speaks and spells,

Crying *What I do is me; for that I came.*

I say more: the just man justices;
Keeps grace: that keeps all his goings graces;
Acts in God's eye what in God's eye he is—
Christ—for Christ plays in ten thousand places,
Lovely in limbs, and lovely in eyes not his
To the Father through the features of men's faces. —Gerard Manley Hopkins

The Shepherd

How sweet is the Shepherd's sweet lot!
From the morn to the evening he strays;
He shall follow his sheep all the day,
And his tongue shall be filled with praise.

For he hears the lambs' innocent call,
And he hears the ewes' tender reply;
He is watchful while they are at peace,
For they know when their shepherd is nigh. —William Blake

The Lamb

Little lamb, who made thee?
Dost thou know who made thee?
Gave thee life & bid thee feed
By the stream & o'er the mead;
Gave thee clothing of delight,
Softest clothing, wooly bright;
Gave thee such a tender voice,
Making all the vales rejoice?
Little lamb, who made thee?
Dost thou know who made thee?

Little Lamb, I'll tell thee,
Little Lamb, I'll tell thee:
He is called by thy name,
For he calls himself a Lamb.
He is meek and he is mild;
He was once a little child.
I a child & thou a lamb,
We are called by his name.

> Little Lamb, God bless thee!
> Little Lamb, God bless thee! —William Blake

Let us imagine a candidate in theology who enters into that phase of life when he is "seeking." And what is he seeking? Well, we would suppose it is the "kingdom of God" (Matthew 6:33). But we would be wrong. No, he is seeking a parish, a livelihood, a living—this is sought first and foremost and becomes the absolute.

A year passes, and by now he is nearly worn out from seeking. He is not really seeking the absolute of faith ("seek first the kingdom and everything else shall be added to you") but is seeking everything else as the absolute. The young man seeks and finds a wife, and eventually is appointed to a parish.

On the day he is to be installed the young man selects for his gospel text: "Lo, we have left all and followed thee." His message is, essentially, that followers of Jesus must be prepared to leave everything behind.

Some time later, preaching on the text, "Seek first the kingdom," the young man is preaching before his former Dean and his Bishop. He delivers an eloquent sermon, and afterwards as the Dean is speaking to the Bishop the Dean asks, "So, what did you think of the sermon?"

The Bishop responds, "It was top rate."

"Yes," responds the Dean, "but if we were to judge the sermon based on the correspondence between the preacher's life and his message? I could not free myself from the thought that this young man—who in many ways represents all of us—could entirely be said to have left everything to seek first the kingdom."

"Not a requirement," answered the Bishop.

"But that was what he talked about," responded the Dean. "It is a doctrine that has to be attended to, purely and without pretense."

And so this is the way that Christendom differs from Christianity—which is the absolute. —Søren Kierkegaard (1813–1855) [19]

But the truth is it is not Jesus as historically known, but Jesus as spiritually arisen with men, who is significant for our time and can help it. Not the historical Jesus, but the spirit which goes forth from Him and in the spirits of men strives for the new influence and rule, is that which overcomes the world.

The abiding and eternal in Jesus is absolutely independent of historical knowledge and can only be understood by contact with His spirit which is still at work in the world. In proportion as we have the Spirit of Jesus we have the true knowledge of Jesus. —Albert Schweitzer, *The Quest of the Historical Jesus*, 399

He comes to us as One unknown, without a name, as of old, by the lake side, He came to those men who knew Him not. He speaks to us the same word: "Follow thou me!" and sets us to the tasks which He has to fulfill for our time. He commands. And to those who obey Him whether they be wise or simple, He will reveal Himself in the toils, the conflicts, the sufferings, which they shall pass through in His fellowship, and, as an ineffable mystery, they shall learn in their own experience Who He is. —Albert Schweitzer, *The Quest of the Historical Jesus*, 401

APPENDIX

Chronological List of Jesus Traditions and Writings

Estimated Year	Early Christian and Related Writings
40–60	Passion Narrative
40–80	Lost Sayings Gospel Q
50–60	1 Thessalonians
50–70	Philippians
50–60	Galatians
50–60	1 Corinthians
50–60	2 Corinthians
50–60	Romans
50–60	Philemon
50–80	Colossians
50–90	Gospel of Thomas
50–95	Book of Hebrews
50–120	Didache
50–140	Oxyrhynchus 1224 Gospel
65–80	Gospel of Mark
70–100	Epistle of James

70–120	Egerton Gospel
70–160	Gospel of Peter
70–200	Testaments of the Twelve Patriarchs
80–100	2 Thessalonians
80–100	Ephesians
80–100	Gospel of Matthew
80–110	1 Peter
80–120	Epistle of Barnabas
80–130	Gospel of Luke
80–130	Acts of the Apostles
80–140	1 Clement
80–150	Gospel of the Egyptians
80–150	Gospel of the Hebrews
80–250	Christian Sibyllines
90–95	Apocalypse of John
90–120	Gospel of John
90–120	1 John
90–120	2 John
90–120	3 John
90–120	Epistle of Jude
93	Flavius Josephus
100–150	1 Timothy
100–150	2 Timothy
100–150	Titus
100–150	Apocalypse of Peter
100–160	Gospel of the Ebionites
100–160	Gospel of the Nazareans
100–160	Shepherd of Hermas
100–160	2 Peter

100–200	Odes of Solomon
105–115	Ignatius of Antioch
110–140	Polycarp to the Philippians
110–140	Papias
110–160	Oxyrhynchus 840 Gospel
111–112	Pliny the Younger
115	Suetonius
115	Tacitus
120–140	Basilides
120–160	Valentinus
120–180	Apocryphon of John
120–180	Gospel of Mary
120–180	Dialogue of the Savior
120–180	Gospel of the Savior
120–180	Second Apocalypse of James
120–180	Trimorphic Protennoia
130–140	Marcion
130–160	2 Clement
130–170	Gospel of Judas
130–200	Epistle of Mathetes to Diognetus
140–150	Epistula Apostolorum
140–160	Ptolemy
140–160	Isidore
140–170	Infancy Gospel of James
140–170	Infancy Gospel of Thomas
140–180	Gospel of Truth
150–160	Martyrdom of Polycarp
150–160	Justin Martyr
150–200	Acts of Peter

150–200	Acts of John
150–200	Acts of Paul
150–200	Acts of Andrew
150–225	Acts of Peter and the Twelve
150–225	Book of Thomas the Contender
150–250	Fifth and Sixth Books of Esra
150–300	Coptic Apocalypse of Paul
150–300	Melchizedek
150–400	Acts of Pilate
150–400	Anti-Marcionite Prologues
170–175	Diatessaron
170–200	Gospel Harmony
170–200	Muratorian Canon
170–200	Treatise on the Resurrection
170–220	Letter of Peter to Philip
175–180	Athenagoras of Athens
175–185	Irenaeus of Lyons
175–185	Theophilus of Caesarea
180	Passion of the Scillitan Martyrs
180–185	Theophilus of Antioch
180–185	Acts of Apollonius
180–250	First Apocalypse of James
180–250	Gospel of Philip
182–202	Clement of Alexandria
185–195	Maximus of Jerusalem
185–195	Polycrates of Ephesus
188–217	Talmud
197–220	Tertullian
200–210	Apollonius

200–220	Caius
200–225	Acts of Thomas
200–300	Coptic Apocalypse of Peter
203	Acts of Perpetua and Felicitas
203–250	Origen
390–425	Liber Graduum

NOTES

INTRODUCTION

1. Albert Schweitzer, *The Quest of the Historical Jesus*, trans. W. Montgomery (New York: Macmillan, 1926), 6.

1. THE WORD MADE FLESH

1. James M. Robinson, ed., *The Nag Hammadi Library* (New York: HarperCollins, 1978).

2. For a classic collection and rendering of these many early apocryphal works, consult M. R. James, *The Apocryphal New Testament* (Oxford University Press, 1924). This work contains other early gospels, lost "heretical books," alternative Acts of the Apostles, early epistles, various apocalyptic writing (which the early church, in times of persecution, wrote with profusion), and, of course, various infancy gospels and narratives.

3. Ibid. (my paraphrase).

4. "The First Epistle of Clement," in *The Ante-Nicene Fathers*, ed. A. Roberts and J. Donaldson (Edinburgh: T. & T. Clark, 1885).

5. For a much deeper exploration of Gnosticism, read Elaine Pagels, *The Gnostic Gospels* (New York: Random House, 1979), and also Hans Jonas, *The Gnostic Religion* (Beacon Press, 1958). The classic Gnostic library collection is James Robinson, ed., *The Nag Hammadi Library* (HarperCollins, 1978).

6. "Irenaeus: Against Heresies," in *The Ante-Nicene Fathers*, ed. A. Roberts and J. Donaldson (Edinburgh: T. & T. Clark, 1885).

7. "Clement of Alexandria," in *The Ante-Nicene Fathers*, ed. A. Roberts and J. Donaldson (Edinburgh: T. & T. Clark, 1885) (my paraphrase).

8. Ibid.

9. This quote from the *Gospel of the Egyptians* (James, *The Apocryphal New Testament*) is an example of the allegorical style that Clement and Origen employed. Attributed to Jesus, the metaphor is unique and may describe the passions or anything associated with weakness or subservient roles. The original meaning has been lost, but the metaphor as used is consistent with the metaphors recorded in the gospel—and which have no literal meaning: i.e., "You are the salt of the earth," "You are the light of the world."

10. "Clement of Alexandria."

11. Ibid.

12. Ibid.

13. Ibid.

14. Steven Fanning, *Mystics of the Christian Tradition* (London: Routledge, 2001), 25.

15. "Origen: Against Celsus,"in *The Ante-Nicene Fathers*, ed. A. Roberts and J. Donaldson (Edinburgh: T. & T. Clark, 1885).

16. "Origen: Origen's Commentary on John," in *The Ante-Nicene Fathers*, ed. A. Roberts and J. Donaldson (Edinburgh: T. & T. Clark, 1885).

17. Ibid.

18. Ibid.

19. James, *Apocryphal New Testament*.

20. "The Gospel according to Peter," in *The Ante-Nicene Fathers*, ed. A. Roberts and J. Donaldson (Edinburgh: T. & T. Clark, 1885). This volume also contains a Gospel parallel of the four canonical gospels and the Gospel according to Peter, with special emphasis on the Passion narrative comparison.

21. Elaine Pagels, *The Gnostic Gospels* (New York: Random House, 1979), 142.

22. For a better understanding of the work of the Jesus Seminar, read *The Five Gospels*. Also note how these scholars work at comparing words that may have been original with Jesus to those teachings which may have been later extrapolations by the early church or subsequent commentary, etc. *The Gospel of Thomas* has many of the same teachings as the New Testament Gospels— with some parables and teachings that scholars believe may well have originated with Jesus but are not found in the New Testament.

23. Robinson, *The Nag Hammadi Library*. These three sayings are part of a collection of 114 that make up *The Gospel of Thomas*.

24. John Dominic Crossan, *The Historical Jesus: The Life of a Mediterranean Jewish Peasant* (New York: HarperCollins, 1991), 428.

25. J. B. Lightfoot, trans., "The Shepherd of Hermas," in *Excluded Books of the New Testament*, trans. J. Barber, J. B. Lightfoot, M. R. James, and H. B. Swete (London: Eveleigh Nash & Grayson, 1927).

2. THE JEWISH JESUS

1. Aboth de Rabba Nathan, 6.
2. Ibid., 23–25.
3. Ibid., 27.
4. Ibid., 28.
5. Aggadat Berishit 31.
6. Bernard Pick, *Jesus in the Talmud: His Personality, His Disciples and His Sayings* (Chicago: Open Court, 1913), 39–40. Note that this reference in the Talmud suggests that Jesus was hanged after being stoned. Also, the reference to the "eve of the Passover" is in accordance with the chronology of the Gospel of John, which differs from the synoptic Gospels (Matthew, Mark, Luke) on this point.
7. "Justin Martyr: From 'Dialogue with Trypho' with excerpts from 'Apology,'" in *The Ante-Nicene Fathers*, ed. A. Roberts and J. Donaldson (Edinburgh: T. & T. Clark, 1885).
8. Tertullian, "De Spectaculis," in *The Ante-Nicene Fathers*, ed. A. Roberts and J. Donaldson (Edinburgh: T. & T. Clark, 1885).
9. Pirke Aboth 3:9, author translation.
10. Ibid., 3:15, author translation.
11. Ibid., 3:8, author translation.
12. Ibid., 3:16, author translation.
13. Ibid., 4:5, author translation.
14. Ibid., 4:7, author translation.
15. Ibid., 4:9, author translation.
16. Ibid., 4:10, author translation.
17. Ibid., 4:11, author translation.
18. Ibid., 4:21, author translation.
19. Ibid., 4:27, author translation.
20. Aboth de Rabba Nathan.
21. Shabbat 31.
22. William Whiston, *The Complete Works of Flavius Josephus* (1867; repr., Grand Rapids, MI: Kregel Publications, 1960).

3. THE CHURCH SPEAKS

1. See the appendix for a chronological listing of the Jesus material through the first three centuries: canonical as well as these other books and the important writings of the church fathers.

2. James O. Hannay, *The Wisdom of the Desert* (London: Methuen, 1904). Unless otherwise noted in italics, all of the desert fathers material in this chapter is from this source. I also translated some of the stories directly from the *Patrologia Graeca*, volume 65, which was compiled by J. P. Migne, Paris, 1858. When directly translated, these are cited as "my translation."

3. My translation from the Greek.

4. Ibid.

5. Ibid.

6. R. A. Kitchen and M. F. G. Parmentier, trans., *The Book of Steps: The Syriac Liber Graduum*, Cistercian Studies 196 (Kalamazoo, MI: Cistercian Publications, 2004).

4. ISA AND MUHAMMAD

1. Hadith refers to the extra-Qur'anic "traditions" of the Prophet Muhammad—his words and deeds—as collected by his followers. In this work I use "hadith" to refer also to the various stories and traditions about Jesus—some referenced to Muhammad and others not.

5. "THE JESUS OF THE SOUL"

1. All three are Persian words for "silk."

2. Javad Nurbakhsh, *Jesus in the Eyes of the Sufis* (New York: Khaniqahi-Nimatuallahi Publications, 2012).

3. Ibid.

4. Ibid.

5. Abu Hamed Ghazali, *Ehya al-olum* (Tehran: Hosain Khadiw Jam, 1981).

6. Mojdeh Bayat and Mohammad Ali Jamnia, *Tales from the Land of the Sufis* (Boston: Shambhala, 1994).

7. Ibid.

8. John Miller and Aaron Kenedi, eds., *God's Breath* (New York: Marlowe, 2000).

9. Nurbakhhsh, *Jesus in the Eyes of the Sufis*.

10. Ibid.

11. Ibid.

6. FROM THE FAR EAST

1. For further study, see Mary Pat Fisher, *Living Religions: An Encyclopaedia of the World's Faiths* (London: I. B. Tauris, 1997); Jeaneane Fowler, *An Introduction to the Philosophy and Religion of Taoism* (Eastbourne: Sussex Academic Press, 2005); Henri Maspero, *Taoism and Chinese Religion*, trans. Frank A. Kierman Jr. (Amherst: University of Massachusetts Press, 1981); Julian F. Pas and Man Kam Leung, *Historical Dictionary of Taoism* (Lanham, MD: Scarecrow Press, 1998); or Brock Silvers, *The Taoist Manual* (Honolulu: Sacred Mountain Press, 2005). Also, Martin Palmer, *The Elements of Taoism* (Shaftesbury, UK: Element, 1991), particularly pages 1–24 and 65–74, contains insightful information about the origins of religious Taoism.

2. *The Essential Tao*, trans. Thomas Cleary (New York: HarperCollins, 1991).

3. For further study , see Ray Riegert and Thomas Moore, *The Lost Sutras of Jesus* (Berkeley, CA: Ulysses Press, 2003) , 2–28 ; and Martin Palmer, *The Jesus Sutras* (New York: Ballantine, 2001), 39–55 .

4. P. Y. Saeki, *The Nestorian Documents and Relics in China*, 2nd ed. (Tokyo: Maruzen, 1951). The Gospel sutras throughout are taken from this translation unless otherwise noted.

5. Lao Tzu, *Tao Teh Ching*, trans. James Legge (Stepney, Australia: Axiom, 2001).

6. Ibid.

7. Paraphrased from *The Teaching of Buddha* (Tokyo: Bukkyo Dendo Kyokai [Society for the Promotion of Buddhism], 1993).

8. Paraphrased from Caroline A. F. Rhys Davids, ed. and trans., *Stories of the Buddha: Being Selections from the Jataka* (London: Chapman & Hall, 1929).

9. *The Teaching of Buddha*.

10. Ibid., various selections.

11. Albert Joseph Edmunds, *Buddhist and Christian Gospels* (Philadelphia: Innes & Sons, 1914), 54.

12. *The Teaching of Buddha*, selections, 378.

13. Ibid.

14. Ibid.

15. Ibid.

16. Ibid.
17. Ibid.
18. Ibid.
19. Ibid.
20. Ibid.
21. Ibid.
22. Ibid.
23. Ibid.
24. Ibid.
25. Ibid.
26. Ibid.
27. Ibid.

7. JESUS AS THEY SAW HIM

1. Albert Schweitzer, *The Quest of the Historical Jesus* (London: A. & C. & Black, 1910), 4.

2. Ibid., 399.

3. John Dominic Crossan, *The Historical Jesus: The Life of a Mediterranean Jewish Peasant* (HarperSanFrancisco, 1991), page xxi. The three quotes here are from Crossan's translation of *The Gospel of Thomas* and found among Crossan's list of teachings that he believes were original to Jesus.

4. William Whiston, trans., *Complete Works of Flavius Josephus* (Edinburgh: William Nimmo, 1867; new ed., Grand Rapids, MI: Kregel Publications, 1960). This famous quote from the works of Josephus was likely a later addition. Josephus was born in 37 CE of a priestly family of the Hasmoneans and at an early age set out to learn about the three major sects within Judaism—the Sadducees, Pharisees, and Essenes. At one point he became involved in the political work with the Roman Empire, but later, during the Jewish revolt of 66 CE, he led Jewish forces against Roman occupation and for some six weeks held out against a superior Roman legion in the fortress of Jotapata, only to surrender in July of 67 CE. After the destruction of Jerusalem and the temple in 70 CE, Josephus returned to Rome with Titus, received Roman citizenship, and was commissioned to write a history of the Jewish people.

5. M. R. James, *The Apocryphal New Testament* (Oxford: Clarendon, 1924), 273. This selection is from the *Acts of Paul*, a book that Tertullian says was composed shortly before his time by a church elder who wanted to honor Paul. Though based on certain portions of the *Acts of the Apostles* and containing some quotes from the Gospels, the book was also used by certain Gnostic sects. The book was probably written around 160 CE.

6. Ibid., 487. This excerpt from *The Epistle of the Apostles* consists of a summary of the Gospel miracles, some basic teachings of Jesus, and an early creedal confession expressing faith in the Trinity. Presented as a revelatory summary that Jesus gave directly to the apostles, this work likely dates to the years before Clement of Alexandria, who also quotes from this work (or another used as the source): "But the saints of the Lord shall inherit the glory of God, and his power. Tell me what glory, O blessed one. That which eye hath not seen nor ear heard, neither hath it come upon the heart of man; and they shall rejoice in the kingdom of their Lord forever. Amen." (*Protrept*, 113, Clement of Alexandria.) The work, though orthodox in its summary, was not widely known beyond the third century but likely dates back to the years circa 160 CE.

7. Ibid., 169. This gospel, noted in Jerome's "Commentary on Matthew" as being among the spurious gospels that include the gospels of the Egyptians, Thomas, Matthias, the Twelve, Basilides, and Apelles, notes the gospel of Bartholomew as a Gnostic text. This gospel, like many others of this variety, is based upon a "revelation" or conversation with Jesus, usually apocalyptic in tone, and deals heavily with the dichotomy of body and spirit and the path to paradise. This gospel is also introduced by noting that what follows are "mysteries" that Jesus is revealing to the apostles—secrets that, if followed, will lead to the heavenly realm. Only a few find this path, however, and the Gnostic tendencies in this gospel, in particular, are wholly evident.

8. So-called papyri discovered at Oxyrhynchus, Egypt, 1897 and 1903, respectively—both believed to contain text from the *Gospel of the Hebrews*—a gospel quoted by some ante-Nicene fathers and possibly one of the earliest Christian writings. Though fragmentary, these papyri contain predominantly teachings of Jesus, much in the same vein as *The Gospel of Thomas*, and may indicate a variant teaching tradition of Jesus largely preserved in Egypt but not found in other sources outside this region. The quotes here—along with the others preceding—are from James, *The Apocryphal New Testament*, 25–30.

9. Translated by Philipp Vielhauer and George Ogg, in Wilhelm Schneemelcher, ed., *New Testament Apocrypha: Gospels and Related Writings* (Louisville, KY: John Knox Press, 1992).

10. From A. Roberts and J. Donaldson, eds., *The Ante-Nicene Fathers* (Edinburgh: T. & T. Clark, 1885). This text is fascinating for its unique teaching on forgiveness. Jerome seems to use the quote to make a point on the "seventy times seven" extrapolation found in the New Testament Gospels.

11. From Roberts and Donaldson, *The Ante-Nicene Fathers*, an intriguing resurrection account not found in the canonical Gospels, perhaps preserved because of the prominent role that James the Just (the brother of Jesus) had in the first-generation Christian community.

12. R. A. Kitchen and M. F. G. Parmentier, trans., *The Book of Steps: The Syriac Liber Graduum*, Cistercian Studies 196 (Kalamazoo, MI: Cistercian Publications, 2004).

13. Ephram lived in Syria in the fourth century. His commentary on the *Diatessaron* is an important source of Jesus material and extant quotes based on the harmony of the four Gospels.

14. From Margoliouth.

15. Ibid.

16. Ibid.

17. John C. Pope, trans., *Seven Old English Poems* (Indianapolis: Bobbs-Merrill, 1966). *The Dream of the Rood* first appeared in manuscript form in the tenth century but is likely much older. This Old English poem, attributed most commonly to either Caedmon or Cynewulf, imagines the cross (rood) speaking about the experience of the crucifixion of Jesus. In this poem, Christ is imagined as a conquering hero-warrior who willingly takes his place on the cross, victorious over the pain and anguish. At its heart, the poem reveals a common image of Jesus near the turn of the first millennium, when Christian conquest of the Holy Lands necessitated a warrior-king. The poem is also hopeful by the end, imaging how Christ was victorious over hell and death.

18. George Herbert wrote this poem in 1633, imagining Christ as one devoted to the work of redemption. Like many poems of this era, Jesus has changed from conquering hero to object of devotion.

19. Søren Kierkegaard, prolific theologian and essayist, was a remarkable storyteller and frequently embedded parables into his writing. The parable here is my paraphrase based on one such parable found in *Judge for Yourselves!* (Princeton, NJ: Princeton University Press, 1944).

GLOSSARY

Alem (Arabic). Muslim cleric.

Aya (Arabic). A sign or parable; in the Qur'an, a manifestation of God in the world.

Batin (Arabic). The inner meaning of the Qur'an.

Boddhisatva (Sanskrit). A person destined to achieve enlightenment.

Brahman. The fundamental and absolute principle of the cosmos in Vedic and Upanisadic religion.

Buddha. An enlightened person.

Buddhism. A religion originating in the Indian subcontinent based on the beliefs, teaching, and practices attributed to Siddhartha Gautama—more commonly known as the Buddha.

Christ (Greek). Meaning "the Anointed One" or in Hebrew, "Messiah"; in Christian terminology refers to Jesus and is sometimes used by Muslims to honor Jesus, whom they regard as the last prophet before Muhammad.

Dharma (Sanskrit). Originally the fundamental law or natural condition of all things. But also the practices and doctrines of a particular religious system.

Disciple (Greek). "Learner." In Christian usage, a follower of Jesus.

Dhikr (Arabic). To remember God in accordance with the Qur'an, and to the Sufi a recitation of the name of God as a mantra.

Dukkha. "Suffering" in Buddhist philosophy.

Fana (Arabic). For the Sufi to be ecstatically absorbed into God.

Gospel (Greek). Meaning "Good News," the proclamation of God's redemption through Jesus. As writing, there are four Gospels in the New Testament (in traditional order: Matthew, Mark, Luke, and John).

Goy (Hebrew). A non-Jew; a Gentile.

Hadith (Arabic). The traditions or oral collection of sayings or stories attributed to the prophet Muhammad.

Hajj (Arabic). The pilgrimage to Mecca which each Muslim is required to make at least once in a lifetime.

Holy Spirit. God who is present and continuing the work of Jesus Christ in the world (in classic Christian theology, the "third person" of the Trinity: Father, Son, and Holy Spirit).

Imam (Arabic). Most commonly used by Sunni Muslims to refer to a cleric or leader, but in traditional Islam, a descendant of Ali, Muhammad's son-in-law.

Incarnation. God taking on human form.

Islam (Arabic). Literally, surrender to God.

Jina. A conqueror or honorary title of Buddha.

Kabah (Arabic). The cube-shaped black granite shrine in Mecca dedicated to Allah.

Kalam (Arabic). Muslim theological debates about the meaning of the Qur'an or other theological topics.

Karma (Sanskrit). In Buddhist thought, the "action" or "work" that drives the cycle of birth and death (*samsara*).

Mary. The mother of Jesus. In Christianity and Islam, the Virgin.

Messiah (Hebrew). "The Anointed One." In Greek, *Christ*.

Mishnah (Hebrew). The code of Jewish law—originally oral—which was collated, edited, and recorded by the early rabbis and is the largest part of the Talmud (the Oral Law).

Nirvana. In Buddhism, the highest level of consciousness or happiness that one can attain.

Patriarchs. The term used by Jews, Christians, and Muslims for Abraham, Isaac, and Jacob, the ancestors of faith.

Pir (Arabic). A spiritual director for Muslim mystics.

Prophet. One who proclaims God's message to humanity.

Samsara. In Buddhism, the cycle of birth and death.

Shahadah (Arabic). The Muslim confession of faith: "I bear witness that there is no God but Allah, and that Muhammad is his Messenger."

Shari'a (Arabic). The Islamic holy law.

Shema (Hebrew). The Jewish confession of faith: "Listen, O Israel; Yahweh is our God, Yahweh is One" (Deuteronomy 6:4).

Shi'a (Arabic). The adherents of Ali, *Shi'is*, who believe that Ali ibn Abi Talib (son-in-law and cousin of the prophet Muhammad) and his descendants—the *imams*—are the true leaders of the Islamic people.

Sufi, Sufism (Arabic). The mystical practitioners of Islam. Historically, these were ones who wore wool (*sufi*) like the Prophet Muhammad and practiced an ascetic form of Islam.

Sunnah, Sunni (Arabic). The majority group of Muslims who practice Islam based solely on the Qur'an, the Hadith, and the Shari'a rather than devotion or adherence to the teachings of an *imam* or community leader (per the *Shi'a*).

Sutra (Sanskrit). A religious discourse.

Talmud (Hebrew). Meaning "study" or "learning." The huge collection of oral law and commentary as collected and edited by the early rabbis.

Tao. Meaning "path," "way," or "principle."

Tao Te Ching. The principle book relating the "way," or Tao; attributed to Lao Tzu.

Tannaim (Hebrew). The rabbis who were first responsible for collecting and editing the material that became the Mishnah (Talmud).

Tikkun (Hebrew). Restoration.

Torah (Hebrew). The Mosaic (Moses) law as found in the first five books of the Bible: Genesis, Exodus, Leviticus, Numbers, Deuteronomy.

Yahweh (Hebrew). The four-letter (YHWH) name for God as found in the Hebrew Bible. In Jewish tradition, the name was pronounced only once a year by the high priest in the ancient Jerusalem Temple on Yom Kippur (the day of atonement); when read in the Bible, the Hebrew word for "Lord" (ADONAI) was substituted.

BIBLIOGRAPHY

GENERAL

Abdullah, Allama Sir, and Al-Mamum Al-Suhrawardy. *The Sayings of Muhammad*. New York: Citadel, 1990.

Armstrong, Karen. *A History of God: The 4000-Year Quest of Judaism, Christianity and Islam*. New York: Knopf, 1993.

Ausubel, Nathan. *A Treasure of Jewish Folklore*. New York: Crown, 1948.

Bayet, Mojdeh, and Mohammad Ali Jamnia. *Tales from the Land of the Sufis*. Boston: Shambhalah, 1994.

Buber, Martin. *Tales of the Hasidim*. New York: Schocken, 1948.

Bukkyo Dendo Kyokai. *The Teaching of Buddha*. Tokyo: Bukkyo Dendo Kyokai, 1966.

Cistercian Publications. *The Sayings of the Desert Fathers*. Kalamazoo, MI: Cistercian Publications, 1972.

Fadiman, James, and Robert Frager. *Essential Sufism*. Edison, NJ: Castle, 1997.

Frankel, Elllen. *The Classic Tales: 4000 Years of Jewish Lore*. Northvale, NJ: Jason Aronson, 1989.

Funk, Robert, and Roy Hoover. *The Five Gospels*. New York: Polebridge, 1993.

Gaster, Moses. *The Exempla of the Rabbis*. London: Asia, 1924.

Hewitt, James. *Parables, Etc*. Vol. 2, no. 11, 1984.

Kornfield, Jack, and Christina Feldman. *Soul Food*. New York: HarperCollins, 1996.

Levin, Meyer. *Classic Hassidic Tales*. New York: Viking, 1975.

Merton, Thomas. *The Wisdom of the Desert*. New York: Norton, 1988.

Miller, John, and Aaron Kenedi, eds. *God's Breath*. New York: Marlowe, 2000.

Miller, Robert J. *The Complete Gospels*. Sonoma, CA: Polebridge, 1994.

Nomura, Yushi. *Desert Wisdom*. Maryknoll, NY: Orbis, 2001.

Novak, Philip. *The World's Wisdom*. New York: HarperCollins, 1995.

The New Revised Standard Version of the Bible (NRSV). Oxford University Press, 1989

Outcalt, Todd. *Candles in the Dark: A Treasury of the World's Greatest Parables*. Wiley, 2002.

Shah, Idries. *The Exploits of the Incomparable Mulla Nasrudin*. London: Octagon, 1983.

———. *The Magic Monastery*. London: Octagon, 1981.

———. *The Pleasantries of the Incredible Mulla Nasrudin*. New York: Penguin Putnam, 1968.

———. *The Subtleties of the Inimitable Mulla Nasrudin*. London: Octagon, 1989.

Silverman, William. *Rabbinic Wisdom and Jewish Values*. New York: Union of American Hebrew Congregations Press, 1971.

Theophane the Monk. *Tales of a Magic Monastery*. New York: Crossroad/Continuum, 1981.
Waddell, Helen. *The Desert Fathers*. New York: Vintage, 1998.
Zerah, Aaron. *The Soul's Almanac*. New York: Tarcher/Putnam, 1998.

JEWISH

Bialik, Hayim Nahman, and Yehoshua Hana Ravnitzky, eds. *Sefer Ha-Aggadah*. Tel Aviv: Dvir, 1936.
Charlesworth, James H., and Loren L. Johns. *Hillel and Jesus: Comparative Studies of Two Major Religious Leaders*. Minneapolis: Fortress, 1997.
Donfried, Karl, and Peter Richardson, eds. *Judaism and Christianity in First Century Rome*. Eugene, OR: Wipf and Stock, 1998.
Edersheim, Alfred. *Sketches of Jewish Social Life in the Time of Christ*. Grand Rapids, MI: Eerdmans, 1979.
Fitzmeyer, Joseph A. *The Semitic Background of the New Testament*. Grand Rapids, MI: Eerdmans, 1997.
Gianotti, Charles R. *The New Testament and the Mishnah: A Cross Reference Index*. Grand Rapids, MI: Baker, 1983.
Instone-Brewer, David. *Traditions of the Rabbis from the Era of the New Testament*. Vols. 1 and 2. Grand Rapids,MI: Eerdmans, 2004.
Kaddushin, Max. *The Rabbinic Mind*. New York: Jewish Theological Seminary, 1962.
Montefiore, C. G., and Lowe, H., eds. *A Rabbinic Anthology*. New York: Schocken, 1974.
Moore, George. *Judaism in the First Centuries of the Christian Era*. 3 vols. Oxford: Oxford University Press, 1927–1930.
Schurer, Emil. *The Jewish People in the Time of Jesus*. New York: Schocken, 1978.
Scott, J. Julius. *Jewish Backgrounds of the New Testament*. Grand Rapids, MI: Baker, 1995.
Zeitlin, Irving M. *Jesus and the Judaism of His Time*. Boston: Polity, 1988.

EARLY CHRISTIANITY, GNOSTICISM, AND THE CHURCH FATHERS

Chadwick, Henry. *The Early Church*. London: 1967.
Elliott, J. K. *The Apocryphal New Testament*. Oxford: Clarendon, 1993.
Grillmeier, Aloys. *Christ in Christian Tradition: Apostolic Age to Chalcedon*. New York: Sheed and Ward, 1965.
James, M. R. *The Apocryphal New Testament*. Oxford: Oxford University Press, 1955.
Layton, Bentley. *The Gnostic Scriptures*. Garden City, NY: Doubleday, 1995.
———. *Nag Hammadi Codex II, 2–7, Volume 1*. Leiden: Brill, 1989.
Louth, Andrew. *The Origins of the Christian Mystical Tradition: From Plato to Denys*. Oxford: Oxford University Press, 1981.
Pagels, Elaine. *The Gnostic Gospels*. New York: Random House, 1979.
Payne, Robert. *The Holy Fire: The Story of the Fathers of the Eastern Church*. New York: Harper, 1957.
Richardson, Cyril C., ed. and trans. *Early Church Fathers*. Philadelphia: Westminster, 1953.
Roberts, Alexander, and James Donaldson, eds. *The Ante-Nicene Fathers: Translations of the Fathers down to A.D. 325*. Edinburgh: T. & T. Clark, 1885.
Wake, William. *The Suppressed Gospels and Epistles of the Original New Testament of Jesus Christ*. London: Hancock, 1863.

ISLAM AND SUFISM

Armstrong, Karen. *Muhammad: A Biography of the Prophet*. San Francisco: Harper, 1992.
Hodgson, Marshall. *The Venture of Islam: Conscience and History in a World Civilization*. Chicago: University of Chicago Press, 1974.
Jafri, H. M. *Origins and Early Development of Shia Islam*. London: Longman, 1981.
Khalidi, Tarif. *The Muslim Jesus: Sayings and Stories in Islamic Literature*. Cambridge, MA: Harvard University Press, 1991.
Margoliouth, D. S. *The Early Development of Mohammedanism*. New York: Scribners, 1914.
———. *Mohammedanism*. New York: Henry Holt, 1911.
Nurbakhsh, Javad. *Jesus in the Eyes of the Sufis*. London: Khaniqahi Nimatullahi Publications, 1992.
Rahman, Fazlur. *Islam*. 2nd ed. Chicago: University of Chicago Press, 1979.
Robson, James. *Christ in Islam*. London: John Murray, 1929.

TAOISM AND BUDDHISM

Armstrong, Karen. *Buddha*. New York: Viking/Penguin, 2000.
Borg, Marcus. *Jesus and Buddha: The Parallel Sayings*. Berkeley, CA: Ulysses Press, 1997.
Cleary, Thomas. *The Essential Tao*. San Francisco: HarperCollins, 1991.
Easwaran, Eknath. *The Dhammapada*. Tomales, CA: Nilgiri Press, 1985.
Legge, James, trans. *Tao Teh Ching*. Stepney, Australia: Axiom, 2001.
Moule, A. C. *Christians in China before the Year 1550*. London: Society for Promoting Christian Knowledge, 1930.
Ni, Hua-Ching. *The Complete Works of Lao Tzu*. Los Angeles, CA: Seven Star, 1979.
Palmer, Martin. *The Elements of Taoism*. Shaftesbury, UK: Elements, 1991.
———. *The Jesus Sutras*. New York: Ballantine, 2001.
Riegert, Ray, and Thomas Moore. *The Lost Sutras of Jesus*. Berkeley, CA: Ulysses Press, 2003.
Saeki, P. Y. *The Nestorian Documents and Relics in China*. Tokyo: Academy of Oriental Culture, 1937.

INDEX

Acts, book of, 22, 68, 69
Acts of Paul, 208
Aleben, 176, 177
al-Ghazali, 159, 205
Allegory, 24
Arius, 32, 33, 35
Athanasius, 32, 33, 35
Attar, 155, 169

Bartholomew, gospel of, 210
Bede, Venerable, 213
Blake, William, 214
Buddha, 171, 188, 189, 190, 191, 196, 199, 203, 204
Buddhism, 177, 178, 185, 188, 195, 203

Celsus, 25
Cheng, Chao, 172, 173
Chuang-Tzu, 171, 172, 175, 186
Clement, 17, 18, 35
Clement, of Alexandria, 20, 21, 22, 23, 84, 210
Confucian, 172, 177
Constantine, 32, 71, 72
Corinthians, books of, 44, 89
Creed, 33, 34, 82

Desert Fathers, 72, 74, 75, 77, 78, 81
Dhammapada, 199
Diatessaron, 83, 84, 85, 88, 212
Didache, 35, 84, 86, 88

Docetism, 28

Egyptians, gospel of, 22
Epistle, of the Apostles, 209
Essenes, 74

Faith, 4

Galatians, book of, 44
Gnosticism, 19, 29, 31, 72

Hadith, 96, 97, 99, 106, 111, 112, 114, 120, 121, 122, 123, 125, 126, 127, 128, 129, 130, 131, 132, 133, 134, 135, 137, 139, 148, 168, 212
Hajj, 96, 146
Hebrews, gospel of the, 27
Herbert, George, 213
Hermas, Shepherd of, 35, 37–41, 84
Hillel, 61, 62, 63, 64, 67
Hinduism, 185
Hopkins, Gerard Manley, 205, 207, 212

Infancy Gospels, 15, 16
Irenaeus, 19, 20, 84
Islam, 95, 96, 99, 106, 107, 111, 147, 151, 152, 179; Five Pillars, 97, 151

Jataka, 196, 197
Jerome, 28, 211

INDEX OF CITATIONS

Bible: Exodus 12:4-13, 45; Psalm 2:1-4, 7-8, 102; Psalm 46:10, 186; Matthew 3:13-15, 103; Matthew 5-7, 126–137; Matthew 5:4, 202; Matthew 5:7, 55; Matthew 5:8, 201; Matthew 5:9, 63; Matthew 5:10, 55; Matthew 5:17, 63; Matthew 5:19, 55; Matthew 5:27, 202; Matthew 5:28, 55; Matthew 5:29, 55; Matthew 5:34, 60; Matthew 5:37, 56; Matthew 5:40, 56; Matthew 5:44, 43, 202; Matthew 6:1, 56, 171, 187; Matthew 6:6, 187; Matthew 6:11, 201; Matthew 6:12, 171, 187; Matthew 6:14, 56; Matthew 6:18, 60; Matthew 6:19-20, 202; Matthew 6:22-23, 202; Matthew 7:1, 60, 63; Matthew 7:2, 56; Matthew 7:4, 56; Matthew 7:13, 60, 186; Matthew 7:25, 57, 201; Matthew 9:17, 60; Matthew 9:37, 57; Matthew 10:37, 201; Matthew 11:29-30, 171, 201; Matthew 13:57, 124; Matthew 13:44, 71; Matthew 14:24-32, 197; Matthew 20:33-35, 123; Matthew 22:15-22, 65; Matthew 22:30, 57; Matthew 23:12, 57; Matthew 25:41, 201; Matthew 28:11-15, 49; Matthew 28:19, 203; Mark 3:19-22, 48; Mark 4:2-8, 198; Mark 7:24-25, 198; Mark 10:17-18, 104; Mark 10:25, 124; Mark 12:29-31, 63, 187; Mark 16, 12–13; Luke 1:1-4, 4; Luke 5:31, 123; Luke 6:29, 203; Luke 6:36, 187; Luke 9:24-25, 186; Luke 14:17, 60; Luke 16:10, 60; Luke 16:13, 187; Luke 17:21, 186; Luke 20:25, 59; Luke 21:6, 123; Luke 23:43, 125; John 1:14, 186; John 3:6, 186; John 3:7, 124, 187, 201; John 8:32, 202; John 14:2, 63; John 15:17, 124; John 19:38-42, 66; John 21:25, 5, 9; Acts 5:33-39, 68; Acts 18:24-27, 22; 1 Corinthians 1:22-23, 44; 1 Corinthians 10:28-29, 89; Galatians 2:15-16, 44; Galatians 3:10, 44; Galatians 3:13, 44; Galatians 4:21, 44; Galatians 5:2, 44

Jataka 190, 197

Qur'an 2:190-193, 113
Qur'an 3:45-48, 100
Qur'an 3:49, 99
Qur'an 3:50, 99
Qur'an 4:157, 103
Qur'an 5:75, 100
Qur'an 5:116-118, 95, 101
Qur'an 19:30-35, 100
Qur'an 43:63-65, 103
Qur'an 55:26-27, 151
Qur'an 112: 1-4, 103

Talmud: Aboth, Pirke 1:12, 63; Aboth, Pirke 1:14, 63; Aboth 2:1, 55; Aboth 2:5, 63; Aboth 2:7, 63; Aboth 2:8, 63;